DUTY AND CHOICE

The Evolution of the Study of Voting and Voters

Devoted to exploring elections as the central act in a democracy, *Duty and Choice: The Evolution of the Study of Voting and Voters* is animated by a set of three overarching questions: Why do some citizens vote while others do not? How do voters decide to cast their ballots for one candidate and not another? How does the context in which citizens live influence the choices they make? Organized into three sections focused on turnout, vote choice, and electoral systems, the volume seeks to provide novel insights into the most pressing questions for scholars of vote choice and voting behaviour. In addition to featuring several prominent Canadian scholars, the collection includes chapters by leading scholars from the United States and Europe.

PETER JOHN LOEWEN is a professor in the Department of Political Science and the Munk School of Global Affairs and Public Policy at the University of Toronto.

DANIEL RUBENSON is an associate professor in the Department of Politics and Public Administration at Ryerson University.

Duty and Choice

The Evolution of the Study of Voting and Voters

EDITED BY PETER JOHN LOEWEN AND DANIEL RUBENSON

UNIVERSITY OF TORONTO PRESS
Toronto Buffalo London

ISBN 978-1-4426-4924-8 (cloth)   ISBN 978-1-4426-2664-5 (paper)

Publication cataloguing information is available from Library and Archives Canada.

This book has been published with the help of a grant from the Federation for the Humanities and Social Sciences, through the Awards to Scholarly Publications Program, using funds provided by the Social Sciences and Humanities Research Council of Canada.

University of Toronto Press acknowledges the financial assistance to its publishing program of the Canada Council for the Arts and the Ontario Arts Council, an agency of the Government of Ontario.

Canada Council   Conseil des Arts
for the Arts   du Canada

ONTARIO ARTS COUNCIL
CONSEIL DES ARTS DE L'ONTARIO
an Ontario government agency
un organisme du gouvernement de l'Ontario

Funded by the   Financé par le
Government   gouvernement
of Canada   du Canada

Canada

Contents

Part II: Vote Choice

Part III: Electoral Systems

Tables

Figures

Foreword

Notes for an Address to a Symposium Celebrating André Blais's Sixty-Fifth Birthday

STÉPHANE DION

I know, the language of this symposium is English. But since we are at Université de Montréal, I will begin my address in French, as a tip of the hat to my former colleagues in the university's Political Science Department.

Those of you in the department who are not among the youngest will remember that years ago, in another century, André and I had decided to organize an English-only symposium, here at Université de Montréal. Alarmed by this precedent, the Assembly of the Political Science Department ordered us to explain ourselves.

Bravely, André declared, "Stéphane will explain." Thanks a lot, André!

So I explained: "This symposium will not be held in English. It will be held in Scientific Esperanto!"

So my address today will take place in Scientific Esperanto.

And don't worry. This won't be long. My speech will take less time than it would take to read one page of André Blais's endless curriculum vitae.

I am very honoured – and thankful – that Daniel Rubenson and Peter Loewen selected me to give these introductory remarks, but I don't see how I can be of any help to you today.

If the idea is to comment on André Blais's scientific writings, *you* are the experts. I have been away from academia too long. So I really don't have the credentials to say meaningful things about his prolific writings.

And if I'm supposed to speak about the man, well, that makes me a bit uncomfortable. André and I are very modest, private men; our respect for one another's privacy certainly helped forge our friendship over the years.

But let's see what I can do; we'll see how far it goes.

Last summer I had a tennis appointment with a friend of mine. Since I was close to being late, I explained to him that I had been delivering a speech to my party's grassroots where I mentioned that, according to several political science studies, attack advertising does indeed dissuade supporters of the targeted political party from casting their ballots. My friend's answer was, "Since you mention it, the most recent studies show that this effect is almost non-existent."

Any idea who that friend is?

Some time before that tennis game, I told that same friend that the severity of the Liberal defeat in the 2008 election was all the more disappointing to me because the televised leaders debates had helped us reduce the gap with the Conservatives. And what was my friend's answer? "That's very unlikely: the most recent studies show that TV debates have a minuscule impact on voters."

Any idea who that friend is?

How many times has André Blais done that to you? How many assumptions, ideas, hypotheses, theories has he blown out of the water with a stroke of his implacable empirical rigour and indefectible methodological mastery?

Thinking of letting enthusiasm get the better of you? Thinking of saying something more spectacular than rigorous? Thinking of having a bit of fun with ideas and words? Do not fear, Professor Blais is here ... to remind you of your sacred duty to scientific rigour!

I'm telling you: we have to be real masochists to celebrate such a man.

Was he born that way or did he become that way? Is it genetics or socialization? I can't say. But I can tell you he was already like that the first time I dealt with him.

It was September 1974, in Quebec City, at Université Laval. I was a student in his crowded Quantitative Methods class, along with hundreds of other students. It was one of my first political science courses; I thought I understood the subject matter well. But I'll never know if that was the case, and I'll tell you why.

That year, Laval's Political Science Department made two contradictory moves: they decided that mathematics would cease to be an admission prerequisite ... and they hired André Blais as a professor.

Since math was not a prerequisite anymore, the student number exploded. Many of these new students were radicals, Marxists, Leninists, Maoists, and so on. Devastated, the teaching staff unwisely tried to keep the student fauna at bay by showering them with assignments. The inevitable happened: the students rebelled.

In a particularly rocky meeting, one of the protest leaders, named Bruno Blais (unrelated to André), was denouncing the lack of democracy at the university while at the same time striking the blackboard with a brush and yelling, "Silence! Shut up! Shut up!" Well, he got his greatest ovation when he declared, "And the worst of them all is André Blais!"

Then the students decided there would be no exams at the end of the term, arguing that this practice was way too elitist and inappropriate, given our numerous other assignments. The professors, still in shock, gave in to that demand so that the classes could resume. All of the professors but one: André Blais, adamant that his exam be held. But the department went along with the students, and this is why I never wrote that exam.

The following year, André found himself teaching political science at Université de Montréal. Of course, his move had nothing to do with his differing perspective on final exams, or did it?

Notwithstanding that episode, André has always had positive things to say about the teaching he received at Université Laval; he is still especially grateful to one of his former Laval professors, Vincent Lemieux. Likewise, André always speaks highly of his experience as a young professor at the University of Ottawa.

I met André again in 1984, when I was hired to teach political science at Université de Montréal. André welcomed me right away, just like he did so many of his new colleagues. He showered me liberally with good teaching and research tips and, surprisingly, given his seniority, often sought advice from me.

It was not very long before he offered me the opportunity to co-author a paper with him. So I wrote the first draft and gave it to him. After a while, he phoned me. "Do you mind if I change the title?" he asked. "No, not at all." A little later, he phoned again: "Do you mind if I change the first sentence?" "No, just do it." After a while, he sent me his version: every sentence had been changed. Nothing remained of my original text! And the worst of it was that I had to admit that each and every change he made was an improvement!

How often has he done that to you? I'm telling you, what a bunch of masochists we are to be celebrating this man!

Well, years have gone by, and now I wonder: how could I pay a fair tribute to André's distinguished career and accomplishments as a masterful researcher and professor? Should I count the number of books and articles he has written, the number of conferences he has delivered, the number of courses he has taught, the number of master's and doctoral theses he has supervised, the number of universities he has visited, the dollars in research funds he has secured, the number of his citations? Impossible. That's way beyond my mathematical abilities. I told you: I did not write his Quantitative Methods exam at Université Laval.

There was a time when we could find some fault in André's work habits: for a while, when we all used computers to write our papers, he wrote his in longhand and had them typed by support staff. But then, one day, we found that he had become a lot more proficient than most of us in the use of information technology.

Thankfully, André Blais still suffers from one human shortcoming: let's say that he's not the most flamboyant showman in town. His sober body language, uniform tone, and unwavering reserve don't make for the most electrifying speaking performances! But he was quick to recognize this challenge and turn it into an asset. Over the years, André's precise wordsmithing, clear text structures, and concise discourse have made him an effective and compelling speaker. When he's done speaking – whether in a classroom, scientific convention, or media event – you understand exactly what he meant to say, and you will not forget what he said.

André once told me that he wasn't too interested in dealing with the media, that it wasn't a career priority of his. Yet the media love him. They appreciate his sense of nuance and his precise, concise, and informed commentaries.

Precision before all else, mannerisms be damned! Recently André asked me to comment on one of his latest drafts. A typical quote: "Further post-estimation tests show that the Extreme Anxiety model explains significantly more variation in the probability to vote for A in every election, as compared to the Affect-as-Information – Affective Intelligence model. The χ^2 for the difference is 4.12 ($p = .04$) for the Fifth election, 4.00 ($p = .04$) for the "Far AB-Far BC" election and 9.92 ($p = 0.00$) for the "Far AB-Close BC" election."

Well, of course! That's obvious. I couldn't have said it better myself.

Or here's another quote: "The less people are more interested in politics, the more they are less inclined to vote, at least at a 0.5 coefficient!"

Ok, I invented that one.

So, precision before all else: that's André ... Or is it? Well, no, that's not André. For André Blais, it's not precision first, it's generosity first. Generosity and dedication to his students, assistants, colleagues, co-authors; and an absolute dedication to his wife, Suzanne, and their four children. André Blais is the ultimate team player and family man!

But here I am, getting personal when I said I wouldn't. So let me conclude by saying that this conference is a wonderful idea and that I will try to stay around, because I'm sure to learn a lot from you. I'm sure of that because if you were chosen to deliver a presentation at a Conference for André Blais, you must be very, very good indeed.

Thank you. Merci.

DUTY AND CHOICE

The Evolution of the Study of Voting and Voters

1 Duty and Choice: The Evolution of the Study of Voting and Voters

PETER JOHN LOEWEN, DANIEL RUBENSON,
AND MAXIME HÉROUX-LEGAULT

Introduction

Elections are the central act in a democracy. It is in these contests that citizens select their leaders and these leaders go on to shape the future of a city, a state, or a country. Elections matter and so do the choices individuals make during these events.

Citizens make two important decisions in every election. First, they decide whether to participate. Once this decision is made, citizens must decide for whom to vote. Both of these decisions are made within the context and under the influence of some set of electoral rules.

1. Why do some citizens vote while others do not?
2. How do voters decide to cast their ballots for one candidate and not another?
3. And how does the context in which citizens live influence the choices they make?

This volume is dedicated to answering these three questions.

In the chapters that follow, these questions are explored in turn. We first explore why some individuals choose to vote while others abstain. The effect of prosocial attitudes such as altruism on political participation is examined in chapter 2 by Kam, Cranmer, and Fowler. In chapter 3, Dawes, Loewen, and Arsenault present evidence for how "behavioural anomalies" such as self-control problems and ambiguity aversion are related to turnout. Green's chapter 4 focuses on recent field experimental work on social pressure and turnout. In chapter 5, which bridges the terrain between turnout and vote choice, Godbout and Turgeon examine whether voters have different preferences compared to non-voters.

We then explore how voters decide for whom to vote. Nadeau, Bélanger, and Jérôme take up the classic question of how the economy affects vote choice. Then in chapter 7 Fournier, Cutler, and Soroka examine the issue of campaign effects and analyse heterogeneous effects across different types of voters. Garand and Xu take the study of vote choice to a new arena by studying the effects on vote choice of government employment.

Finally, we explore how electoral systems matter for these decisions. In part III, Anderson studies the impact of party system polarization and the number of parties on attitudes of democratic legitimacy. The chapter by Lachat looks at the psychological effects of electoral systems on voter behaviour. The question of strategic voting and how electoral systems affect it is the topic of Aldrich and Stephenson's chapter.

The individual citizen is central to all of this. Individuals decide whether to vote in an election and who weigh up the choices in front of them. In what follows, we lay out some of what we know about how individuals make choices, in particular what we have learned over the last sixty years of research in electoral behaviour. We then discuss our current understanding of how the nature of the alternatives presented to the citizen – and crucially the structure of those alternatives in different electoral systems – affects the choices the citizen makes. We conclude by highlighting the contributions of each chapter in this volume to our understanding of both the sense of duty felt by the citizen and the nature of the choices she makes.

The Citizen

Early accounts of the citizen as voter were at once simple and elegant. In *An Economic Theory of Democracy*, Downs (1957) describes a rational actor whose preferences are complete (in that, for example, she can choose among A, B, and C) and transitive (in that if she prefers A to B, and B to C, she must prefer A to C). When presented with alternatives, this rational citizen would choose whatever option gave her the most utility. She knew the positions of political parties and the policies that placed them in those positions. In short, this citizen was no fool.

In this telling, the citizen faced costs to vote and so would do so only if the expected benefits of voting exceeded those costs. This (and later seminal work by Riker and Ordeshook 1968) raised an important paradox. If the likelihood of any single vote being decisive is so small, then the expected benefits of voting must also be tiny. While the costs of voting are not substantial, they are also not zero. So why then would the rational citizen vote? By Downs's reckoning, the voter must love democracy and vote for that reason. Riker and Ordeshook offered similar possibilities, as did others in later work (see Blais 2000 for a comprehensive review). The citizen was rational, but she was also given over at least a bit to moral or dutiful considerations. Downs's (1957) conception of the citizen provided a helpful framework not only for understanding citizens, but also for comprehending the behaviour of parties. Following on Hotelling (1929), Downs conceived of parties occupying a single ideological dimension. Given rational voters choosing between these alternatives, there are strong incentives for the number of political parties to winnow to two, and for parties to converge on the median voter. For Downs, the rationality of parties reflected the rationality of the citizen.

It was not long before both conceptions came up against their limits. In the case of the citizen, there was not only the problem of non-zero turnout. There was also the unlikely proposition that the voter was both purely instrumental and fully informed. In the case of the parties, the possibility of multidimensional competition and the improbability of equilibrium under such systems reduced the usefulness of Downs's (1957) account (Adams, Merrill, III, and Grofman 2005; Enelow and Hinich 1984). But of course voter turnout can still be explained by a rational choice approach. There is little in such an account that is counter to explaining turnout per se; it is the strictly narrow definition of rationality and its application to turnout that seems incompatible.

A contemporary account of the citizen drew an almost entirely different picture. Closely observing and surveying real voters in Erie County, Ohio, in the 1940 election, the Columbia School authors Lazarsfeld, Berelson, and Gaudet (1944) found voters who had largely decided who would get their support before the campaign even began. If there was action over the campaign, it was over the decision to cast a ballot.

Thus the citizen was not merely an individual (however rational), but an individual embedded in a group. And it was these groups that not only motivated the citizen to vote, but also informed her preferences. These groups – whether ethnic, religious, or economic – could then become the focus of analysis, and parties could then be understood not to be competing so much for the support of individual voters, but for groups of voters. Such an approach found purchase elsewhere, not least in Canada, where vote choice has long been structured along lines of both religious beliefs (with Protestants voting disproportionately for conservative parties and Catholics for the Liberal Party) and ethnicity (with ethnic minorities and immigrants voting disproportionately for the Liberal Party) (Blais 2005; Johnston et al. 1992). Similar classifications certainly present in other locales as well, if less importantly than the effects of another grouping, namely class (Butler and Stokes 1969). If the picture of the citizen present in the Columbia account is a rich one, it was still not complete. Indeed, the missing element from such an account is, in retrospect, an obvious one: the story left little room for politics and campaigns. If vote choice was largely set by one's social milieu, and if such settings are slow to change, then why would we observe any volatility between elections?

This puzzle was somewhat solved by the work of the "Michigan school." Beginning in 1960, Campbell et al. began to forward a conception of the citizen that could explain both long-term stability and short-term volatility in vote choice. Under this telling, the citizen was likely to identify with one party or another. Such partisan identification came from early life experiences and an early understanding of the citizen's place and the place of others like her in her social milieu.

This had several important downstream effects, not least in that it acted as a "filter" through which new political events and information would be processed. This explains a certain baseline of stability in vote choice, as voters have a standing position, and this position influences how they experience current political events. Still farther downstream, they allowed for the influence of other factors, such as the evaluation of current politicians, issues, and events.

This model has been subject to some debate, both over its applicability in other countries (LeDuc 1981), over time, and over the nature of partisanship (Fiorina 1981). However, this account stands up as perhaps the most comprehensive, if not the most parsimonious. In this telling, the citizen's engagement with politics is one of long-standing dispositions, short-term politics, and occasional shocks generated by the political system.

This is also a conception that added important information to the story of how the citizen decided to vote. Partisan identification makes voting easier – by eliminating the difficulty of making a choice each time – and more meaningfully increasing the voter's engagement with parties and concern for the outcome.

These three conceptions – Downsian, Columbia, and Michigan, for lack of other labels – proved both rich and long lasting. In many ways our modern understanding of citizen participation in electoral democracy rests on these building blocks. We now understand, for example, that for at least some voters spatial reasoning proves very important for both vote choice and voter turnout (Delli Carpini and Keeter 1997; Clarke et al. 2009; Jesse 2008). We also appreciate more fully both the degree to which voters are embedded within social networks (Sinclair 2012) and the extent to which their concern for other people in their group matters for their decision to be an active political citizen (Dawes, Loewen, and Fowler 2011; Loewen 2010). There also exists a rich literature, dating back to Key (1949), on how geography and differences in the social and political environment affects civic participation and political behaviour (e.g., Alesina and La Ferrera 2000; Huckfeldt 1979; Oliver 2000; Wong et al. 2015). Likewise, work on both behavioural genetics (e.g., Fowler, Baker, and Dawes 2008) and personality (Mondak 2010) has shown that both basic political preferences and the propensity to participate has a basis both in genetic inheritance from parents and the development of traits early in life.

We have also come to understand, though perhaps not as fully, just how important the electoral system is for the citizen. We understand electoral systems to be the collection of rules that determine how citizens vote (in particular how they indicate their preferences on the ballot) and how those votes are translated into seats (Blais and Massicotte 2002).

The translation of votes into seats has perhaps proved to be the richest for research, and several empirical regularities have been uncovered. Principal among these regularities is that more proportional electoral systems – where the share of seats parties receive more closely matches the votes they received – produce more parties, more minority governments, and higher voter turnout (Blais and Massicotte 2002; Cox 1997; Duverger 1959). There is also some evidence that parties in such systems exhibit greater ideological diversity (Horowitz 1990; Lijphart 1991). Finally, the translation of votes into seats invites citizens to engage in different voting strategies. In particular, we have come to understand how so-called strategic voting – the casting of a vote for a party other than your preferred one – exists in every electoral system, but takes different forms (Blais, Loewen, and Bodet 2002; Cox 1997; Fredén 2014).

For all of this progress, however, there remain several gaps in the literature, both within each set of questions (Who votes? For whom? And how does context matter?) and, perhaps most importantly, between them. For example, the study of voter turnout has not yet determined definitively when citizen rationality outweighs common decision-making anomalies. It has similarly not yet resolved how much heterogeneity there is within citizens on this score. Similarly, we know much less than we could about how the individual heterogeneity matters for vote choice, once citizens decide to enter the ballot box. Who responds to campaigns, for example, is an open and active line of research. Finally, we know much less about how electoral systems further condition these heterogeneities. There are, then, outstanding questions that cannot be answered by only looking within one of these sets of questions. We need to instead understand how citizens differ one from another and then understand how where they live makes these differences matter less or more. The chapters that follow go some way to answering these questions.

We believe that in order to better understand electoral democracy, a research program is needed that makes connections between the three sets of questions of participation, vote choice, and institutional context. While each chapter in this volume contributes on its own, taken together they begin to shed light on the connections between these three crucial dimensions of electoral democracy.

The research reported in these chapters also speaks to methodological and substantive developments in the study of voting and political behaviour more generally. Two threads stand out. First is the turn to randomized experiments in political science to better understand causation. For example, in chapter 4 Green provides an extensive review and discussion of field experimental work on social pressure and turnout. Chapter 2 by Kam, Cranmer, and Fowler, and chapter 3 by Dawes, Loewen, and Arsenault also use experiments embedded in surveys to get at behavioural measures, as opposed to merely attitudinal ones. Political science has always been a discipline that borrows from other fields of study. This trend is, if anything, increasing. In particular, several of the contributors here integrate tools and approaches from psychology and behavioural economics with the study of political phenomena.

Outline of the Book

The book is divided into three parts, reflecting the three main themes discussed above. The first part deals with turnout – the decision to cast a ballot. Part II examines questions related vote choice. The final chapters in part III present work on electoral systems and their effects. Of course, as discussed above, these themes and questions are not mutually exclusive and there is much work in tying them together.

Part I: Voter Turnout

There has been a considerable focus on the effect of civic duty in turnout. Recently, however, field experimental work has begun to explore the role of social pressure. Donald Green's chapter argues that the effects of social pressure appear to be much stronger than proponents of civic duty suggest, but that they also depend on a strong assertion of the norm of civic duty. This pattern suggests a possible synthesis of the civic duty and social pressure hypotheses: social pressure works when norms of civic duty are made salient.

If individuals are self-interested and if their vote is very unlikely to sway an election, why do they vote? Recent evidence suggests that individuals vote because they are altruistic and care about the outcome of elections for other citizens. In this chapter, Fowler et al. argue that if altruistic individuals see promise of a net societal gain from political outcomes, they should be more likely to participate. When the potential gains are purely distributive, however, altruists may be no more likely to participate than egoists. Empirically, they first show that dictator game[1] behaviour predicts support for humanitarian norms and donations to Hurricane Katrina victims, suggesting that dictator game allocations are valid measures of altruism. Next, they demonstrate that this measure of altruism predicts general participation in politics, suggesting that past results with students may be generalizable to a broader population. Moreover, they find that the dictator game allocations provide an independent contribution to explaining variation in participation, above and beyond self-reported attitudes towards helping others. Consistent with the argument that altruists participate only when they think doing so will make everyone better off, In chapter 2, Kam, Cranmer, and Fowler uncover no relationship between altruism and voter turnout in an election where the outcome is distributive and where it is not clear that either political outcome will produce a net societal gain. They conclude by considering the relationship between altruism and other less adversarial forms of political participation.

Dawes, Loewen, and Arsenault in chapter 3 likewise takes up the question of why individuals vote if their ballot cannot be expected to make a difference. They partially explain this paradox by considering individuals' "behavioural anomalies" or cognitive mistakes when they make decisions. Some of these mistakes are related to how accurately individuals assess the likelihood of an event, such as the chance that it will be decisive in an election. Other mistakes are related to individuals' ability to take an action in the present that has a benefit in the future, such as voting today when their preferred party will not take power and implement its policies until the future. Dawes, Loewen, and Arsenault argue that three different anomalies – ambiguity aversion, insensitivity to sample size, and self-control problems – should be related to voter turnout. Then, using data from Sweden, the United States, the United Kingdom, and Canada, they show that self-control problems and ambiguity aversion are related to voter turnout in the expected direction.

Godbout and Turgeon take up the question of the partisan effects of turnout. Voter turnout is declining around the world. As fewer citizens vote, scholars and political observers alike have raised concerns that the political preferences of voters are more likely to be represented than those of non-voters. Their chapter 5 takes on this important question by comparing the partisan and policy preferences of voters and non-voters in Canada. Using over twenty years of survey data from the Canadian Election Studies (1988–2008), Godbout and Turgeon show that there is indeed a significant difference in the political attitudes expressed by these two groups. Specifically, they find that non-voters are more conservative on certain issues and more likely to hold anti-system views than voters. These findings and the econometric techniques used to uncover them thus raise important questions for those who have previously argued that there are no important differences between voters and non-voters.

Part II: Vote Choice

The contribution from Nadeau, Bélanger, and Jérôme examines the effect of the economy on vote choice. Specifically, chapter 6 looks at the relationship between local economic conditions and the vote in national elections in Canada. The authors show that regional economic conditions, namely the provincial unemployment rate, have an impact on vote choice, which is combined with the more important factor of national economic conditions. The authors also make an argument about the varying influence of local economic conditions, cross-nationally reflecting variation in the political and economic importance of regional governments.

Fournier, Cutler, and Soroka's chapter 7 asks whether and how election campaigns have heterogeneous effects across different types of voter. Building on the Converse-McGuire-Zaller model of opinion change, They propose that campaigns should disproportionately affect the voting decisions of voters who are both ambivalent and attentive. The model is tested on campaign events, advertising, debates, and media coverage with rolling cross-section survey data from two Canadian elections. Analyses suggest that the impacts of these real, measured campaign forces are indeed limited to voters who have both high levels of information and are also somewhat ambivalent, or cross-pressured, in their vote choice. These results thus deepen our understanding of political behaviour in a campaign; they also support Zaller's claim that his theory of attitude change applies to election campaigns.

Garand and Xu explore the degree to which government employees differ from other citizens in their political behaviour. The authors build on the work of André Blais and other scholars to reconsider the effects of government employment on vote choice. Previous research based on theories of government growth suggests that government employees differ from other citizens in their political and policy attitudes, levels of voter participation, and the candidates and political parties for whom they vote. As a result they play an important role in shaping government spending and taxation decisions. In chapter 8, Garand and Xu use survey data from the United States, Canada, and other Western democracies to consider the degree to which government bureaucrats differ from other citizens in their vote choices. Their findings suggest that there remains considerable empirical support for this component of the bureau voting theory, i.e., in comparison to individuals not employed in the public sector, government employees tend to vote for liberal parties and candidates. This pattern is consistent across countries and found in the United States, Canada, and other Western democracies.

Part III: Electoral Systems

Scholars are divided over the question of whether polarized pluralism is good for or inimical to democratic legitimacy. In his chapter 9, Anderson argues that this divide is due to the common conation of different dimensions of the electoral supply – party system polarization and the number of parties that require theoretical and empirical separation and specification. Using data from twenty-four democracies around the world, Anderson shows that party system polarization and number of parties strongly and separately influence the attitudes of those citizens who have incentives to take a negative view of the political system. Countries' macro-level supply of choices and individuals' predispositions interactively shape citizen consent such that distinct partisan offerings diminish the negative views within disenchanted segments of the electorate hold. These results paint a more positive picture of the consequences of electoral fragmentation than is common among students of democracy.

Electoral systems have mechanical and psychological effects. Much is known about the mechanical effect, i.e., the disproportionality between parties' shares of votes and seats. However, psychological effects on parties' and voters' behaviour are more difficult to capture. Lachat's chapter 10 examines which factors influence the relative importance of the electoral system effects. The analysis focuses on Switzerland, comparing the outcomes of the PR election of the National Council and of the majoritarian election of the Council of States – the two houses of the Swiss federal parliament. Both institutional and partisan factors are considered: district magnitude, the presence and number of incumbents and small party challengers, and coordination failures within the left-wing or right-wing political camp.

In chapter 10 by Aldrich and Stephenson, the authors examine the incidence of strategic voting cross-nationally, thereby also allowing them to investigate differences in strategic voting across electoral and party system type. They find that behaviour consistent with what we might define as strategic voting is quite widespread. The authors' evidence suggests that both individual and institutional factors affect the extent of strategic voting. In terms of individual level effects, it is particularly political sophistication, partisanship, and political participation that drive strategic behaviour. When it comes to the institutional setting, electoral systems and, relatedly, the number of parties are what matter. However, the authors conclude with a call for more theorizing, as their results are somewhat puzzling in light of current theory on strategic voting.

The chapters in this volume cover a lot of ground substantively and methodologically. However, they all deal with questions of central importance to the study of democratic politics and are connected by a concern with how individuals behave in elections: Why do they vote?

What explains the choices they make at the ballot box? How do the rules of the game – electoral systems – condition this behaviour? These questions are, of course, also the focus of a vast body of research produced by André Blais, to whom this volume is dedicated.

NOTE

1 The dictator game is a canonical game in behavioural economics used to measure altruism. In the basic set-up a player receives an endowment of money and has the option to give some amount away or to keep all of it. The person receiving the money will never know it came from the player, and the player will not know the identity of the receiver. Any money that is given away is a measure of pure altruism, since the player is giving it up with no expectation of receiving anything in return, not even credit for being nice.

References

Adams, James F., Samuel Merrill, III, and Bernard Grofman. 2005. *A Unified Theory of Party Competition: A Cross-National Analysis Integrating Spatial and Behavioral Factors.* Cambridge: Cambridge University Press.

Alesina, Alberto, and Eliana La Ferrera. 2000. "Participation in Heterogeneous Communities." *Quarterly Journal of Economics* 115 (3): 847–904.

Blais, André. 2000. *To Vote or Not to Vote? The Merits and Limits of Rational Choice.* Pittsburgh, PA: University of Pittsburgh Press.

– 2005. "Accounting for the Electoral Success of the Liberal Party in Canada." *Canadian Journal of Political Science* 38 (4): 821–40.

Blais, André, Peter Loewen, and Marc André Bodet. 2002. "Strategic Voting." In *Voters' Veto: The 2002 Election in New Zealand and the Consolidation of Minority Government,* edited by Jack Vowles, Peter Aimer, Susan Banducci, Jeffrey Karp, and Raymond Miller, 68–84. Auckland: Auckland University Press.

Blais, André, and Louis Massicotte. 2002. "Electoral Systems." In *Comparing Democracies 2: New Challenges in the Study of Elections and Voting,* edited by Lawrence LeDuc, Richard G. Niemi and Pippa Norris, 40–69. London: Sage.

Butler, David, and Donald Stokes. 1969. *Political Change in Britain: Forces Shaping Electoral Choice.* New York: St Martin's.

Campbell, Angus, Philip E. Converse, Warren E. Miller, and Donald E. Stokes. 1960. *The American Voter.* Ann Arbor: University of Michigan Press.

Clarke, Harold D., David Sanders, Marianne C. Stewart, and Paul Whiteley. 2009. *Performance Politics and the British Voter*. Cambridge: Cambridge University Press.

Cox, Gary W. 1997. *Making Votes Count: Strategic Coordination in the World's Electoral Systems*. Cambridge: Cambridge University Press.

Dawes, Christopher T., Peter John Loewen, and James H. Fowler. 2011. "Social Preferences and Political Participation." *Journal of Politics* 73 (3): 845–56.

Delli Carpini, Michael X., and Scott Keeter. 1997. *What Americans Know about Politics and Why It Matters*. New Haven, CT: Yale University Press.

Downs, Anthony. 1957. *An Economic Theory of Democracy*. New York: Harper and Row.

Duverger, Maurice. 1959. *Political Parties: Their Organization and Activity in the Modern State*. Paris: A. Colin.

Enelow, James M., and Melvin J. Hinich. 1984. *The Spatial Theory of Voting: An Introduction*. Cambridge: Cambridge University Press.

Fiorina, Morris P. 1981. *Retrospective Voting in American National Elections*. New Haven, CT: Yale University Press.

Fowler, James H., Laura A. Baker, and Christopher T. Dawes. 2008. "Genetic Variation in Political Participation." *American Political Science Review* 102 (2): 233–48.

Fredén, Annika. 2014. "Threshold Insurance Voting in PR Systems: A Study of Voters' Strategic Behavior in the 2010 Swedish General Election." *Journal of Elections, Public Opinion & Parties* 24 (4): 473–92.

Horowitz, Donald L. 1990. "Comparing Democratic Systems." *Journal of Democracy* 1 (4): 73–9.

Hotelling, Harold. 1929. "Stability and Competition." *Economic Journal* 39 (1): 41–57.

Huckfeldt, Robert. 1979. "Political Participation and the Neighborhood Social Context." *American Journal of Political Science* 23 (3): 579–92.

Jesse, Stephen A. 2008. "Partisan Bias, Political Information and Spatial Voting in the 2008 Presidential Election." *Journal of Politics* 72 (1): 327–40.

Johnston, Richard, André Blais, Henry E. Brady, and Jean Crete. 1992. *Letting the People Decide: Dynamics of a Canadian Election*. Cambridge: Cambridge University Press.

Key, V.O. 1949. *Southern Politics in State and Nation*. Knoxville: University of Tennessee Press.

Lazarsfeld, Paul F., Bernard Berelson, and Hazel Gaudet. 1944. *The People's Choice: How the Voter Makes Up His Mind in a Presidential Election*. New York: Duell, Sloan and Pearce.

LeDuc, Lawrence. 1981. "The Dynamic Properties of Party Identification: A Four-Nation Comparison." *European Journal of Political Research* 9 (3): 257–68.

Lijphart, Arend. 1991. "Constitutional Choices for New Democracies." *Journal of Democracy* 2 (1): 72–84.

Loewen, Peter John. 2010. "Antipathy, Affinity, and Political Participation: How Our Concern for Others Makes Us Vote." *Canadian Journal of Political Science* 43 (2): 661–87.

Mondak, Jeffery J. 2010. *Personality and the Foundations of Political Behavior.* Cambridge: Cambridge University Press.

Oliver, J. Eric. 2000. "America City Size and Civic Involvement in Metropolitan." *American Political Science Review* 94 (2): 361–73.

Riker, William H., and Peter C. Ordeshook. 1968. "A Theory of the Calculus of Voting." *American Political Science Review* 62:25–42.

Sinclair, Betsy. 2012. *The Social Citizen: Peer Networks and Political Behavior.* Chicago: University of Chicago Press.

Wong, Cara, Jake Bowers, Daniel Rubenson, Mark Fredrikson, and Ashlea Rundlett. 2015. "Maps in People's Heads as a New Measure for Context." Working paper.

PART I

Voter Turnout

.

2 Altruism, Participation, and Political Context

CINDY D. KAM, SKYLER J. CRANMER, AND
JAMES H. FOWLER

Sometimes the world is messy, and the most parsimonious explanation is wrong.
                                                                    – Jon Elster[1]

Is a theory of political participation that is based solely on self-interest realistic enough to be useful? Social scientists often start with the simple assumption that human beings are driven by self-interest. While this axiom helps simplify otherwise complex strategic interactions, it falls short in explaining a wide range of political phenomena, including two of the dominant foci of behavioural research: public opinion and political participation (Citrin and Green 1990; Mansbridge 1990b, 1990c; Sears and Funk 1990, 1991). In research on public opinion, scholars have searched for the impact of self-interest. Instead of discovering that self-interest is the guiding foundation of policy preferences, it instead appears to be the exception, found in narrow, circumscribed instances (e.g., Campbell 2002; Citrin and Green 1990; Green and Cowden 1992; Sears and Citrin 1985). In research on political participation, predictions from models based solely on self-interest often contradict observed behaviours (e.g., Aldrich 1993; Downs [1957] 1985; Feddersen and Pesendorfer 1996; Ledyard 1982; Myerson 2000; Palfrey and Rosenthal 1985). In the well-known paradox of participation, people actually do turn out in large numbers to vote, protest, or otherwise support a political cause despite the fact that an individual decision to do so has essentially no effect on the political outcome. In response to this paradox, a growing literature suggests an alternative to the self-interested rationale for political behaviour.

We argue that altruism, or a willingness to pay a personal cost to provide benefits to others, can help to explain why some people participate in the political process (Dawes et al. 2012; Dawes, Loewen, and Fowler 2011; Edlin, Gelman, and Kaplan 2007; Fowler 2006; Fowler and Kam 2007; Jankowski 2002, 2004; Loewen 2010). If individuals incorporate benefits to others in their decision, then the potentially minuscule effect of their own action on a political outcome is counterbalanced by the very large number of people who might benefit from it.[2]

However, we argue that the link between altruism and participation may be contingent. Political stakes and political contests evoke multiple motivations and multiple interpretations. If a political outcome appears to have no effect on net benefits to society and/or is merely redistributive (shifting costs or benefits from one party to another), then altruists will gain nothing from investing time and resources in politics and thus will participate no more than individuals who are self-interested. An exception to this rule may occur if one side of a contest is considered disadvantaged over the other and thus deserving of support; altruists may be more likely to act on behalf of those who are perceived to be more deserving of help in that case.[3] We therefore expect the relationship between altruism and participation to be *context-dependent*. Although altruists will generally participate in politics more than individuals who are primarily self-interested, they are likely to participate more only in those circumstances where they think they have a chance to help others.[4]

We test our expectations using the "dictator" game (Forsythe et al. 1994). In our implementation of the dictator game, subjects divide 10 one-dollar bills between themselves and an anonymous individual, and the amount they donate is used as a measure of altruism. Subjects are then asked a number of questions regarding their socio-economic status, political attitudes, support for humanitarian norms, and participation behaviour. Early studies used this technique to study the relationship between altruism and participation (Dawes, Loewen, and Fowler 2011; Fowler 2006; Fowler and Kam 2007), but they focused exclusively on student populations. Later studies expanded the range of subjects (Loewen 2010) and here we also study a non-student population to see if the relationship between altruism and participation holds in a population with more demographic variance than the typical population of "college sophomores." While we do not have a random sample representative of the population as a whole, use of a non-student sample provides support for a somewhat broader claim of generalizability. Moreover, unlike previous studies, we use both self-reported

and *validated* turnout to tie behaviour in the dictator game to participation in political life. Research that connects measures derived from
behavioural economics (such as dictator game behaviours) to political
phenomena is relatively hard to find. The work that does link dictator game behaviours with political phenomena uses self-reported measures, which are prone to intentional or accidental misreporting. Here
we go beyond this existing work by incorporating validated turnout
behaviour, thus alleviating the concern that people may misrepresent
their participation.

We first establish that there is a positive relationship between dictator game giving and political participation in a non-student population,
adding evidence to support the claim that previous results for students
apply to a general population. Second, we show that dictator game giving provides added-value in explaining political participation, above
and beyond self-reported attitudes towards helping others. Third, we
argue that the link between altruism and political life can depend upon
how political stakes are framed, and we provide suggestive evidence in
this regard. When electoral issues are framed as distributive contests,
where costs and benefits are merely shifted from one party to another
and where there is no clear way to connect political activity with making everyone better off, altruists participate no more than egoists.

Regard for Others and Political Life

Empirical conundrums and unexpected acts of selflessness have exposed cracks in the foundational assumption of self-interest. They have
also stimulated academic inquiries into altruism across several disci-
plines, including the biological sciences – where the actions of para-
sites, ants, bees, and guppies are the focus of analysis[5] – and the social
sciences of psychology, sociology, economics, and, at a more halting
pace, in political science.

In psychology, the study of prosocial behaviour enjoyed its heyday
in the 1960s and 1970s, with research focusing on the conditions under
which individuals help others.[6] In the ensuing decades, psychologists
continued to investigate the developmental, cognitive, and emotional
mechanisms underlying why people help others, as well as the situa-
tional determinants of helping behaviours (for a comprehensive review, see Dovidio et al. 2006). Sociologists have examined, among
other things, the causes and consequences of voluntary acts such as
blood and organ donation and civic volunteering as well as disaster

assistance, focusing to a greater degree than psychologists on the creation and maintenance of social norms and relying to a lesser degree on experimental research (Piliavin and Charng 1990; Simmons 1991). Even economists have incorporated the notion of regard for others in their models (e.g., trying to explain decisions to contribute to charitable causes; see, e.g., Schokkaert 2006 for an extensive review of this literature) and in behavioural economics (e.g., in understanding non-equilibrium behaviour in experimental markets, public goods, ultimatum, and dictator games; for reviews, see Camerer 2003; and Fehr and Schmidt 2006).[7]

In political science, sustained research on altruism is harder to find. Monroe's (1998) remarkable work on Jewish rescuers during the Second World War has provided the field with the most comprehensive, and most moving, depiction of altruism (but, ironically, the protagonists themselves would probably have disagreed with the notion that they were engaging in *political* acts). The political science literature, generally, has focused on the applicability, reach, and limitations of the self-interest principle. Where self-interest fails, a variety of other considerations come to the forefront, including partisanship, group membership, values, ideology, and duty. A general concern for others and a willingness to sacrifice for others – altruism – has held a substantially less central role in political science – and we think this is a mistake.[8]

It is a mistake because altruism can be observed in a wide range of contexts (Fehr and Fischbacher 2003; Piliavin and Charng 1990). As such, we think its consequences should be observable in political life as well. We argue that altruism, which we define as the willingness to pay a personal cost to provide benefits to others,[9] is a critical component of the calculus of participation and is missing in traditional self-interested models. Models of participation assuming only instrumental self-interest posit that individuals are expected to participate in order to secure a benefit, B, if their preferred outcome is realized. However, the probability, P, that a given individual will affect an outcome is generally extremely small. Thus, typically the individual cost, C, of participating (e.g., time and effort) is greater than the expected benefit of participation: $C > PB$. In this typical case, rational and purely self-interested individuals will not participate; clearly, this prediction contradicts the observed phenomena of large-scale participation.[10]

We argue that the policy outcomes of political actions do affect individual decision-making. A growing number of scholars (Dawes, Loewen, and Fowler 2011; Edlin, Gelman, and Kaplan 2007; Fowler 2006; Fowler and Kam 2007; Jankowski 2002, 2004) are explicitly including in the calculus of participation the argument that an individual cares about the impact of policies on others as well as themselves. Although a single participatory act may have little effect on a political outcome, the number of people who benefit may be quite large. Thus, those who exhibit sufficient concern for the welfare of others may be willing to engage in costly political participation. Moreover, as people become more concerned for the welfare of others, they should experience greater benefits when political outcomes portend improvements for the welfare of others generally. Thus, altruists will generally be more likely to participate than individuals who are self-interested.

We see the inclusion of altruism into the calculus of participation as more than simply adding a new variable to an existent model. Including altruism in the calculus represents a fundamental theoretical shift away from the self-interest axiom, which has dominated models of participation since their inception in our discipline. We believe that incorporating altruism into the way we think about individual participation in politics is not a final tweak to the canonical model, but rather the first step towards a modern, realistic, and predictive successor to the self-interested model.

Further, we believe that the role of altruism in political participation is context-dependent. We argue that political outcomes can have two effects: (1) they can change the average level of welfare of members of the polity, inducing a societal "net benefit" and/or (2) they can favour particular social and political groups, transferring resources from one part of the society to the other. When altruists believe outcomes affect the average level of welfare in the society, they may believe their actions have the potential to make a large group of individuals better off. Under these conditions we expect altruists to participate more than egoists. However, when they believe that political outcomes have no effect on net welfare and are merely redistributive, then they may believe their actions will make some better off at the same time they make others worse off. Consequently, under these conditions we do not expect to see a distinction between altruists and egoists. Thus, the connection between altruism and political participation may depend upon how the outcomes of political contests are understood.

Finding Altruists among Dictators

Our study contributes to existing empirical work by adopting an innovative measure of altruism and expanding the population of study beyond convenience samples of undergraduates. Previous attempts to examine the relationship between other-regarding behaviour and participation have relied on questions in the National Election Study (NES) pilots. Knack (1992) creates an index of "social altruism" from questions about charity, volunteer work, and community involvement on the 1991 NES Pilot Study and finds a positive relationship between the index and voter turnout. However, the questions used in the index are very close to those used by scholars who argue that the *civic skills* derived from organizational involvement (not the altruistic motivations that lead to it) enhance political participation (Verba, Schlozman, and Brady 1995). Jankowski (2004) finds a relationship between voter turnout and "humanitarian" norms from questions on the 1995 NES Pilot Study. For example, turnout correlates with answers to the question "One of the problems of today's society is that people are often not kind enough to others." These questions certainly reflect expectations about the altruism of others, but it is not clear how they relate to the respondent's own willingness to *bear costs* to provide benefits to others.

While the findings in Knack (1992) and Jankowski (2004) are supportive of the relationship between altruism and political participation, they both rely on respondents' *expressed* preferences for helping others. In neither case do respondents actually experience a cost in order to give a benefit to someone else. In contrast, preferences for helping others are *revealed* in what experimental economists call the "dictator game" (Forsythe et al. 1994). In this game, the experimenter gives player 1 a certain amount of money and then asks the subject to divide that money between herself and player 2. If player 1 is motivated only by her own economic gain, she should keep all the money for herself and allocate nothing to player 2. However, this is not what players normally do. In a survey of dictator game results, Camerer (2003) shows that the mean allocation to player 2 ranges from 10% to 52%. Anonymity conditions tend to decrease the mean allocation, but even in the most anonymous treatments (Hoffman et al. 1994) about 40% of the allocations still exceed 0.

Subjects in our study consist of 112 non-student citizens residing in Yolo County, California. These individuals were recruited at Farmers' Markets and grocery stores in Davis and an adjoining town, from February through May of 2006. The sampling frame was restricted to citizens over the age of eighteen with a permanent residence in Yolo County. Upon approaching the booth, potential subjects were asked if they were residents of Yolo County. They were asked to provide a name, and the researcher looked up the name to determine whether the individual had voted in the previous special election, was registered but did not vote in the previous special election, or was not registered to vote in Yolo County. The subject was classified as one of these three types and assigned a subject identification number to indicate which "type" each was.

These subject identification numbers were written in invisible ink and were unnoticeable from the subject's point of view. Only the researcher knew which "type" the individual was.

Subjects then received a folder containing a set of written instructions. First, they were instructed to play an anonymous version of the dictator game. Each subject received two opaque envelopes. One contained 10 one-dollar bills, and the other was empty. They were instructed to decide how many one-dollar bills they would like to share with an anonymous individual and to put those one-dollar bills into the "small envelope." Subjects were told that their decisions were completely anonymous and that the anonymous recipient would never be able to find out the subject's identity. They were also informed that they would be returning the small envelope to a clear plastic box on display (it contained many, many envelopes). There was no apparent identifying information of any kind on the small envelope, in order to maximize subjects' sense of anonymity in playing the dictator game. After playing the dictator game, subjects then completed a brief questionnaire. Again, to maximize conditions of anonymity, no identifying information of any kind appeared on the survey. Each subject received five dollars for participating in the study, in addition to whatever each chose to keep from the dictator game. The complete instructions appear in the appendix.

Complete anonymity in playing the dictator game and in filling out the surveys would have made it impossible for us to conduct individual-level analyses, however. As we mentioned, there was no *apparent* identifying information on the dictator game envelopes or on the surveys. To enable us to match the dictator game behaviours with the survey responses, subject identification numbers were attached to the dictator game envelopes and to the survey responses in invisible ink.

Subjects in this study were more heterogeneous than student samples used in previous work. They ranged in age from twenty-three to eighty-two, with a mean age of forty. About 58% of subjects were female; 75% were white. Despite the attempt to recruit from all walks of life, the subject pool reflects the fact that some recruitment occurred in a college town: 38% of our subjects had graduate degrees and 41% had bachelor's degrees.

Figure 2.1 displays the distribution of dictator game behaviours among our sample. The distribution is trimodal – a bit out of the ordinary compared with previous research. Early research typically found modes at 0 and at 5, but not at 10 (Camerer 2003). But that research also relied almost exclusively on student samples. Hence, with this design, we reveal slightly different patterns of giving, using a non-student sample.

Table 2.1 provides pairwise correlations between dictator game behaviours and demographics available in the questionnaire.

We see that only two correlations are statistically distinguishable from zero: women give more than men (which is consistent with the literature – Eckel and Grossman 1998),[11] and individuals with higher incomes give more than individuals with lower incomes (which contradicts findings in student populations where high-income individuals tend to give less – Carpenter, Verhoogen, and Burks 2005).[12]

Results from the literature on giving in the dictator game indicate that, while several factors might explain giving, dictator game

Figure 2.1 Dictator Game Behaviours

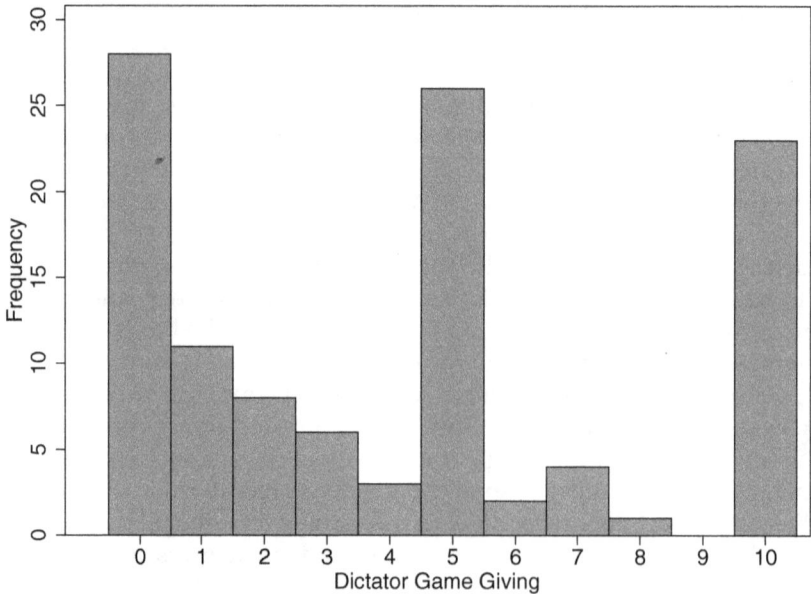

Table 2.1 Pairwise Correlations between Altruism and Individual-Level Characteristics

	Pearson Correlation with Altruism
Age	0.145
Female	0.189*
Income	0.205*
Education	0.150
Non-white	−0.050
Religious attendance	0.117
Partisanship	−0.011
Strength of partisanship	−0.015

Note: All variables coded from 0 to 1.

See appendix for details on variable coding

*$p < 0.10$

allocations may be a good proxy for individual altruism.[13] Indeed, two of the leaders in the field, Camerer and Fehr (2004) write, "Dictator games measure pure altruism" (73), and the utility function used in Andreoni and Miller (2002) to explain behaviour in the dictator game yields a monotonic relationship between the equilibrium allocation in the dictator game and the weight a player places on the other player's utility. In other words, the more a player cares about the well-being of others, the more she will allocate to the other player in the dictator game.[14]

We tested the relationship between dictator giving and altruism by asking respondents four items that represent humanitarianism, which Feldman and Steenbergen (2001) define as "the belief that people have responsibilities toward their fellow human beings and should come to the assistance of others in need" (659). Dictator game allocations and a scale constructed from these questions correlate positively at 0.29 ($p < 0.01$), and in multiple regression dictator game behaviours significantly predict self-reported humanitarianism scores.[15] As a second test, we asked respondents if they had made a personal contribution for Hurricane Katrina relief (the catastrophic hurricane occurred six to nine months prior to the fielding of our study), if they were considering making one, or if they were not considering making one at this time.

People who gave more in the dictator game were more likely to have contributed for Hurricane Katrina relief (or to have considered giving) than those who kept more to themselves (correlation = 0.13, $p < 0.01$), and again this result is robust to inclusion of multiple controls. These two sets of analyses suggest that our altruism measure is, indeed, correlated with what we theoretically believe it should be related to.

Altruism and Political Participation

Our next intention is to establish a baseline relationship between altruism and political participation. Our dependent variable consists of an additive scale of nine political acts, rescaled to range from 0 (none) to 1 (all nine). These political acts include both electoral (contributed to or worked on a campaign), governmental (contacted a public official; participated in a non-work-related protest; contributed to a political organization; been a member of a political organization), and community (been a member of a local board; attended local meetings; worked with others in the community) participation.[16]

Subjects were asked to indicate which acts they had participated in, within the past two years. We begin with a simple model that regresses political participation on altruism, and then we add a series of control variables commonly found in the literature on political participation (see, e.g., Verba, Schlozman, and Brady 1995).

As shown by the OLS estimates in table 2.2, our measure of altruism strongly predicts political participation. This effect is substantial in the bivariate case and withstands the inclusion of a series of control variables.[17]

Our design also enables us to determine the extent to which there is added-value in including dictator game behaviours, compared with the more easily implemented self-reporting questions on humanitarianism and charitable giving. How well do the dictator game behaviours perform, compared with the self-reported measures of humanitarianism or Katrina contributions instead, in predicting political participation? To find out, we re-estimated our models, substituting the humanitarianism scale and Katrina contribution response for the dictator game behaviours, and then substituting the Katrina contribution for the dictator game behaviours.

The results in table 2.3 show that humanitarian norms significantly predict political participation. Katrina contributions are positively, but not significantly, associated with political participation. Most importantly, when all three are included in the model that predicts political

Table 2.2 Dictator Game Behaviour and Political Participation

	Political participation	Political participation
Dictator Game	0.226***	0.179***
Behaviour	0.067	0.067
Age		0.321***
		0.104
Female		−0.033
		0.049
Income		0.076
		0.077
BA degree		−0.003
		0.063
Advanced degree		−0.057
		0.069
Non-white		−0.107*
		0.058
Religious		−0.014
Attendance		0.068
Strength of		0.094
Partisanship		0.084
Intercept	0.253***	0.167**
	0.037	0.077
$p > F$	0.001	0.001
N	111	110

Note: Table entry is the OLS regression coefficient with standard error below.

Dependent variable consists of the number of political acts completed in the last two years, rescaled to range from 0 (none) to 1 (all nine).

***$p < 0.01$; **$p < 0.05$; *$p < 0.10$

participation, only the coefficient on dictator game behaviours remains statistically distinguishable from zero. This model attests to the added-value obtained from looking to a less conventional measure of altruism. Our dictator game measure requires respondents to sacrifice some material benefits to the self in order to help an anonymous other. As

Table 2.3 Comparing the Effects of Dictator Game Behaviour and Attitudes towards Helping Others

	Including dictator game behaviours	Including human- itarian norms	Including Katrina contribution	Combined model
Dictator game	0.179***			0.151**
Behaviour	0.067			0.070
Humanitarian		0.280*		0.190
Norms		0.142		0.145
Katrina			0.058	0.024
Contribution			0.058	0.057
Age	0.321***	0.314***	0.300***	0.304***
	0.104	0.107	0.113	0.110
Female	−0.033	−0.015	−0.017	−0.040
	0.049	0.050	0.052	0.051
Income	0.076	0.108	0.113	0.076
	0.077	0.077	0.078	0.077
BA degree	−0.003	0.006	−0.002	0.005
	0.063	0.065	0.066	0.064
Advanced degree	−0.057	−0.034	−0.038	−0.040
	0.069	0.071	0.073	0.071
Non-white	−0.107*	−0.111*	−0.105*	−0.102*
	0.058	0.059	0.061	0.059
Religious	−0.014	−0.003	0.018	−0.020
Attendance	0.068	0.069	0.069	0.069
Strength of	0.094	0.046	0.080	0.063
Partisanship	0.084	0.088	0.089	0.087
Intercept	0.167**	0.008	0.173**	0.030
	0.077	0.122	0.082	0.121
$p > F$	0.001	0.002	0.001	0.001
N	110	109	109	109

Note: Table entry is the OLS regression coefficient with standard error below.

Dependent variable consists of the number of political acts completed in the last two years, rescaled to range from 0 (none) to 1 (all nine).

***$p < 0.01$; **$p < 0.05$; *$p < 0.10$

such, it is less prone to the problem that "talk is cheap." In other words, it is easier for the less altruistic to make themselves look more altruistic when it comes to espousing humanitarian norms and reporting charitable contributions – doing so is an essentially costless act. Dictator giving, even in the low-stakes game that we created, provides additional discriminatory power – it is harder for the less altruistic to dress as altruists when it means immediately depriving themselves of cash in hand. On the whole, respondents will appear more altruistic when responding to attitudinal questions than to the dictator game, because egoists will be pressured to give the socially desirable response for the attitudinal questions but will feel cross-pressured by self-interested motives when it comes to the dictator game.

Our findings suggest that the positive relationship between political participation and altruism, as measured through dictator game behaviours, holds beyond the "narrow database" (Sears 1986) of student samples. With this sample of non-student adults, we find that altruism significantly predicts political participation across an array of acts. Moreover, dictator game giving provides independent leverage in predicting political participation, even when more conventional measures of other-regardingness are controlled.

Altruism, Turnout, and Political Context

So far we have demonstrated the criterion validity of dictator game behaviours: that dictator game allocations correlate with conventional measures of other-regardingness. We have also shown that altruism predicts participation across a wide-ranging series of acts, where individuals are reporting on behaviour within the last two years. Finally, we have found that dictator game behaviours make an independent contribution to explaining variation in political participation – a contribution that is unmatched by self-reported measures of humanitarianism and charitable giving.

We designed an aspect of our study to gain purchase on an additional research question, one that focuses on the extent to which features of political life resonate or repulse altruists and egoists. In so doing, we are extending existing theory; we seek to elaborate upon the simple question of whether or not altruism predicts participation, to examine the conditions under which altruism does or does not spur action in political life. As such, this theoretical extension aims to build a more comprehensive model of political participation – one that incorporates both individual predispositions and political context.

To do so, we took advantage of an unusual election. Recall that when subjects approached the booth to participate in our study, the researcher identified their turnout status in the recent November 2005 special election held in the state of California. Each subject was assigned a subject identification number that indicated whether he or she had voted, was registered but had not voted, or was not listed on the county voting rolls. While the special election featured some state-wide ballot propositions (each of which failed, most by a landslide) and a local school board election, the centrepiece of the election was a local ballot proposition called Measure X. In the city of Davis, turnout on Measure X was quite high for an off-year election: 60.7%, comparable to the turnout in the October 2003 California Recall election (68%) and comparable to turnout in the 2002 midterm elections (61%).[18]

Measure X asked voters to determine whether a parcel of farmland should be rezoned for residential and commercial use. Developers proposed to build just under 2,000 residential units and a set of shopping centres on a 400-acre plot of land. Measure X was a serious and highly divisive political issue. It received front-page lead story attention in the town's local paper nearly every day in November leading up to the election, as well as five days in October and four days in September. It was the single most expensive political campaign ever run in the city of Davis (*Davis Enterprise*, 2 November 2005). It generated far more letters to the editor than any other issue at stake in the election: in the week preceding the election, excerpts from ninety-five letters *just on Measure X* were printed in the paper.

Measure X supporters and opponents lobbed an array of arguments back and forth; most focused on who would stand to gain and who would stand to lose as a consequence of the proposed development. One central concern in the city of Davis is affordable housing: the median home price at the time was $540,000. Supporters of Measure X pointed out that at least 1% of the developed homes would be affordable housing units (which would be available at a rate of fourteen units per year, over the course of ten years). Opponents of Measure X countered that any affordable housing units would be dominated by large, million-dollar homes. The local paper's most prominent columnist and political pundit noted that even if affordable housing units were made available in the new development, "the average $667,000 Davis homeowner is scared to death that a home comparable to his may be built ... for $400,000" (*Davis Enterprise*, 8 November 2005). The columnist went on to point out that the more affordable the units in the new development were, "the more homeowners will vote against the project and the more renters will vote in favor" (*Davis Enterprise*, 8 November 2005). On balance, the city's assessment of Measure X was that the impact of the developed housing was "fiscally neutral" (*Davis Enterprise*, 21 September 2005), and the city's financial director was paraphrased as advising voters to evaluate the project "for its amenities rather than what it might do to the city budget" (*Davis Enterprise*, 5 October 2005). In other words, there was no consensus on whether voting for or against Measure X would produce a societal benefit.

Another issue of contention concerned the environmental impacts of the proposed housing development. Supporters of Measure X argued that the environmental impacts would be mitigated in various ways; for example, through the use of solar energy in the developed homes, the protection of wetlands, the construction of bike paths to minimize car use. The key designer of the Measure X project had received Sierra Club endorsement and international acclaim for the environmentally friendly design of a prior, smaller-scale project in the 1970s. Opponents argued that the environmental impacts were negative due to worsened air quality and increased traffic experienced by those living near the proposed development; further, the local Sierra Club took a stand against Measure X. There were strong arguments on both sides, and there was no clear sense of whether Measure X would hurt or harm the environment.

A key campaign event occurred one month prior to the election, when Trader Joe's, a well-known West Coast–based specialty food store, announced it would set up shop in the proposed development. Homes in the town were blanketed with wine-bottle-shaped flyers proclaiming that Trader Joe's was coming to Davis. The city had been courting the food store for several years, to no avail. The local paper's most prominent columnist wryly remarked, "Here comes Trader Joe's ... no, I am not making this up ... but yes, there is a catch ... the catch is, if you want a Trader Joe's in Davis, you have to vote 'YES' on Measure X" (*Davis Enterprise*, 6 October 2005). Another element to the Measure X campaign, then, was a promise of clear benefits for the self-interested (budget-conscious foodies obsessed with Trader Joe's) in the town. This, too, makes the stakes of Measure X quite distinct from typical political contests.

The campaigns for and against Measure X fought over who would stand to gain and who would stand to lose. Many of the gains would be experienced by people who eventually might be candidates for residing in the proposed development; many of the losses would be experienced by people living near the proposed development. Nearly every argument about potential benefits to the public was countered; as one local columnist summarized, "[Measure X] is a very mixed bag" (*Davis Enterprise*, 25 October 2005). Much of the debate was distributive: about how the proposed development would shift benefits to some individuals at a cost borne by others. The League of Women Voters, which took a public position on all of the state-wide propositions and has regularly endorsed national, state, and local candidates, publicly stated that it took no position on Measure X. The local Audubon Society, similarly, publicly stated that it took no position on Measure X. In addition, the campaign included key themes that would trigger self-interested considerations. The fact that a "Yes" vote would open the door to Trader Joe's locating in town provided a clear opportunity for individuals to translate self-interested preferences into their decision of whether and how to vote. And the spectre of more affordable housing highlighted different costs and benefits for homeowners and renters. As a local political pundit predicted, "There is a large, very silent group of voters who are thinking with their pocket books. No one will admit to such a selfish motive, but trust me, it's out there. The size of this voting bloc will determine whether Measure X passes or fails" (*Davis Enterprise*, 19 October 2005). In the end, voters overwhelmingly defeated Measure X, with 41.2% of voters supporting it and 58.7% opposing it.

We are interested in whether the core finding that altruists participate more in political life than egoists holds within a divisive, distributive political context drenched with self-interested appeals such as the one surrounding Measure X. We suspected the answer would be no, since the political stakes were framed in such starkly redistributive, egoistic ways. To identify the effect of altruism on voter turnout in this election we estimate a model using validated vote as the dependent variable, where a value of 1 indicates validated turnout in the November 2005 special election, and 0 indicates all others.

In the bivariate regression in table 2.4, altruism is not a significant predictor of validated vote. After including a series of controls, altruism is still not a significant predictor of validated vote. To determine if our results were a function of how we coded the dependent variable, we re-estimated the relationship between turnout and altruism, using two alternative models. Recall that the first version assigns a value of one to all subjects whose vote could be validated and a value of zero to all others. In the next model, we recoded the dependent variable to a value of 0 if registered but did not vote, 1 if registered and voted, with all others dropped from the analysis, on the idea that we might want to examine the propensity to vote among those who already were registered. These results appear in the second set of estimates, and still, altruism fails to predict turnout.[19]

Finally, we included a self-reported measure of turnout, acquired in the survey. We assign a value of 1 to those who are "sure" they voted, and a value of 0 to all others. These estimates appear in the third set of results, and altruism continues to be an insignificant predictor of turnout. If our altruism measure were solely a function of social desirability, then we would have expected to see a strong and significant relationship between dictator game behaviour and self-reported turnout. This, however, is not the case. While the relationship is positive, it is not distinguishable from zero. Moreover, when we restrict the analysis to those who were registered voters, altruism still does not significantly predict self-reported turnout in the special election.[20]

Notice, too, that we have a hard time predicting voter turnout using these models. All of the bivariate models are insignificant (judging by the p-value on the χ^2 test). However, the addition of individual-level covariates such as age, religious attendance, and partisanship significantly contributes to explaining variation in the dependent variable, across most of the models. This suggests that lack of power is not the issue.

What's the difference? Why does altruism fail to distinguish voters from non-voters in this special election? We believe there are two possible explanations. The first is that the tenor of the campaign disillusioned and dismayed altruists, turning them away from participating in the election, while it simultaneously drew in egoists. The second explanation is that altruists participated at the "normal" level, but egoists turned out at an unusually high rate.

Our data suggest some gentle support for the first interpretation. The average level of altruism among non-registered subjects is 0.35, whereas the average altruism among registered subjects (regardless of whether they turned out in the election) is 0.43. This difference, while not statistically distinguishable from zero, is consistent with our initial story about altruism and participation in political life in general: altruists are more prepared to participate in political life.

However, among those who were registered to vote, the average level of altruism among those who stayed home was 0.46, whereas the average altruism among those who turned out in the special election was 0.42. These small differences, combined with our small sample size, make any statistical conclusions difficult; however, the data are suggestive in this regard. What these results indicate is that although altruism may provide a general propensity to participate in political life, the nature of political debate may attenuate this relationship.

Altruism and the Adversarial Electoral Arena

The results reported above are consistent with a story about how political life generally encourages altruists to participate in politics, but particular contexts can attenuate that link. The results might also be interpreted more generally as reflecting the limits of how altruism predicts participation in the electoral system. Fowler (2006), for example, reports that the effect of altruism on turnout in a partisan primary depends upon strength of partisanship. On its own, altruism does not predict turnout in the primary; strength of partisanship provides the lens through which the benefits to electoral contests can be understood.

To determine whether it is the nature of electoral contests or this specific election that hampers the connection between altruism and participation, we re-analysed the political participation data, categorizing the nine acts into three groups – campaign-based, local issue–based, political organization–based – as well as two separate acts: protesting and contacting a public official. We find that altruism does not significantly predict participation in electoral politics (campaign contributions or campaign work). It does, however, significantly predict participating in local issues (attending meetings, working on a local issue, and volunteering on a board) and organizational participation (membership and contributions), and it significantly predicts contacting a public official and participating in a protest.[21]

Electoral contests are marked by winners and losers, and such political outcomes can be seen as zero-sum where one side loses, while the other wins. Other political acts may be less vulnerable to being cast in distributive terms: working with others on a local issue, or contacting a public official, or belonging to a political organization. These acts are less overtly conflictual and thus might be more amenable to altruistic motivations.

Table 2.4 Dictator Game Behaviours and Turnout in a Special Election

	Validated vote: All subjects 1 if voted, 0 otherwise		Validated vote: Registered voters 1 if voted, 0 otherwise		Self-report: All subjects 1 if sure voted, 0 otherwise		Self-report: Registered voters 1 if sure voted, 0 otherwise	
Dictator game	0.034	−0.116	−0.195	−0.268	0.362	0.497	0.118	0.404
Behaviour	0.327	0.405	0.374	0.472	0.353	0.404	0.412	0.476
Age		0.040***		0.019		0.036***		0.028*
		0.011		0.013		0.012		0.015
Female		−0.027		−0.130		−0.151		−0.329
		0.308		0.369		0.304		0.393
Income		0.136		0.260		−0.821*		−1.444**
		0.471		0.558		0.481		0.601
BA degree		−0.170		−0.063		0.082		−0.208
		0.361		0.414		0.369		0.473
Advanced		0.325		0.487		0.326		0.409
degree		0.412		0.462		0.420		0.507
Non-white		−0.304		−0.389		−0.007		0.457
		0.350		0.410		0.347		0.486
Religious		−1.145***		−0.736		−0.830**		−0.649
Attendance		0.433		0.488		0.417		0.522
Partisanship		−1.591***		−2.308**		−1.174		−2.158**
		0.663		0.903		0.828		0.930
Intercept	0.212	0.199	0.684	1.783	0.474	0.186		2.099
	0.181	0.636	0.217	0.825	0.188	0.670		0.924
lnL	−75.832	−56.592	−53.364	−41.646	−64.554	−56.496	−42.274	−35.582
$p > \chi2$	0.917	0.000	0.603	0.012	0.303	0.070	0.774	0.159
N	112	111	91	90	112	111	91	90

Note: Table entry is the probit regression coefficient with standard error below.

***$p < 0.01$; **$p < 0.05$; *$p < 0.10$

Conclusion

Harold Lasswell (1936) famously described politics as "who gets what, when, how." According to Lasswell, the political process is fundamentally defined in distributive terms. This is one view of politics and the political process, but it is clearly not the only one. We believe altruism is an important variable to study *precisely because we think political life is not always viewed this way by ordinary citizens.* For the less sceptical (e.g., the broad class of theorists and empiricists who are believers in the "classical theory of democracy"), political life could be an arena in which political actors work towards the common or public good – or, at the very least, political life might be motivated by considerations beyond the distributive gains accruing to the self.

As such, we began this enterprise with an interest in identifying ways that political participation might be considered instrumental. We did so by considering the possibility that individuals incorporate non-self-interested incentives into their decisions about whether to participate in political life. Our altruism theory suggests that individuals gain utility from political participation when participatory acts provide benefits to others, even when conducting those acts imposes a personal cost.

We have gone beyond existing research by testing the criterion validity of dictator game behaviours. By showing that dictator game behaviours correlate well with humanitarian norms and charitable contributions, we lend support to the interpretation of dictator game giving as a measure of altruism, which we conceptualize as a willingness to bear personal costs to improve the welfare of others. We have extended previous research, too, by observing dictator game behaviours among a non-student sample and by showing that the findings reported elsewhere regarding the relationship between altruism and political participation replicate beyond student subjects to non-students. Altruism, that is, how people play the dictator game, predicts participation across a variety of acts. Moreover, how people play the dictator game provides an independent contribution, over and above that of self-reported attitudes, in explaining variation in participation. As such, our work illustrates the utility of incorporating measures from behavioural economics into models of participation.

Finally, we extend existing work by suggesting that the effect of altruism might be contingent upon circumstance. By situating our research within an actual political contest, we suggest that in political contests where the stakes are distributive and where it is not clear that

Table 2.5 Dictator Game Behaviour and Electoral, Local, and Organizational Politics

	Electoral acts	Local acts	Organizational acts	Contact public official	Protest
Dictator game	0.149	0.526***	0.410*	0.806**	0.780**
Behaviour	0.190	0.197	0.228	0.392	0.387
Age	0.018***	0.013**	0.003	0.031***	0.009
	0.005	0.005	0.006	0.011	0.010
Female	−0.240*	−0.116	0.067	−0.408	0.233
	0.140	0.145	0.169	0.291	0.288
Income	0.339	0.018	0.402	0.017	0.075
	0.222	0.230	0.267	0.443	0.449
BA degree	−0.073	−0.054	−0.107	0.450	0.258
	0.178	0.184	0.214	0.369	0.375
Advanced	−0.163	−0.516**	−0.117	0.535	0.234
degree	0.196	0.203	0.236	0.398	0.403
Non-white	−0.176	−0.307*	−0.445**	−0.509	0.188
	0.166	0.172	0.200	0.344	0.339
Religious	−0.205	0.208	0.125	−0.290	−0.202
Attendance	0.195	0.202	0.234	0.405	0.395
Strength of	0.338	0.174	−0.042	−0.147	−0.233
Partisanship	0.295	0.305	0.354	0.589	0.700
Partisanship	0.296	−0.004	0.257	−0.269	1.508
	0.355	0.368	0.427	0.714	0.929
Intercept	−0.375	0.097	0.570	−1.332**	−2.475***
	0.302	0.313	0.363	0.618	0.691
$p > F$	0.000	0.001	0.003	0.146	0.070
N	110	110	110	110	110

Notes: Columns 1–3: Table entry is the OLS regression coefficient with standard error below. Columns 4–5: Table entry is the probit regression coefficient with standard error below.

***$p < 0.01$; **$p < 0.05$; *$p < 0.10$

either political outcome will garner a net gain to society, altruism does not predict turnout. These results hold whether we use a validated vote measure or a self-reported vote measure. Granted, we have selected a unique case in which to investigate our theory; while perhaps not an inscrutable test case, we suggest that our work satisfies the characteristics of a "plausibility probe," an analysis that "strengthen[s] the prospects" of a theory, but that requires more rigorous, cross-case testing before the theory can be validated (Eckstein 1975, 112). This study of the special election over Measure X has provided us with a stronger footing for arguing that the relationship between altruism and political participation may depend upon how political stakes are framed.[22]

Altruism is likely to have broader applications beyond political participation, and our innovative measures might serve other researchers' purposes in this regard. At a very general level, altruism might have implications for individuals' understandings of politics and subsequent beliefs about political processes. Altruists may see politics as a forum for the production of policies to improve the public good, and thus they might favour political processes that enhance participation and dialogue, over adversarial rules (Mansbridge [1980] 1983). Altruists might oppose policies that are targeted at specific groups and instead favour policies that are more generally applied, much as humanitarians might (Feldman and Steenbergen 2001). Altruists may be more willing to withstand present-day inconveniences to invest in improvements for the future – e.g., in order to protect the environment for future generations. Moreover, features of political life (like specific types of political debate and campaign appeals) may suppress or activate altruistic motivations.

Altruism, as we have described it, refers to a general regard for others – regardless of who they are. This, no doubt, is an extreme form of other-regardingness – one extreme point on a continuum of regard, anchored on the one side by concern for the self and anchored on the other by concern for others, generally. Group perspectives – considerations of group-based identity, group solidarity – fall in between in this view. For the egoist, the "social moron," to use Amartya Sen's phrase (1990, 37), the universe encompasses the individual, period; the outside world is a "warre of every man against every man" (Hobbes [1651] 1904, 85). Moving further along this continuum, the social world for the ethnocentric is categorized into virtuous ingroups deserving praise and assistance and dastardly outgroups deserving disdain and scorn (Sumner [1906]

2002; Kinder and Kam 2009). Moving still further along to the end of the continuum, for the altruist, or the "cosmopolitan" to use Nussbaum's (1996) phrase, all human beings become part of the relevant community or ingroup, and a concern for others, generally, supplants the ingroup/outgroup biases of ethnocentrism. Up to this point, we have treated altruism and egoism as distinct categories – but they are probably better viewed as points on a continuum. Exploring these conceptual relationships – and determining the extent to which and the conditions under which political entrepreneurs, political institutions, and political contexts can activate the predispositions of citizens located along this continuum – would be an important and useful extension to our work. In short, we urge readers to take seriously the notion that when some individuals contemplate political life, they encounter and embrace the notion that political processes and political outcomes are valuable not because of the benefits they promise to the self, but because of the benefits they portend for others.

Appendix: Dictator Game Instructions and Question Text

Sacramento Area Voter Survey

Please read these instructions carefully.

In the envelope with these instructions you will find 10 $1 bills. You must choose how to divide the 10 $1 bills between yourself and an anonymous individual. You may keep all, none, or some of the money – the decision is up to you and will be completely anonymous. You will never be able to find out the identity of the anonymous individual, and the anonymous individual will never be able to find out your identity.

If you choose to share some $1 bills, take that number of $1 bills and put them back in the small envelope. We will then mail any money that is in the small envelope to a randomly selected individual in the city of Woodland.

Please seal the small envelope once you have finished.

Once you have sealed the small envelope with any money you may have chosen to share, please answer the enclosed survey.

After you are finished answering the enclosed survey,

- Please seal the survey in the large envelope.
- You will place the small envelope in the clear locked box held by the researcher. This box will not be unlocked until the end of the survey, so we will not be able to identify you with your decisions or survey responses.
- Please return the survey sealed in the large envelope to the researcher.

Thank you very much for your time.

Question Text

Humanitarianism Norms **(Response Options: Five points, Strongly Agree to Strongly Disagree)**

One should always find ways to help others less fortunate than oneself.

It is best not to get too involved in taking care of other people's needs.

A person should always be concerned about the well-being of others.

People tend to pay more attention to the well-being of others than they should.

Additive scale ranging from 0 (Least Humanitarian) to 1 (Most Humanitarian)

Katrina Contribution: Have you personally made a charitable contribution for hurricane (Katrina) relief, are you considering doing so, or is that not something you are considering at this time? (Response Options: Already have made a contribution / Considering doing so / Not considering doing so at this time) *Coded in three categories: 0 (Not considering) to 1 (Already made)*

Participation (Response Options: Yes/No):

In the past two years, have you worked as a volunteer – that is, for no pay at all or for only a token amount – for a candidate running for national, state, or local office?

In the past two years have you contributed money – to an
individual candidate, a political party, a political action committee, or any other organization that supports candidates or
ballot propositions in elections?

In the past two years, have you served in a voluntary capacity –
that is, for no pay at all or for only a token amount – on any
local governmental board or council that deals with community problems and issues such as a town council, a school
board, a zoning board, a planning board, or the like?

In the past two years have you regularly attended meetings of
an official local government board or council?

In the past two years, aside from membership on a board or
council or attendance at meetings, have you informally gotten
together with or worked with others in your community or
neighbourhood to try to deal with some community problem?

In the past two years, aside from contacts made as a regular
part of your job, have you telephoned, written a letter to,
or visited a government official to express your views on a
public issue?

In the past two years, have you taken part in a protest, march,
or demonstration on some national or local issue (other than
a strike against your employer)?

In the past two years, not counting membership dues, have you
given money to any organizations that take stands on any
public issues – either locally or nationally?

In the past two years, have you been a member of any organizations that take stands on any public issues – either locally
or nationally?

Additive scale ranging from 0 (No acts) to 1 (All nine acts)

Self-Reported Turnout: In talking to people about elections, we find
that they are sometimes not able to vote because they're sick,
they're not registered, they don't have the time, or they have
difficulty getting to the polls. Did you happen to vote in the
November 2005 special election? (Response Options: I did not
vote / I thought about voting this time – but didn't / I usually
vote, but I didn't this time / I am sure I voted)
Coded 1 if "sure I voted" and 0 otherwise

Age: **What is your age?** (Open-ended)
Rescaled to range from 0 (23) to 1 (82).

Female: **Are you male or female?** (Response Options: Male/
Female)
Coded 0 if male, 1 if female

Income: Please choose the category that describes the total
amount of income earned in 2004 by your FAMILY. Consider
all forms of income, including salaries, tips, interest and
dividend payments, scholarship support, student loans,
parental support, social security, alimony, and child
support, and others. (Response Options: $15,000 or
under/$15,001 – $25,000/$25,001 – $35,000/$35,001 –
$50,000/$50,001 – $65,000/$65,001 – $80,000/$80,001 –
$100,000/over $100,000)
Coded in eight categories: 0 ($15,000 or under) to 1 (over $100,000)

BA Degree/Adv Degree: What is the highest level of education
that you have completed? (Response Options: Less than a High
School Diploma / High School Diploma / Vocational Training /
Attended College / Bachelor's Degree / Graduate Degree /
Other)
Two Dummies: BA Degree; Adv Degree; all others serve as sup-
pressed reference group

Non-white: Which of the following categories best describes you?
(Response Options: Asian / Black / Hispanic-Latino / Native-
American /White / Other)
Coded 0 if white; 1 for all others.

Religious Attendance: How often do you attend religious ser-
vices? (Response Options: Every week / Almost every week /
Once or twice a month / A few times a year / Never)
Coded in five categories: 0 (never) to 1 (every week)

Partisanship: Generally speaking, do you usually think of yourself as a Republican, a Democrat or what? (Response Options:
Strong Democrat / Democrat / Independent, But Closer to
Democrats / Independent / Independent, But Closer to Repub-
licans / Republican / Strong Republican)

Coded in seven categories: 0 (Strong Republican) to 1 (Strong Democrat)

Strength of Partisanship: *Based on Partisanship question*
Coded in four categories: 0 (Independent) to 1 (Strong Partisan)

NOTES

1 Elster (1990, 45), critiquing the assumption that all human beings are motivated by selfishness.

2 Chapter 3 provides other useful insights into how the effects of these basic
factors for turnout matter differently between individuals.

3 For example, Eckel and Grossman (1998) manipulate the target of dictator
games to ascertain the role that altruism might play in these games; they
find that subjects are much more likely to give when the target is the Red
Cross compared with an anonymous individual. Perceptions of deserving-
ness can increase expressions of altruism.

4 See Mansbridge (1990b, 21–2) for a more extended discussion of how
institutions and political contexts can activate self-interested versus other-
regarding motivations.

5 Darwin's "survival of the fittest" doctrine suggests that self-interested
organisms will have the greatest fitness (or chance of survival): "Natural
selection appears to be a process that promotes selfishness and stamps out
altruism" (Sober and Wilson 1998, 3). At the group level, Darwin's doctrine
does not fare so well, as Darwin himself noted. Groups in which certain
members are willing to engage in altruistic acts heighten the group's
overall fitness, suggesting there is some evolutionary advantage to altruism within groups. Here, note that *altruism* as it is defined by evolutionary
biologists does not require intention – merely an act by which an individual organism "increases the fitness of others and decreases the fitness
of the actor" (17). For a review of the evolutionary biologists' approach to
altruism, see Sober and Wilson (1998).

6 This research on why people offer help (or fail to offer help) to others
was stimulated by the Kitty Genovese incident, in which a young woman
was brutally attacked on the street, in view or within earshot of at least
thirty-eight bystanders, and was eventually killed. Not a single bystander
intervened. See Dovidio et al. (2006, 19–20) for a discussion. Prosocial
behaviour incorporates a wide variety of acts, including *helping* (in which

an individual performs an act that benefits someone else), *altruism* (which, in the formulation of Dovidio et al., requires benevolent intention and assistance provided without the expectation of benefits to the self), and *cooperation* (where more than one individual works to produce a common good that is beneficial to more than a single actor).

7 In their stunning set of cross-cultural experiments in fifteen small-scale societies, Henrich et al. (2004) report that "there is no society in which experimental behavior is even roughly consistent with the canonical model of self-interested actors" (5).

8 Work by Wilson and Banfield (1963, 1964, 1971) is relevant here, although the specific term *altruism* is not used. Instead, Wilson and Banfield suggest that individuals are either "public-regarding" or self-oriented in their dispositions towards politics, as evidenced, say, by support for public good provision or willingness to pay taxes for the provision of public goods that benefit others.

9 Defining altruism is a subject of ongoing controversy – one we do not intend to resolve here. Some scholars require motivation, intent, and sacrifice; one foundational definition defines altruism as "behavior carried out to benefit another without anticipation of rewards from external sources" (Macaulay and Berkowitz 1970, 3). Some definitions require a successful outcome for the target; others merely intent. Others say an altruistic act is any act in which "the actor could have done better for himself had he chosen to ignore the effect of his choice on others" (Margolis 1982, 15), thus an altruistic act "need not have zero or negative value to the actor" (15). Some equate altruism with any form of other-regardingness (including group-based preferences – Margolis 1982). Others restrict altruism to refer to a willingness to help anyone, regardless of who they are (Monroe 1998). Finally, some definitions of altruism require that the motivation be *strictly* other-oriented: acts that benefit others but driven by egoistic motivations (say, alleviation of guilt, or feeling better about oneself, or mood maintenance) do not count as altruism (see, e.g., a discussion by Simmons 1991, 6). Andreoni's (1990) discussion of "pure" and "impure" altruism allows for this distinction: under pure altruism, individuals "care about the well-being of others" (Meier 2006, 18). For impure altruism, individuals are motivated by the "warm glow" that they themselves receive from conducting the altruistic act: "People care not only about the utility of the recipient but receive some private goods benefit from their pro-social behavior *per se*" (19). For a parallel discussion from the psychological literature, see Karylowski's (1982) typology of "exocentric" and "endocentric" sources of altruism. The former refers to concern for others; the latter to concern for the self.

A characteristic of altruistic behaviour (which makes it distinct from, say, group favouritism) is that altruistic individuals do not generally restrict their altruistic actions to those that will benefit specific groups. Altruists tend to identify with humanity generally rather than any specific subgroup (Monroe 1998).

10 This is typically referred to as the paradox of voting, but its properties extend easily to other political acts. Riker and Ordeshook (1968) proposed a modification of the related "calculus of voting" by introducing a D term to capture the benefit to the self of fulfilling one's personal "duty." This approach specifies that individuals gain utility through the expressive act of participation. In this model, the participatory act is not instrumental; that is, utility derived from fulfilling a duty is unrelated to the policy outcome and the benefits it might import.

11 But see Andreoni and Vesterlund (2001), who explore the gender dynamics of price elasticities.

12 Higher rates of giving in our sample might be consistent with the possibility that altruism functions as "a luxury good, being chosen with proportionately greater frequency as resources rise" (Mansbridge 1990a, 259). The argument is similar to that made for post-materialist values (Inglehart 1971). Note, though, that altruism still emerges among those who are not well-off; Carpenter, Verhoogen, and Burks (2005) report that students who come from families with higher incomes tend to give less in the dictator game. See Mansbridge (1990a, 259) for a discussion of other exceptions.

13 Another explanation for excess giving is that subjects do not understand the game and are just making random allocations. Andreoni and Miller (2002) address this concern by examining within-subject patterns of choices in their series of dictator games with different payoffs. They find that 98 per cent of the subjects make choices that are consistent with the general axiom of revealed preferences across eight treatments, suggesting that most of them understand the game and are not choosing randomly.

14 This is not to say that the same individual will always play the dictator game in the same fashion. Generosity in dictator game giving is sensitive to a number of manipulable features of the game, including the conditions of anonymity, the recipient of the allocation (whether the recipient is anonymous or known, identified as an individual or an organization, etc.). See Meier (2006) for a discussion.

15 A similar significant relationship between dictator game giving and humanitarianism items is reported by Fong (2007), who correlates N-player dictator game giving by student subjects with items that are similar (though not identical) to those that we use.

16   Although some participation researchers argue for analysing not just the quantity of participation but the type of participation (e.g., Leighley 1995), many other participation researchers (e.g., Verba, Schlozman, and Brady 1995) analyse an individual's underlying propensity to be politically engaged, and hence they construct indices of participation based on disparate acts. Existing literature thus gives us some justification in combining the participation variables into a single dimension. The additive scale ranges from 0 to 9 acts, with a mean of 3.13, standard deviation of 2.42. For the nine items, Cronbach's $\alpha = 0.78$. Factor analysis yields an eigenvalue for the first factor of 2.62. The second factor trails far behind, at a value of 0.49, falling below the Kaiser criterion of 1. We conclude that the items can, indeed, be combined into a single scale.

17   Part of our contribution is examining dictator game behaviours among a non-student sample. In order to go beyond captive student samples and to entice non-students to participate in the study, we felt it necessary to design a very brief questionnaire. This trade-off produces an admittedly short list of controls that omits several covariates that might be both related to altruism and predictive of participation (e.g., information, civic skills, efficacy). We note that Fowler and Kam (2007) analyse a similar set of variables (drawn from a student sample) and show that the inclusion of information, civic skills, and efficacy (among other control variables) does little to the substantive and statistical significance of altruism in predicting political participation.

18   To preserve anonymity, the specific subject identification number was never attached to an identifying name. Instead, subjects were assigned ID numbers in the 100 series (e.g., 101, 102, etc.) if the county listed them as having voted in the 2005 November special election; in the 200 series if the county listed them as registered but not having voted; and in the 300 series if they were not listed on the rolls. In hindsight, had we attached an identifying tag between the subject's name and the ID number, we would have been able to validate voting behaviour in previous elections. Unfortunately, our design does not enable us to go beyond the November 2005 special election.

19   Ideally, we would have estimated a selection model to account for the systematic processes that predict (1) registration and (2) turnout. Unfortunately, we lack the requisite measures to properly identify such a model. Sartori's (2003) binary-selection model that allows for identical predictions in both selection and outcome models did not converge.

20   This dependent variable provides us with another opportunity to deal with the question of whether our dictator game behaviour largely reflects

social desirability rather than sincere regard for others. Because we have both validated and self-reported turnout, we can generate a measure of "misremembering" that reflects whether there is a social desirability bias in the respondent's answer. This measure is coded 1 for respondents who said they voted (but did not) and 0 for all others (those who said they did not vote but actually did are assigned a value of 0 because this is not the socially desirable response). A probit regression that includes dictator game allocations alone yields a coefficient of 0.298, standard error of 0.374, and p-value of ~0.43. Even after inclusion of the series of control variables, dictator game allocations are still not significantly related to social desirability bias.

21 We have grouped the nine acts into theoretically relevant categories. In models where we estimated the effect of altruism on each act separately, altruism was not a significant predictor for either of the electoral acts (the probit coefficients are 0.18, s.e. = 0.38, p ~0.64, and b = 0.28, s.e. = 0.43, p ~0.53 for campaign contributions and campaign work, respectively). Altruism is a significant predictor for two of the three local acts (its effect is moderate though not statistically distinguishable from zero for attending local meetings, b = 0.41, s.e. = 0.48, p ~0.39). It is a statistically significant predictor for one of the two organizational acts (its effect is moderate though not statistically distinguishable from zero for organizational membership, b = 0.42, s.e. = 0.36, p ~0.24).

22 An experimental design that manipulates the frame of particular electoral contexts could validate the theory; we strongly encourage such follow-up work.

References

Aldrich, John H. 1993. "Rational Choice and Turnout." *American Journal of Political Science* 37 (1): 246–78.

Andreoni, James. 1990. "Impure Altruism and Donations to Public Goods: A Theory of Warm-Glow Giving." *Economic Journal (London)* 100 (June): 464–77.

Andreoni, James, and Lise Vesterlund. 2001. "Which Is the Fair Sex? Gender Differences in Altruism." *Quarterly Journal of Economics* 116:293–312.

Andreoni, James, and John Miller. 2002. "Giving According to GARP: An Experimental Test of the Consistency of Preferences for Altruism." *Econometrica* 70 (2): 737–53.

Camerer, Colin F. 2003. *Behavioral Game Theory: Experiments in Strategic Interaction*. Princeton: Princeton University Press.

Camerer, Colin F., and Ernst Fehr. 2004. "Measuring Social Norms and Preferences Using Experimental Games: A Guide for Social Scientists." In *Foundations of Human Sociality: Economic Experiments and Ethnographic Evidence from
Fifteen Small-Scale Societies*, edited by Joseph Henrich, Robert Boyd, Samuel
Bowles, Colin Camerer, Ernst Fehr, and Herbert Gintis, 55–95. Oxford: Oxford University Press.

Campbell, Andrea Louise. 2002. "Self-Interest, Social Security, and the Distinctive Participation Patterns of Senior Citizens." *American Political Science
Review* 96 (3): 565–74.

Carpenter, Jeffrey, Eric Verhoogen, and Stephen Burks. 2005. "The Effects of
Stakes in Distribution Experiments." *Economics Letters* 86 (3): 393–8.

Citrin, Jack, and Donald Philip Green. 1990. "The Self-Interest Motive in
American Public Opinion." *Research in Micropolitics* 3:1–28.

Dawes, Christopher T., Magnus Johannesson, Erik Lindqvist, Peter
John Loewen, Robert Ostling, Marianne Bonde, and Frida Priks.
2012. "Generosity and Political Preferences." IFN Working Paper no.
941, 21 November. SSRN, https://papers.ssrn.com/sol3/papers.
cfm?abstract_id=2179522.

Dawes, Christopher T., Peter J. Loewen, and James H. Fowler. 2011. "Social
Preferences and Political Participation." *Journal of Politics* 73 (3): 845–56.

Dovidio, John F., Jane Allyn Piliavin, David A. Schroeder, and Louis A.
Penner. 2006. *The Social Psychology of Prosocial Behavior*. Mahwah, NJ: Lawrence Erlbaum Associates.

Downs, Anthony. (1957) 1985. *An Economic Theory of Democracy*. New York:
Harper. Reprint.

Eckel, Catherine C., and Philip J. Grossman. 1998. "Are Women Less Selfish
Than Men? Evidence from Dictator Experiments." *Economic Journal (London)*
108 (448): 726–35.

Eckstein, Harry. 1975. "Case Study and Theory in Political Science." In *Handbook of Political Science*, edited by Fred I. Greenstein and Nelson W. Polsby,
79–138. Reading, MA: Addison-Wesley.

Edlin, Aaron, Andrew Gelman, and Noah Kaplan. 2007. "Voting as a Rational
Choice: Why and How People Vote to Improve the Well-Being of Others."
Rationality and Society 19 (3): 293–314

Elster, Jon. 1990. "Selfishness and Altruism." In *Beyond Self-Interest*, edited by
Jane J. Mansbridge, 44–52. Chicago: University of Chicago Press.

Feddersen, Timothy J., and Wolfgang Pesendorfer. 1996. "The Swing Voter's
Curse." *American Economic Review* 86 (3): 404–24.

Fehr, Ernst, and Urs Fischbacher. 2003. "The Nature of Human Altruism."
Nature 425 (6960): 785–91.

Fehr, Ernst, and Klaus M. Schmidt. 2006. "The Economics of Fairness, Reciprocity, and Altruism: Experimental Evidence and New Theories." In *Handbook of the Economics of Giving, Altruism, and Reciprocity*, edited by Serge-Christophe Kolm and Jean Mercier Ythier, 1:615–91. Amsterdam: Elsevier.

Feldman, Stanley, and Marco Steenbergen. 2001. "The Humanitarian Foundation of Public Support for Social Welfare." *American Journal of Political Science* 45 (3): 658–77.

Fong, Christina M. 2007. "Evidence from an Experiment on Charity to Welfare Recipients: Reciprocity, Altruism, and the Empathic Responsiveness Hypothesis." *Economic Journal (London)* 117 (522): 1008–27.

Forsythe, Robert, Joel L. Horowitz, N.E. Savin, and Martin Sefton. 1994. "Fairness in Simple Bargaining Experiments." *Games and Economic Behavior* 6 (3): 347–69.

Fowler, James H. 2006. "Altruism and Turnout." *Journal of Politics* 68 (3): 674–83.

Fowler, James H., and Cindy D. Kam. 2007. "Beyond the Self: Social Identity, Altruism, and Political Participation." *Journal of Politics* 69 (3): 811–25.

Green, Donald Philip, and Jonathan A. Cowden. 1992. "Who Protests: Self-Interest and White Opposition to Busing." *Journal of Politics* 54:471–96.

Henrich, Joseph, Robert Boyd, Samuel Bowles, Colin Camerer, Ernst Fehr, Herbert Gintis, and Richard McElreath. 2004. "Overview and Synthesis." In *Foundations of Human Sociality: Economic Experiments and Ethnographic Evidence from Fifteen Small-Scale Societies*, edited by Joseph Henrich, Robert Boyd, Samuel Bowles, and Colin Camerer, Ernst Fehr, and Herbert Gintis, 8–54. Oxford: Oxford University Press.

Henrich, Joseph, Robert Boyd, Samuel Bowles, Ernst Fehr, and Herbert Gintis. 2004. "Introduction and Guide to the Volume." In *Foundations of Human Sociality: Economic Experiments and Ethnographic Evidence from Fifteen Small-Scale Societies*, edited by Joseph Henrich, Robert Boyd, Samuel Bowles, Colin Camerer, Ernst Fehr, and Herbert Gintis, 1–7. Oxford: Oxford University Press.

Hobbes, Thomas. (1651) 1904. *Leviathan*. Edited by A.R. Waller. Cambridge: Cambridge University Press. Reprint.

Hoffman, Elizabeth, Kevin A. McCabe, Keith Shachat, and Vernon L. Smith. 1994. "Preferences, Property-Rights, and Anonymity in Bargaining Games." *Games and Economic Behavior* 7 (3): 346–80.

Inglehart, Ronald. 1971. "The Silent Revolution in Europe: Intergenerational Change in Post-Industrial Societies." *American Political Science Review* 65 (4): 991–1071.

Jankowski, Richard. 2002. "Buying a Lottery Ticket to Help the Poor: Altruism, Civic Duty, and Self-Interest in the Decision to Vote." *Rationality and Society* 14 (1): 55–77.

– 2004. "Altruism and the Decision to Vote: Explaining and Testing High Voter Turnout." Paper presented at the Annual Meetings of the American Political Science Association, Chicago, IL.

Karylowski, Jerzy. 1982. "Two Types of Altruistic Behavior: Doing Good to Feel Good or to Make the Other Feel Good." In *Cooperation and Helping Behavior*, edited by Valerian J. Derlaga and Janusz Grzelak, 397–413. New York: Academic.

Kinder, Donald R., and Cindy D. Kam. 2009. *Us against Them: Ethnocentric Foundations of American Public Opinion*. Chicago: University of Chicago Press.

Knack, Stephen. 1992. "Social Altruism and Voter Turnout: Evidence from the 1991 NES Pilot Study." 1991 NES Pilot Study Reports.

Lasswell, Harold D. 1936. *Who Gets What, When, and How*. New York: McGraw-Hill.

Ledyard, John O. 1982. "The Paradox of Voting and Candidate Competition." In *Essays in Contemporary Fields of Economics: In Honor of Emanuel T. Weiler*, edited by George Horwich and James P. Quirk, 57–80. West Lafayette, IN: Purdue University Press.

Leighley, Jan E. 1995. "Attitudes, Opportunities and Incentives: A Field Essay on Political Participation." *Political Research Quarterly* 48 (1): 181–209.

Loewen, Peter John. 2010. "Antipathy, Affinity and Political Participation: How Our Concern for Others Makes Us Vote." *Canadian Journal of Political Science* 43:661–87.

Macaulay, J.R., and L. Berkowitz. 1970. *Altruism and Helping Behavior*. New York: Academic.

Mansbridge, Jane J. (1980) 1983. *Beyond Adversary Democracy*. Chicago: University of Chicago Press. Reprint.

– 1990a. "Expanding the Range of Formal Modeling." In *Beyond Self-Interest*, edited by Jane J. Mansbridge, 254–63. Chicago: University of Chicago Press.

– 1990b. "The Rise and Fall of Self-Interest in the Explanation of Political Life." In *Beyond Self-Interest*, edited by Jane J. Mansbridge, 3–22. Chicago: University of Chicago Press.

–1990c. "Self-Interest in Political Life." *Political Theory* 18 (1): 132–53.

Margolis, Howard. 1982. *Selfishness, Altruism, and Rationality*. Cambridge: Cambridge University Press.

Meier, Stephan. 2006. *The Economics of Non-Selfish Behavior*. Cheltenham, UK: Edward Elgar.

Monroe, Kristen Renwick. 1998. *The Heart of Altruism*. Princeton: Princeton University Press.

Myerson, Roger B. 2000. "Large Poisson Games." *Journal of Economic Theory* 94 (1): 7–45.

Nussbaum, Martha C. 1996. "Patriotism and Cosmopolitanism." In *For Love of Country: Debating the Limits of Patriotism*, edited by Joshua Cohen, 2–18. Boston: Beacon.

Palfrey, Thomas R., and Howard Rosenthal. 1985. "Voter Participation and Strategic Uncertainty." *American Political Science Review* 79 (1): 62–78.

Piliavin, Jane Allyn, and Hon-Wen Charng. 1990. "Altruism: A Review of Recent Theory and Research." *Annual Review of Sociology* 16:27–65.

Riker, William H., and Peter C. Ordeshook. 1968. "A Theory of the Calculus of Voting. " *American Political Science Review* 62 (1): 25–42.

Sartori, Anne E. 2003. "An Estimator for Some Binary-Outcome Selection Models without Exclusion Restrictions." *Political Analysis* 11:111–38.

Schokkaert, Erik. 2006. "The Empirical Analysis of Transfer Motives." In *Handbook of the Economics of Giving, Altruism, and Reciprocity*, edited by Serge-Christophe Kolm and Jean Mercier Ythier, 1:127–81. Amsterdam: Elsevier.

Sears, David O. 1986. "College Sophomores in the Laboratory: Influences of a Narrow Data Base on Social Psychology's View of Human Nature." *Journal of Personality and Social Psychology* 51 (3): 515–30.

Sears, David O., and Jack Citrin. 1985. *Tax Revolt: Something for Nothing in California*. Cambridge, MA: Harvard University Press.

Sears, David O., and Carolyn L. Funk. 1990. "The Limited Effect of Economic Self-Interest on the Political Attitudes of the Mass Public." *Journal of Behavioral Economics* 19 (3): 247–71.

Sears, David O., and Carolyn L. Funk. 1991. "The Role of Self-Interest in Social and Political Attitudes." *Advances in Experimental Social Psychology* 24:1–91.

Sen, Amartya K. 1990. "Rational Fools: A Critique of the Behavioral Foundations of Economic Theory." In *Beyond Self-Interest*, edited by Jane J. Mansbridge, 25–43. Chicago: University of Chicago Press.

Simmons, Roberta G. 1991. "Presidential Address on Altruism and Sociology." *Sociological Quarterly* 32 (1): 1–22.

Sober, Elliott, and David Sloan Wilson. 1998. *Unto Others: The Evolution and Psychology of Unselfish Behavior*. Cambridge, MA: Harvard University Press.

Sumner, William Graham. (1906) 2002. *Folkways: A Study of Mores, Manners, Customs, and Morals*. Mineola, NY: Dover Publications.

Verba, Sidney, Kay Lehman Schlozman, and Henry E. Brady. 1995. *Voice and Equality: Civic Voluntarism in American Politics*. Cambridge, MA: Harvard University Press.

Wilson, James Q., and Edward C. Banfield. 1963. *City Politics*. Cambridge, MA: Harvard University Press.

– 1964. "Public-Regardingness as a Value Premise in Voting Behavior." *American Political Science Review* 58 (4): 876–87.

– 1971. "Political Ethos Revisited." *American Political Science Review* 65 (4): 1048–62.

3 Behavioural Anomalies Explain Variation in Voter Turnout

CHRISTOPHER DAWES, PETER JOHN LOEWEN, AND GABRIEL ARSENAULT

Introduction

Individuals regularly diverge from the courses of action prescribed by expected utility theory or rational choice prescriptions. Some individuals exhibit very high discount rates. Such individuals will take a payment today when an appreciably larger payment a short time later is offered. Others make decisions that suggest a misunderstanding of probability theory. Examples abound, and not only among those who purchase lottery tickets. Such divergences – collectively termed *behavioural anomalies* – are widespread and consistently present. Indeed, they lie at the centre of various behavioural and psychological approaches to social science. Nevertheless, theories of voter turnout have largely ignored the regularity with which citizens do not behave according to the dictums of expected utility. This may not be for the better. As we show in this chapter, such anomalies help explain variation in the decision to vote, an action central to the study of politics and a question central to political science (and especially the work of Blais 2000).

The apparent paradox of voter turnout has been a central challenge to political science at least since Downs (1957), and certainly since Riker and Ordeshook (1968) presented their calculus of voter turnout. Why do individuals choose to vote in elections, in particular when their vote cannot be thought to be decisive, and when the expected benefits of voting are thus so small? The answer, following Riker and Ordeshook, is that citizens experience personal gratification by voting and fulfilling their sense of civic duty.[1] While Riker and Ordeshook's model does highlight this problem and propose a solution, its greater function is organizational (Clarke and Primo 2011). Their offering collects in one model several factors thought to explain voter turnout, namely the probability of being decisive (which encompasses the empirical regularity of competition increasing turnout); the benefits of election (which captures among other things the empirical regularity of higher turnout in more consequential elections); the sense of a duty to vote (which potentially covers several different psychological effects); and the costs of casting a ballot (which can cover both the costs incurred in casting a ballot and the costs incurred in preparing to make a decision). This model, then, brings together several empirical regularities of voter turnout.

Our own reading of the literature suggests that most investigation has occurred around the C, P, and D terms (Blais 2000 provides a comprehensive review). Comparatively less work has been undertaken on the comparative effects of election benefits, or B. There are a few exceptions, namely work on social preferences and voter turnout (Edlin, Gelman, and Kaplan 2007; Fowler and Kam 2007; Fowler 2006; Loewen 2010; Dawes, Loewen, and Fowler 2011). This work has demonstrated that concern for others reduces the degree to which benefits are discounted by the probability of being decisive, allowing benefits to drive the decision to vote. To the extent that P has been investigated, it has typically been in the context of the effects of the competitiveness of an election, i.e., as something exogenous to individuals, though there are important exceptions (Blais and Rheault 2010).

Here we explicitly consider anomalies related to the P and B terms at the level of individual voters, rather than at some higher, aggregate level. We thus ask not how exogenous variation in the benefits of an election or the probability of being decisive matter for an election. Instead, we look to differences between individuals that matter for these terms. In doing so, we build on recent work that recognizes the potentially central role of such individual differences for political participation and political behaviour more generally (e.g. Fowler et al. 2011; Mondak 2010).

We focus on three behaviour anomalies: ambiguity bias, sensitivity to sample size, and self-control problems. In what follows, we explain each of these anomalies and draw out their relationship to the traditional vote calculus. We then describe our subjects, measures, and models.[2] We then present our results from a series of Swedish subjects and a series of replications in the United States and Great Britain. We then conclude. To anticipate, we find broad support for the claim that behavioural anomalies partially explain the decision to participate in elections. In particular, we find that individuals who exhibit self-control problems – measured through procrastination in paying bills and through high discount rates – are less likely to vote. We replicate this finding in an American and British context.

P Anomalies

We consider two anomalies related to probability in the vote calculus. The first is ambiguity aversion; the second is insensitivity to sample size. Individuals who exhibit ambiguity aversion reveal a preference for known risks over unknown risks. When confronted with a choice in which probabilities are either certain or uncertain, individuals with ambiguity aversion are more likely choose certain probabilities, even if this decision is less optimal according to expected utility theory. The classic task to draw out ambiguity aversion, as first proposed by Ellsberg (1961), is to allow individuals to participate in a lottery in which they can choose an outcome based on some number of red balls or a larger number of yellow and black balls, all placed in the same Greek urn.[3] The exact number of yellow balls (and thus black balls) is not specified, only that there is a larger combined number of yellow and black balls than red balls. An individual who is ambiguity averse will choose the lower expected payoff of the red ball. Ambiguity aversion may be negatively related to voter turnout in the cases where an individual has uncertainty over the outcome of an election, or the differences between parties or the potential coalition formations are uncertain (see Ghirardato and Katz 2006). In such scenarios, individuals are not comparing certain choices. Instead, they are left to estimate the likelihoods that one party will win over another (and by extension, how likely that party is to win). Those who are averse to such uncertainty might be less likely to vote. However, we think the more relevant application of ambiguity aversion is simply that individuals will avoid making such probabilistic judgments. Since ambiguity aversion is likely correlated with a reduced ability to properly evaluate probabilistic information, those who demonstrate ambiguity aversion will, *ceteris paribus*, be more likely to cast a ballot.[4]

Insensitivity to sample size is an anomaly in which an individual displays a lack of understanding of the law of large numbers. The classic example is provided by Kahneman and Tversky (1972) in which respondents are asked which of two hospitals – one of which delivers a large number of babies each day and the other a small number – is more likely to deliver an unusually large share of baby boys in a given day. Those who ignore size of a sample fail to appreciate that larger samples are less likely to produce large deviations from the mean than smaller samples. Those sensitive to the sample size will factor this into their decision-making. Therefore, we posit that insensitivity to sample size may be positively correlated with voter turnout, as those who are less familiar with basic statistical principles will overestimate their own probability of being decisive, *ceteris paribus*.

B Anomalies

We consider two measures of an anomaly related to the benefits of an election. The two measures are closely related and follow on earlier work on the relationship between self-control and turnout (Fowler and Kam 2006; Loewen and Dawes 2011). The first measure of self-control problems is excessive discounting; individuals prefer an immediate payment over future payments of a substantially larger value. The second measure is self-reported procrastination: individuals put off paying a cost now, instead accepting a larger cost in the future. The logic by which both of these anomalies are related to vote choice are the same as those expressed in Fowler and Kam (2006) and Loewen and Dawes (2011). Elections ask individuals to incur costs now – through both information search and attention as well as through the actual physical costs of voting. Because elections generally lead to parties that have different policies with different material winners and losers, voters do stand to realize some benefits from the election of their preferred party. However, they only realize these benefits in the future, sometimes years after the election. Accordingly, voters are asked to trade off costs now for a stream of benefits later. Individuals who more steeply discount future payoffs will thus be less likely to vote, because the ratio of costs to benefits will be greater. We note that this applies with equal felicity to a turnout calculus which incorporates benefits accrued to others (Loewen 2010), provided those benefits are in the future. It also applies to models of turnout in which the benefit of voting is the maintenance of democracy, provided that maintenance occurs at some future date.

We expect, *ceteris paribus*, that those individuals who exhibit greater discount rates and/or greater procrastination will be less likely to vote.

Data and Methods

Our study relies on the Swedish Twin Registry, the largest twin registry in the world. The survey we use (called SALTY) was administered on this sample from the fall of 2008 to the spring of 2010. We include approximately 9,000 subjects who completed the survey. The instrument asked subjects whether they voted in the last Swedish general parliamentary election in 2006. SALTY subjects were matched to administrative records in order to include measures of their income and years of education. A more detailed description of the sample and the SALTY survey can be found in Cesarini et al. (2010).

Measures

We make use of four sets of questions designed to measure our key predictors. Ambiguity aversion relies on a modified version of Ellsberg's urn problem. Subjects are told that the urn is filled with thirty red balls and sixty yellow and black balls, whose proportion is unknown. They are then given a choice between a lottery of paying 900 kronar for a red ball, 1,000 kronar for a yellow ball, or 1,000 kronar for a black ball.[5] Those who are ambiguity averse would choose the red ball lottery, despite choosing a yellow or black ball both having a higher expected value. Those who choose the red ball are classified as ambiguity averse. We create a dichotomous measure of this, with the averse reading 1 and the non-averse reading 0.

Closely following Kahneman and Tversky (1973), insensitivity to sample size is measured by asking subjects in which hospital, large or small, is it more likely that 60% of babies born would be boys. Those who responded that this would occur in a large hospital were classified as insensitive to sample size and given a value of 1 on a dichotomous variable.

Discounting is measured by asking subjects whether they would choose an immediate payoff of 5,000 kronar today or another, larger amount in a week. Subjects were presented with three larger amounts: 5,500, 6,000, or 7,000 kronar. We created a categorical variable ranging from 0 to 3, where the variable indicates how many times a subject chose an immediate reward.

Procrastination is measured by asking respondents how often they fail to pay their bills on time. Subjects could offer responses ranging from "Never" to "Several Times a Month." These responses are coded dichotomously, where 1 indicates that a subject fails to pay bills on time once every six months or more often.

We note that all of our measures have higher values when the subject does display the anomaly, meaning we expect the ambiguity aversion and insensitivity variables to be positively related to turnout and the self-control variables to be negatively related to turnout.

Models and Specifications

We specify random effects logit models, which account for the fact that observations in our data set are correlated within families. For the time being, we include minimal controls for age, years of education, income, and gender. The models take the form (for individual i in family j where X is a matrix containing the control variables):

$$P(y_i = 1) = logit^{-1}(\alpha_j + \beta_{Anomaly} Anomaly_i + \beta_{X_k} X_{ik})$$

(1)

$$\alpha_j \sim N(0, \sigma^2_{Family})$$

(2)

Principal Results

Our results pertaining to the P term are presented in tables 3.1–3.2. Our results conform to our expectations in one of two cases. Those who exhibit ambiguity aversion are more likely to vote than those who do not. The odds ratio (not reported) suggests that the odds of voting over not voting are 35% larger for those who are ambiguity averse compared to those who are not. By contrast, those who do not reason properly about sample sizes appear less likely to vote in the election, with odds of voting over not voting only 75% as large as those who do not exhibit an insensitivity to sample size. This is plainly contrary to our expectations.

Tables 3.3–3.4 present our results for our B measures. These provide unambiguous support for our expectations. Those who exhibit higher discount rates are less likely to have voted in the parliamentary elections in question. For each immediate payoff that subjects accept, their odds of voting over not voting decrease by 13%. Similarly, those who exhibit more procrastination in their bill payments have odds of turning out over not turning out, which are just 60% as large as those who do not exhibit procrastination. Finally, we note that all of our control variables perform as expected, following conventional turnout models. Turnout increases with income, years of education, and age. It is occasionally higher for men, though never impressively so.

Table 3.1 Ambiguity Aversion and Voter Turnout, Swedish Sample

Variable	Coefficient	(Standard error)
Ambiguity aversion	0.300**	(0.107)
Income	0.250**	(0.074)
Years of education	0.206**	(0.026)
Age	0.035**	(0.012)
Male	0.227†	(0.132)
Intercept	−10.028**	(2.588)
N		9104
Log-likelihood		−1609.143
$X^2_{(5)}$		107.222

Significance levels: †: 10% *: 5% **: 1%

Table 3.2 Insensitivity to Sample Size and Voter Turnout, Swedish Sample

Variable	Coefficient	(Standard error)
Insensitivity	−0.300**	(0.111)
Income	0.221**	(0.073)
Years of education	0.196**	(0.026)
Age	0.032**	(0.012)
Male	0.214	(0.132)
Intercept	−8.-948**	(2.563)
N		9007
Log-likelihood		−1655.051
$X^2_{(5)}$		97.604

Significance levels: †: 10% *: 5% **: 1

Table 3.3 Discounting and Voter Turnout, Swedish Sample

Variable	Coefficient	(Standard error)
Discounting	−0.129*	(0.062)
Income	0.252**	(0.073)
Years of education	0.196**	(0.025)
Age	0.030*	(0.012)
Male	0.269*	(0.130)
Intercept	−10.231**	(2.541)
N		9294
Log-likelihood		−1684.358
$X^2_{(5)}$		98.057

Significance levels: †: 10% *: 5% **: 1%

Table 3.4 Procrastination and Voter Turnout, Swedish Sample

Variable	Coefficient	(Standard error)
Procrastination	−0.520*	(0.220)
Income	0.247**	(0.073)
Years of education	0.204**	(0.026)
Age	0.029*	(0.012)
Male	0.231†	(0.131)
Intercept	−10.063**	(2.542)
N		9419
Log-likelihood		−1717.386
$X^2_{(5)}$		100.387

Significance levels: †: 10% *: 5% **: 1%

Replication Results

We provide partial replication of our positive findings in two different data sets. The first is drawn from a medical study conducted at the University of California San Diego. The second was conducted during the 2010 British General Election by YouGov and administered by Duch and colleagues. The U.S. data allow us to measure both the effects of discounting and ambiguity aversion, while the British data provide just a measure of discounting.

Our U.S. data are drawn from a long-running study of hypertension among approximately 1,000 individuals. Multiple individuals are typically sampled from a nuclear family, and subjects reside principally in Southern California. In the spring of 2010, we surveyed all of these individuals for whom we had current mailing addresses and asked them, among other things, identical versions of the ambiguity aversion and discounting questions posed in the Swedish study. This generated 490 responses, which we matched against the 2009 California voter file.

The measure of turnout we present is the number of 2008 elections in which the subject participated. There were three such elections: presidential primary, direct primary, and the general election. After discarding subjects with missing records, we are left with approximately 350 subjects.

Our British data are drawn from the Cooperative Campaign Analysis Project, an initiative spearheaded by Duch and colleagues and fielded by YouGov. The study includes a multiple wave survey in which different research teams buy different modules. Research teams share common questions. We placed a small number of questions in a post-election wave, including a discounting question in which subjects could choose between an immediate payoff of survey points[6] or a payoff one month in the future. As with the Swedish and American data, we sum the total number of choices for the immediate payoff. However, given the large number of choices in this set-up (twelve), we take the log of the sum.

Tables 3.5 and 3.6 present our results for ambiguity aversion and discounting. As can be seen, there is no replication of the result for ambiguity aversion. Indeed, the standard errors dwarfs the coefficient, while other variables perform as expected. There is, however, a clear effect for discounting, such that subjects with less self-control are less likely to vote. A similar replication appears in the British data. According to the results in table 3.7, those with the highest observed rate of discounting have odds of turning out only 49% as high as those with the lowest observed discount rates. In probability terms, this translates into a decrease from 0.785 to 0.647. This is a substantively impressive effect and larger than that exhibited in Sweden.

Table 3.5 Ambiguity Aversion and Voter Turnout, U.S. Replication

Variable	Coefficient	(Standard error)
Ambiguity aversion	0.099	(0.257)
Income	0.073†	(0.042)
Years of education	0.154†	(0.081)
Age	0.096**	(0.011)
Male	0.345	(0.292)
N	348	

Significance levels: †: 10% *: 5% **: 1%

Table 3.6 Discounting and Voter Turnout, U.S. Replication

Variable	Coefficient	(Standard error)
Discounting	−0.385**	(0.150)
Income	0.045	(0.043)
Years of education	0.143†	(0.083)
Age	0.099**	(0.012)
Male	0.231	(0.130)
N	350	

Significance levels: †: 10% *: 5% **: 1%

Table 3.7 Discounting and Voter Turnout, British Replication

Variable	Coefficient	(Standard error)
Discounting	−1.006*	(0.478)
Income	2.441**	(0.561)
Years of Education	1.239*	(0.582)
Age	3.367**	(0.632)
Male	0.039	(0.243)
N	771	

Significance levels: †: 10% *: 5% **: 1%

Conclusion

Individuals differ in the consistency and frequency with which they violate the precepts of expected utility. Such differences have been consistently and widely demonstrated. We argue that these differences should be related to the decision to vote. In doing so, we are effectively advancing two arguments. First, models of voter turnout should take account of not only characteristics of the political environment and individual differences in political preferences and attitudes. They should also take account of perhaps more fundamental predispositions that likely extend beyond the political realm. Second, while admittedly more a matter of analytical organization, we should take as a starting point extant models of turnout as a framework for understanding how these differences will matter for turnout. More specifically, how may these individual differences influence the parameter values in the rational-choice model of voting. We hope this chapter serves as a good illustration of how this approach may be implemented.

Our results are clearly mixed. We find that discounting behaviour affects turnout in the expected fashion and in accordance with previous work. It should be pointed out that our analysis is the first to study time preferences outside of a laboratory setting with a large sample.[7] Moreover, we replicate these findings in two other jurisdictions, both of which have starkly different electoral systems and markedly different political cultures. However, findings around the probability of being decisive are much less clear. This is, perhaps, the logical function of an electoral system in which pivotality is difficult to define, let alone compute (Rheault, Blais, and Godbout 2011; Blais and Rheault 2010). Nonetheless, these results remain to be explained.

We forward four courses of action. First, these discounting results should be replicated in more countries. While each country is unique, Sweden is characterized by a party system that resembles few others, in addition to strong social norms of voting. Indeed, turnout rates over 90% in the absence of compulsory voting underline this exceptionality. Second, we should consider additional behavioural anomalies. The list of these deviations is long and many can be easily extended to questions of voter turnout, vote choice, and more general political preferences. Third, the exploration of these anomalies and their relationship to voter turnout should be sensitive to institutional differences between countries that make some anomalies more relevant than others. For example, as institutional differences lead to differences in the benefits conferred in elections or the likelihood of being pivotal, we should expect the importance of the anomalies related to the B and P terms to vary. Fourth, provided that these anomalies can be shown to consistently explain variation in voter turnout and other political behaviour, we think they may be candidates for mediators of the genetic basis of political participation (Fowler, Baker, and Dawes 2008; Fowler et al. 2011).

NOTES

1 The duty aspect of turnout, we note, has been long neglected but is taken up in recent field experimental work (see Green's review in chapter 4) and the recent review of the political theory of citizen duty and its empirical implications in an unpublished paper by Christopher Achen and André Blais. For work on the origins of individual differences in duty, see Loewen and Dawes (2012).
2 Readers will note that our approach shares a close similarity with that used in the Chapter 3. We use behavioural tasks to recover information about individuals' preferences or beliefs, we then analogize these to a factor in a classic model of turnout, and we then show that these factors in fact do empirically explain variation.
3 An aside: What's a Greek urn? About three hundred euros a week, on average.
4 We are, then, not advancing a specific claim about ambiguity aversion and its relationship to voter turnout. Instead, we are taking evidence of this anomaly as a proxy for an individual's ability to make accurate inferences about the probability of some event.
5 1 krona is approximately equal to 0.15 Canadian dollars.
6 These can be converted to cash.
7 Fowler and Kam (2007) studied 235 undergraduates in a laboratory setting.

References

Blais, André. 2000. *To Vote or Not to Vote? The Merits and Limits of Rational Choice*. Pittsburgh, PA: University of Pittsburgh Press.
Blais, A., and L. Rheault. 2010. "Optimists and Skeptics: Why Do People Believe in the Value of Their Single Vote?" *Electoral Studies* 30 (1): 77–82.
Cesarini, D., M. Johannesson, P. Lichtenstein, O. Sandewall, and B. Wallace. 2010. "Genetic Variation in Financial Decision-Making." *Journal of Finance* 65 (5): 1725–54.

Clarke, Kevin, and David Primo. 2011. *A Model Discipline: Political Science and the Logic of Representations*. Oxford: Oxford University Press.

Dawes, C.D., P.J. Loewen, and J.H. Fowler. 2011. "Social Preferences and Political Participation." *Journal of Politics* 73 (3): 845–56.

Downs, Anthony. 1957. *An Economic Theory of Democracy*. New York: Harper and Row.

Edlin, A., A. Gelman, and N. Kaplan. 2007. "Voting as a Rational Choice: Why and How People Improve the Well-being of Others." *Rationality and Society* 19 (3): 293–314.

Ellsberg, D. 1961. "Risk, Ambiguity, and the Savage Axioms." *Quarterly Journal of Economics* 75 (4): 643–69.

Fowler, J.H. 2006. "Altruism and turnout." *Journal of Politics* 68:647–83.

Fowler, J.H., L.A. Baker, and C.T. Dawes. 2008. "Genetic Variation in Political Participation." *American Political Science Review* 102 (2): 233–48.

Fowler, J.H., and C.D. Kam. 2006. "Patience as a Political Virtue: Delayed Gratification and Turnout." *Political Behavior* 28 (2): 113–28.

– 2007. "Beyond the Self: Altruism, Social Identity, and Political Participation." *Journal of Politics* 69:813–27.

Fowler, J.H., P.J. Loewen, C.T. Dawes, and J. Settle. 2011. "Games, Genes, and Political Participation." In *Man Is by Nature and Nurture a Political Animal*, edited by Rose McDermott and Peter Hatemi, 207–23. Chicago: University of Chicago Press.

Ghirardato, P., and J.N. Katz. 2006. "Indecision Theory: Quality of Information and Voting Behavior." *Journal of Public Economic Theory* 8 (3): 379–99.

Kahneman, D., and A. Tversky. 1972. "Subjective Probability: A Judgment of Representativeness" *Cognitive Psychology* 3 (3): 430–54.

– 1973. "On the Psychology of Prediction." *Psychological Review* 80 (4): 237–51.

Loewen, P.J. 2010. "Affinity, Antipathy, and Political Participation: How Our Concern for Others Makes Us Vote." *Canadian Journal of Political Science* 43 (3): 661–87.

Loewen, P.J., and C.D. Dawes. 2011. "Chrna6 Predicts Voter Turnout. University of Toronto Working Paper.

– 2012. "The Heritability of Duty and Voter Turnout." *Political Psychology* 33 (3): 363–73.

Mondak, J.J. 2010. *Personality and the Foundations of Political Behavior*. New York: Cambridge University Press.

Rheault, L., A. Blais, and J.F. Godbout. 2011. "Probability of Pivotal Outcome in Multi-Candidate Plurality Elections." Université de Montréal Working Paper.

Riker, W.H., and P.C. Ordeshook. 1968. "A Theory of the Calculus of Voting." *American Political Science Review* 62:25–42.

4 Civic Duty and Social Pressure as Causes of Voter Turnout

DONALD P. GREEN

In his learned synthesis of theories and evidence on voter turnout, *To Vote or Not to Vote?*, André Blais (2000) argues that most citizens believe that voting is a civic duty or obligation. With characteristic wit, Blais likens failure to vote as a "venial sin," a misdeed that is wrong but forgivable (92). These feelings of obligation, he argues, cause many people to vote who would otherwise abstain on the grounds that their vote has an infinitesimal chance of altering the outcome. Blais's argument is slightly different from that of Riker and Ordeshook (1968), who argue that the utility derived from doing one's civic duty makes voting rational because it outweighs the expenditure of time and effort. Blais contends that costs and benefits play no role in the voting calculus of people who feel that voting is an obligation. Only those with a weak sense of civic duty base their turnout decisions on instrumental considerations such as convenience and opportunity costs (102).

Blais's evidence for the claim that civic duty is both a proximal cause of voting and a psychological force that overcomes the collective action problem comes from four sources. First, Blais adduces survey evidence from the United States, Canada, United Kingdom, and France to show that most citizens in these countries believe that voting is a duty or obligation (2000, 95). Second, he argues that the support for norms of civic duty expressed in survey responses is more than mere lip service. When students in a German lab are given an opportunity to forgo their right to vote in return for large sums of money, the vast majority refuse (97). Third, he revisits his in-depth interviews with regular voters from Montreal and notes that voters overwhelmingly regard political participation as a civic obligation, although people feel less obligation to vote in low salience elections involving issues to which they feel little

connection. Finally, a multivariate regression of voter turnout on measures of civic duty and other factors shows that a scale measuring commitment to statements such as "It is the duty of every citizen to vote" is
a very strong predictor. In sum, civic duty is a widely recognized norm
that is powerfully correlated with voter turnout.

One of the most important empirical claims in *To Vote or Not to Vote?*
concerns the relationship between civic duty and social pressure. Although the conviction that voting is a civic duty might cause one to feel
guilty about not voting, Blais (2000) argues that the effects of civic duty
are not reducible to instrumental concerns about ostracism by one's
family or peers in the event that one failed to vote (103). Fewer than half
the respondents in his surveys believe that others would disapprove of
them if they were to fail to vote, and this belief does not predict voter
turnout (105). The bottom line of Blais's investigation is that "it is an
internalized sense of duty and not the presence of social pressures that
induces people to vote" (104).

My aim in this chapter is to revisit the claim that civic duty matters while social pressure does not. Since the publication of *To Vote or
Not to Vote?* in 2000, a large experimental literature has emerged in the
domain of voter turnout. Much of this literature evaluates the effectiveness of voter mobilization tactics ranging from door-to-door canvassing to televised public service announcements, but recent years have
witnessed a surge of scholarly interest in what Blais called "social pressure." Instead of gauging the effects of social pressure by asking people
to imagine how others would react if they were to abstain and using
that measure to predict voter turnout, experimental investigations of
social pressure tests its effects by deploying an array of voter mobilization messages that vary in the amount of social pressure they exert. The
causal effect of social pressure is then assessed by comparing the turnout rates of groups that were randomly assigned different messages.

This experimental approach has a number of advantages but also
some important limitations. One advantage is that random assignment
facilitates causal inference. Consider the drawbacks of an observational
study, in which the "treatment" is a feeling, belief, or attitude that was
"assigned" in some unknown way. The correlation between voting and
feelings of civic duty observed in non-experimental research may be
spurious: those who say that voting is an obligation may be more prone
to vote for other unmeasured reasons, such as the fact that they are
in the habit of voting and feel comfortable doing it. Random assignment ensures that the subjects who are assigned the treatment group

have the same expected propensity to vote as those who are assigned to the control group. Another advantage of the experimental approach is that the researcher controls the intervention and can change it in order to test specific theories. The researcher who studies non-experimental data must rely on the treatments that nature provides, and survey measures of those treatments are often unreliable. A third advantage of field experimental studies of voter turnout is that they generally rely on official records of voter turnout, whereas most survey-based observational studies rely on voters' self-reports. Self-reports introduce the possibility of bias because respondents who portray themselves as committed to norms of civic duty may be more inclined to falsely report that they voted in recent elections. Two important limitations of experiments on voter turnout should also be mentioned at the outset. One is that they seldom assess the effects of their interventions on political attitudes (for an exception, see Bedolla and Michelson 2012), and therefore the researcher must make some assumptions when attributing the mobilizing effects of certain treatments to the subjects' thought processes. As we will see below, linking experimental treatments to civic duty and social pressure requires some guesswork. Second, the range of possible treatments, subjects, and electoral contexts is vast, and a great deal of experimentation may be necessary in order to understand when and why an intervention exerts an effect. Experimental science takes mincing steps.

This chapter begins by explaining the theoretical underpinnings of social pressure, as they relate to the calculus of voter turnout. Next, we review the burgeoning literature on social pressure and voter turnout, calling attention to the gaps and anomalies in the experimental database. We conclude by arguing that although the effects of social pressure seem to be much stronger than Blais argued, they also appear to depend on a strong assertion of the norm of civic duty. This pattern suggests a possible synthesis of the civic duty and social pressure hypotheses: social pressure works when norms of civic duty are made salient.

Intrinsic versus Extrinsic Selective Benefits

The collective action problem as applied to the problem of voter turnout may be stated as follows: When each person's contribution to the collective cause is negligible and the outcome can be enjoyed even by people who do not contribute, no individual has an incentive to sacrifice for a collective cause. The fact that large numbers of people do in fact vote has led scholars to posit that "selective incentives" (Olson 1965) induce people to participate in elections. One type of selective incentive is the intrinsic satisfaction that one feels when casting a ballot. Voters may either enjoy the act of voting per se or feel good about themselves for advancing a partisan cause or honouring a civic obligation. Much of the literature on the paradox of voter turnout refers to feelings of civic duty as a possible solution (Riker and Ordeshook 1968). A second type of selective incentive involves extrinsic rewards: people receive side-payments for voting. In electoral systems where bribes and other mate-rial inducements are rare, incentives are thought to be social: voters are rewarded by the approbation of others, while non-voters are criticized or shunned. In other words, people are rewarded or punished accord-ing to whether they comply with social norms (Cialdini and Trost 1985), such as the expectation that citizens ought to participate in elections.

This latter type of selective incentive has recently been the focus of active scholarly investigation. Research on the effects of "social pres-sure" has centred on interventions that play upon a basic human drive to win praise and avoid chastisement. Experimental communications exert social pressure by praising those who uphold norms or scolding those who violate them. Although experimental treatments vary, social pressure communications typically involve some combination of three ingredients: they admonish the receiver to adhere to a social norm, in-dicate that the receiver's compliance will be monitored, and suggest that the monitored behaviour will be disclosed to others.

This identification strategy is quite different from the one that Blais uses. His survey measures ask subjects whether they would anticipate social disapprobation from friends or family in the event they did not vote. One's family and friends are not randomly assigned, and neither are one's perceptions of their reactions to non-voting. The experiments presented below confront subjects with social norms that are enforced by the person sending the experimental message, who in some cases discloses (or threatens to disclose) information about voter turnout to others in the household or neighbourhood.

Social pressure is relatively easy to operationalize in experimental treatments. As the experiments summarized below illustrate, there are many ways of putting voters on notice that their participation in elec-tions is being monitored and disclosed to others. More challenging is the experimental manipulation of civic duty. Creating deep-seated feel-ings of civic obligation is beyond the scope of an ordinary experiment, and even experiments that have randomly exposed high school students to civics classes have found it difficult to enhance commitment to this social norm (Green et al. 2011). Less ambitious and more tractable is the aim of priming norms of civic duty by couching appeals to vote in terms of doing one's civic duty. The complication, however, is that admonishing citizens to do their civic duty both primes their sense of civic obligation and suggests that failure to vote would meet with disapprobation. Although civic duty and social pressure inevitably overlap to some extent, one may fruitfully investigate the interaction between interventions that assert norms and interventions that enforce norms. Do civic duty appeals work without monitoring or disclosure? Do monitoring and disclosure work when little is said about civic duty? As we review the experimental evidence, special attention is paid to the question of whether monitoring and disclosure interact with the forcefulness with which civic duty appeals are made. We will see that monitoring and disclosure have powerful effects only when used in conjunction with strong statements about civic duty.

Social Pressure and Civic Duty: An Overview of Experimental Evidence

Field experiments that test the effects of social pressure date back to Gosnell's (1927) pioneering study of voting in the 1924 election, in which he mailed Chicagoans political cartoons depicting non-voters as unpatriotic "slackers." The idea of revealing to voters that their participation in elections will be monitored dates back at least to Gross, Schmidt, Keating, and Saks (1974), who tested its effects on voter turnout in college campus elections. Decades later, this line of inquiry was revived by Gerber, Green, and Larimer (2008), whose experimental study of social pressure sparked a series of follow-up experiments that shed light on the conditions under which social pressure's effects are large or small. We therefore begin with the Gerber, Green, and Larimer study and discuss how the interpretation of its results has evolved in the wake of subsequent research.

Set in the context of a low-salience 2006 primary election in Michigan, the Gerber, Green, and Larimer (2008) experiment involved five randomly assigned groups, a control group consisting of 100,000 households and four groups of 10,000 households apiece that received a single piece of mail. The first treatment group was reminded that voting is a civic duty. The second group (the "Hawthorne" condition) was told that they were part of a study that would monitor whether they voted but would not contact them further. A third group received the "Self" mailing, which indicated that voting is a matter of public record and presented an official-looking log of whether each member of the household voted in two recent elections. The fourth treatment group received the "Neighbours" mailing, which included not only the voting records of those in the household but also others living on the block. Both the Self and Neighbours mailing also promised a follow-up mailing that updates the voting log with turnout records from the upcoming election.[1] As in all of the field experiments described here, outcomes were measured using official records indicating which subjects actually voted.

The results in table 4.1 show a clear progression: the more social pressure a mailing exerts, the stronger the treatment effect.[2] The control group voted at a rate of 29.7%. The weakest of the treatments, the civic duty mailing, increased turnout to 31.5%.[3] Viewed in isolation, this increase in turnout might seem fairly small, but bear in mind that a slew of large-scale experiments on the effects of direct mail have found it to have negligible effects on turnout. For example, the direct mail experiments reported by Gerber and Green (2000) and Bedolla and Michelson (2012) suggest that mailings that stress the importance of doing one's civic duty ordinarily have effects of 0.5 percentage points or less. Why does the civic duty mailing have roughly three times the effect of the typical piece of voter mobilization mail? What seems to set the civic duty mailer in the Gerber, Green, and Larimer (2008) study apart is its confrontational tone. In contrast to the civic duty mailings distributed by Gerber and Green (2000), which highlight the sacrifices that others have made for the freedoms we enjoy, the mailings in Gerber, Green, and Larimer (2008) lecture the reader: "Why do so many people fail to vote? We've been talking about this problem for years, but it only seems to get worse. The whole point of democracy is that citizens are active participants in government; that we have a voice in government. Your voice starts with your vote. On August 8, remember your rights and responsibilities as a citizen. Remember to vote."

The next arm of the Gerber, Green, and Larimer (2008) experiment assessed the "Hawthorne effect" of alerting voters to the fact that their behaviour will be observed by researchers. This treatment was designed to assess the effects of surveillance without any overt social pressure; recipients of this mailing were assured that they would not be contacted, and the results, drawn from public records, would remain

Table 4.1 Voter Turnout by Assigned Social Pressure Condition (Gerber, Green, and Larimer 2008)

	Experimental group				
	Control (not mailed)	Civic duty (encouraged to vote)	Hawthorne (encouraged & monitored)	Self (encouraged, monitored, shown own past voting)	Neighbours (encouraged, monitored, shown own & others' past voting)
Percentage voting	29.7%	31.5%	32.2%	34.5%	37.8%
N of individuals	191,243	38,218	38,204	38,218	38,201

confidential. This treatment, which involved both researcher surveillance and an injunction to do one's civic duty, proved to be a significantly stronger inducement to vote than civic duty alone. Turnout in this group was, 32.2% which was 2.5 percentage points higher than the control group. In conjunction with a strong injunction to do one's civic duty, surveillance increases turnout.

Much stronger is the Self treatment, which combines a civic duty appeal with two other ingredients: household members' official voter turnout records in previous elections and notification that these records would be updated to reflect turnout in the upcoming election. In other words, the Self mailer accentuates the surveillance message of the Hawthorne mailing by demonstrating that voter turnout is observable in public records and adds a promise to monitor and disclose future behaviour. Individuals sent the Self mailing voted at a rate of 34.5%, which is 4.8 percentage points higher than the control group, implying a 16% increase in turnout. This effect increases substantially when subjects are presented with both their own vote histories and those of the neighbours, again with a promise to update and distribute these vote histories. Individuals sent the Neighbours mailing voted at a rate of 37.8%, which is 8.1 percentage points higher than the control group. This estimated treatment effect is among the strongest ever observed in a large-scale randomized voter mobilization experiment.

Having described the results of the Gerber, Green, and Larimer (2008) experiment, let's now consider how interpretation of the results has evolved in the wake of subsequent experimental research. First, let's rule out the notion that there is something idiosyncratic about the Gerber, Green, and Larimer (2008) results that renders them irre-producible. Gerber, Green, and Larimer (2010) report the results of a follow-up experiment conducted amid Michigan's municipal elections of 2007. The study tested the Civic Duty and Self treatments and found essentially the same results as in 2006. The Self treatment was also used in a 2009 congressional special election in Illinois, again producing sim-ilar results (Sinclair, McConnell, and Green 2012). Mann's (2010) use of the Self treatment in a 2007 Kentucky gubernatorial race generated a similar percentage increase in turnout; the absolute percentage point increase in turnout was smaller as a result of the very low participation rates in his samples (Mann 2010). The only instance in which the Self mailing failed to generate at least the 16% increase in turnout observed in the Gerber, Green, and Larimer (2008) study was the Abrajano and Panagopoulos (2011) study of Hispanic voter mobilization in a special election in Queens. Turnout was extremely low (3.94%) in the control group, and the English-language version of the Self mailer produced a turnout rate of 5.05% (a 28% increase), but the Spanish-language ver-sion produced a turnout rate of only 4.18% (a 6% increase). On average, the two treatments generated a 17% turnout increase. In short, when researchers employed mailings that were similar to the Gerber, Green, and Larimer (2008) treatments, they obtained results that varied no more than would be expected by sampling variability.

Now let's consider some experiments that investigated the effects of alternative treatments. Panagopoulos (2010, 2013) tested the effects of presenting registered voters with the chance to be on an honour roll if public records show that they voted in an upcoming election. In the first study, the mailing promised to publish the names of voters in a local newspaper; the second study presented a list of neighbours with exemplary voting records and invited the voter to join this honoured group by voting in the upcoming gubernatorial election. Both treat-ments produced positive effects, although the second study's effects were about half as large as the Self mailer's effect. Even larger effects, albeit with a large margin of statistical uncertainty, were obtained when mailings threatened to shame non-voters by putting their names in a local newspaper.

One might surmise from these studies that surveillance and disclo-sure have powerful effects on voter turnout, but this interpretation is challenged by three recent experiments. Panagopoulos (2011) sought to develop a version of the Self treatment that made people aware that their participation in elections was being observed but in a friendly, non-confrontational manner. By thanking voters for their participation in a recent election, his mailings reminded voters that voting is observable, but the tone of the mailing is altogether different from the scolding Self mailing. Panagopoulos demonstrates that the Thank You mailing increased turnout in three different electoral settings, with effects that are roughly two-thirds as large as the Self mailing's effect. One interpretation of these results is that revealing vote history in a friendly way exerts less social pressure than the Self mailing, but Panagopoulos also shows that the Thank You mailings are equally effective when recipients are praised for being concerned about public affairs, with no mention of past voting. Evidently, the gratitude effect is distinct from the effects of social pressure, and presenting voters with information about their past votes does not make these mailings more effective.

Two further clues about why the Self mailer works come from experiments that change its ingredients. Matland and Murray (2013) randomly vary whether their mailers present recipients with their vote history in previous elections and find that vote history per se has relatively weak effects on turnout. What makes this finding interesting is that the tone of the mailing is quite different from the Self mailing used by Gerber, Green, and Larimer (2008). The wording of the Self mailing is confrontational, notifying the reader that a "different approach" (i.e., monitoring voter turnout) is needed to get people to do their civic duty; Matland and Murray's mailing does not explain why vote history is being presented, nor do they threaten to update the recipient's voting record. The weak effects they obtain seem to suggest that surveillance is effective only if it is directly linked to a forceful statement about civic duty. A second suggestive piece of evidence on this point comes from a phone-banking experiment conducted by Green, Larimer, and Paris (2010). The sample consisted of voters who had not cast a ballot by early afternoon on Election Day; the treatment was a late afternoon call using a script that emphasized that voter turnout was being monitored:

> Hi. This is (*caller's name*) calling on behalf of Vote 2009. It's Election Day, and we're checking off names as people vote at (*location of polling place*). According to this list, you haven't voted yet – they're open until (*hour*) – are you planning to vote? [Pause for answer] Thanks – I'll let them know.

This treatment seemed to have relatively weak effects. The effect of the treatment on those who were reached by callers was 1.7 percentage points with a standard error of 1.7 percentage points. One interpretation of this result is that monitoring is not sufficient to increase turnout. This script did not mention civic duty, nor did it encourage voting. This experiment did not feature a direct comparison of a monitoring-only treatment with a monitoring-plus-duty treatment, but that test now seems to be the logical next step in this line of experimental inquiry.

Discussion

On the surface, experimental evidence seems to contradict Blais's claim that civic duty causes voter turnout but social pressure does not. A series of large-scale experiments appear to demonstrate that as social pressure mounts, voter turnout rises. This interpretation, however, must be qualified by another set of large-scale experiments that show that social pressure by itself or paired with expressions of gratitude is insufficient to generate substantial gains in turnout. Although a definitive experiment has yet to be conducted, the evidence now seems to suggest that social pressure exerts a powerful effect when combined with a forceful statement about civic obligation. Social pressure appears to work not because surveillance per se intimidates people into voting but rather because it pushes people to act in a manner that is consistent with their convictions about civic duty.

Several fruitful lines of further investigation suggest themselves, some involving new interventions, others involving new methodological procedures, and still others looking at the interaction between treatments and subjects' attributes. First, our conjecture about the interaction between social pressure and civic duty must be tested directly using a series of treatments that vary whether civic duty norms are asserted forcefully and whether they are paired with surveillance and disclosure. A related line of inquiry is to prime feelings of civic duty in more subtle ways to see if social pressure's effects are heightened when voters are thinking about injunctive norms about voting.

Another next step is calibrating effects against one another in a more systematic fashion. One shortcoming of the literature on social pressure is that only some of the studies use an established treatment (such as the Self treatment) as a benchmark to which other treatments are compared. As a result, one cannot tell whether study-to-study variation in estimated effects reflects the treatments, electoral context, or subject pool. A synoptic experiment would enable researchers to compare treatments holding context and subject pool constant.

Context and individual characteristics may moderate the effects of social pressure when intrinsic motivation to participate runs high. Bodet and Gélineau (2014) find, for example, that the Civic Duty mailer failed to raise turnout in a Quebec provincial election, where base rates of voting were comparable to a U.S. presidential election. This finding is echoed by a variety of unpublished proprietary studies in the United States that find various social pressure mailings to have weak effects in presidential elections, especially in battleground states. This pattern suggests that those who might otherwise respond to appeals based on civic duty and social pressure in a low turnout election are already voting in high turnout elections. More systematic exploration of this hypothesis is needed, exposing randomly selected members of the same voter population to social pressure mailings in either high turnout or low turnout contexts.

A further challenge is to link experimental interventions with more detailed measurement of individual attitudes. One practical way to do this would be to initially conduct a large survey that measures civic attitudes; respondents to this survey would then become subjects in a seemingly unrelated experiment testing the effects of social pressure. This type of study would help assess whether, as Blais suggests, those with a high degree of commitment to civic duty norms are less responsive to interventions that affect the calculus of voting. One intriguing possibility is that social pressure appeals work only when directed at people who are committed to the norm of voting, in which case we might conclude that social pressure works not because it imposes additional extrinsic costs on non-voters but rather because it accentuates the intrinsic motivation to vote among those committed to the voting norm.

NOTES

1 Although this feature of the design maximizes the strength of the intervention, it confounds the presentation of an official-looking turnout record (which adds credence to the idea that voting records are going to be monitored) with the disclosure of one's turnout record to others. Below we consider some experiments (e.g., Abrajano and Panagopoulos 2011; Matland and Murray 2013) that present turnout records without promising disclosure of the records to others.

2 All contrasts with the control group are statistically significant at the 5 per cent level.

3 This effect was replicated in another large-scale experiment conducted the
following year, also in Michigan. See Gerber, Green, and Larimer (2010).

References

Abrajano, Marisa, and Costas Panagopoulos. 2011. "Does Language Matter?
The Impact of Spanish versus English-language GOTV Efforts on Latino
Turnout." *American Politics Research* 39 (July): 643–63.
Bedolla, Lisa Garcia, and Melissa R. Michelson. 2012. *Mobilizing Inclusion:
Transforming the Electorate through Get-Out-the-Vote Campaigns.* New Haven,
CT: Yale University Press.
Blais, André. 2000. *To Vote or Not To Vote?* Pittsburgh: University of Pittsburgh
Press.
Bodet, Marc A., and François Gélineau. 2014. "Getting the Message: The
Impact of Social Pressure on Voter Turnout in Quebec Provincial Elections."
Paper prepared for presentation at the Annual Meeting of the American
Political Science Association, Washington, DC, 28–31 August.
Cialdini, Robert B., and Melanie R. Trost. 1998. "Social Influence: Social
Norms, Conformity and Compliance." In *The Handbook of Social Psychol-
ogy*, edited by D.T. Gilbert, S.T. Fiske, and G. Lindzey, 151–92. New York:
McGraw-Hill.
Gerber, Alan S., and Donald P. Green. 2000. "The Effects of Canvassing, Tele-
phone Calls, and Direct Mail on Voter Turnout: A Field Experiment." *Ameri-
can Political Science Review* 94 (3): 653–63.
Gerber, Alan S., Donald P. Green, and Christopher W. Larimer. 2008. "Social
Pressure and Voter Turnout: Evidence from a Large-Scale Field Experiment." *American Political Science Review* 102 (1): 33–48.
– 2010. "An Experiment Testing the Relative Effectiveness of Encouraging
Voter Participation by Inducing Feelings of Pride or Shame." *Political Behavior* 32:409–22.
Gosnell, Harold Foote. 1927. *Getting out the Vote.* Chicago: University of Chicago Press, 1927.
Green, Donald, Peter M. Aronow, Daniel E. Bergan, Pamela Green, Celia Paris,
and Beth I. Weinberger. 2011."Does Knowledge of Constitutional Principles
Increase Support for Civil Liberties? Results from a Randomized Field Experiment." *Journal of Politics* 73 (2): 463–76.
Green, Donald P., Christopher W. Larimer, and Celia Paris. 2010. "When Social
Pressure Fails: The Untold Story of Null Findings." Paper presented at the
68th Annual Meeting of the Midwest Political Science Association, Chicago,
22–5 April.

Gross, Alan E., Michael J. Schmidt, John P. Keating, and Michael J. Saks. 1974. "Persuasion, Surveillance, and Voting Behavior." *Journal of Experimental Social Psychology* 10 (5): 451–60.

Mann, Christopher B. 2010. "Is There Backlash to Social Pressure? A Large-Scale Field Experiment on Voter Mobilization." *Political Behavior* 32:387–407.

Matland, Richard E., and Gregg R. Murray. 2013. "Mobilization Effects Using Mail: Social Pressure, Descriptive Norms, and Timing." *Political Research Quarterly* 67:304–19.

Olson, Mancur. 1965. *The Logic of Collective Action: Public Goods and the Theory of Groups.* Cambridge, MA: Harvard University Press.

Panagopoulos, Costas. 2010. "Affect, Social Pressure and Prosocial Motivation: Field Experimental Evidence of the Mobilizing Effects of Pride, Shame and Publicizing Voting Behavior." *Political Behavior* 32 (3): 369–86.

– 2011. "Thank You for Voting: Gratitude Expression and Voter Mobilization." *Journal of Politics* 73 (3): 707–17.

– 2013. "Positive Social Pressure and Prosocial Motivation: Evidence from a Large-Scale Field Experiment on Voter Mobilization." *Political Psychology* 34 (2): 265–75.

Riker, William H., and Peter C. Ordeshook. 1968. "A Theory of the Calculus of Voting." *American Political Science Review* 62 (1): 25–42.

Sinclair, Betsy, Margaret McConnell, and Donald P. Green. 2012. "Detecting Spillover Effects: Design and Analysis of Multilevel Experiments." *American Journal of Political Science* 56:1055–69.

5 The Preferences of Voters and Non-Voters in Canada (1988–2008)[1]

JEAN-FRANÇOIS GODBOUT AND
MATHIEU TURGEON

Introduction

Voter turnout has been declining in recent years in Canada and in other democracies (Blais et al. 2004). In Canadian federal elections, this trend has greatly accelerated since the 2000 election. Averaging across decades, turnout has gone from 77.2% in the 1960s, to 74.5% in the 1970s, to 73.3% in the 1980s, to 68.3% in the 1990s, and finally to 61.4% in recent years. The lowest turnout ever recorded in Canadian federal elections occurred in 2008 when it reached a meagre 58.8%. To be sure, fewer voters in Canada participate in elections today compared to a generation ago.

There has been extensive scholarly work examining the *sources* of this decline (e.g., Gray and Caul 2000; Pammett and LeDuc 2003), but not much has been done – at least in the Canadian context – on the *consequences* of low turnout on political representation. One notable exception is a contribution by Daniel Rubenson, André Blais, Patrick Fournier, Elizabeth Gidengil and Neil Nevitte (2007). In this work, the authors evaluate the claim made by Lijphart (1997) that higher turnout would benefit parties and policies of the left. Analysing survey data from the 2000 election, they conclude that voters' opinions and preferences are representative of the entire electorate; consequently, universal turnout would not affect election results significantly in Canada. Their finding that turnout does not have a partisan bias is congruent with what has been found in the United States and several other democracies (e.g., Highton and Wolfinger 2001; Lutz and Marsh 2007).

In this chapter we re-examine the claim that turnout can produce a partisan bias in Canada. We argue that although the approach of

Rubenson et al. is a first step in the right direction, there is still room for improvement in order to evaluate this important and consequential claim. Here we propose a weighting scheme that allows for a greater discrimination among the electorate to compare between the preferences of voters and non-voters as measured in surveys of seven different Canadian elections in Canada (1988–2008). We find that voters and non-voters differ more significantly than what was initially reported by Rubenson et al. Moreover, the differences between voters and non-voters are consistent and, contrary to common wisdom, would *not* necessarily benefit parties and policies of the left. We further investigate this trend by focusing on three recent elections (2004–8) and find that non-voters are generally more conservative than voters on issues of relevance to Canadian politics. Not surprisingly, we also show that non-voters have more negative views of political parties and politicians in general. They do not see voting as a civic duty and are generally less satisfied with the way democracy works in Canada. To be sure, our findings indicate rather clearly that voters and non-voters *are* different and that this difference *is* important.

The chapter proceeds as follows. In the first part, we compare the opinions of voters and non-voters by looking at partisanship and voting intentions in the 1988–2008 Canadian Election Studies (CES). We next offer a more detailed analysis of several survey questions related to policy issues in the 2004–2006–2008 CES. We conclude with some general suggestions to further investigate this question.

Turnout and Partisan Bias

Research on voter turnout shows rather clearly that some people are more likely to participate in elections (Blais 2000; Wolfinger and Rosenstone 1980). For example, older, wealthier, and more educated people all have a higher probability of voting (Rosenstone and Hansen 1993). Non-voters are predominantly found in lower socio-economic strata of the population. Presumably, the gap in political participation would favour the more privileged segment of the electorate who hold distinct interests and values than lower socio-economic status voters. If so, election outcomes, and subsequent policy outcomes, would be different if non-voters were to participate in the electoral process (Lutz and Marsh 2007).

The question is, Do voters and non-voters actually hold distinct interests and values? In other words, do they have different political opinions and preferences? Common wisdom has it that citizens from lower socio-economic strata, who are more likely *not* to vote, have a stronger preference for left-of-centre political parties and policies. On the other hand, higher-status citizens, who are more likely to vote, tend to prefer conservative right-of-centre political parties and policies (De-Nardo 1980; Pacek and Radcliff 1995). Thus, if there is any partisan bias associated with low turnout it should cut in a more conservative direction, benefiting parties and policies from the right. In the Canadian context, this would imply that the Conservative Party benefits the most from the decline in voter turnout. The 2011 election results appear to confirm this trend.

Paradoxically, most of the work in this area has failed to demonstrate any significant difference in political opinions and preferences between voters and non-voters. Generally, studies find that higher turnout rates would not systematically alter the results of elections (e.g., Brunell and DiNardo 2004; Highton and Wolfinger 2001; Sides, Schickler and Citrin 2008). The same finding applies to Canada, despite the fact that these two groups differ significantly in their socio-economic characteristics. As stated earlier, a thorough analysis of the 2000 Canadian Election Study by Rubenson et al. indicates that voters and non-voters do not hold different political opinions and preferences. Moreover, the authors also present evidence that universal turnout would not have significantly altered the results of this election.

But are these findings representative of a general trend? In order to answer this question, we must consider the results of more than one election, especially since turnout has decreased dramatically since 2000. As figure 5.1 demonstrates, turnout in Canadian elections reached its historical low in 2008, with 58.8% of the eligible voting population casting a ballot. This study also proposes to improve on the approach adopted by Rubenson et al. to compare the average opinions of voters with the average opinions of non-voters. Specifically, Rubenson and colleagues compare the opinion of members of these two groups in a logistic regression where the dependent variable is turnout, and the independent variables are age, gender, education, income, and country of origin. Each policy issue is then added separately to the model to estimate whether it has a direct impact on the probability of voting. Thus their approach measures whether having different opinions on issues actually influences the probability of voting, whereas the approach presented here directly compares the opinion of voters and non-voters.

Figure 5.1 Voter Turnout in Canada

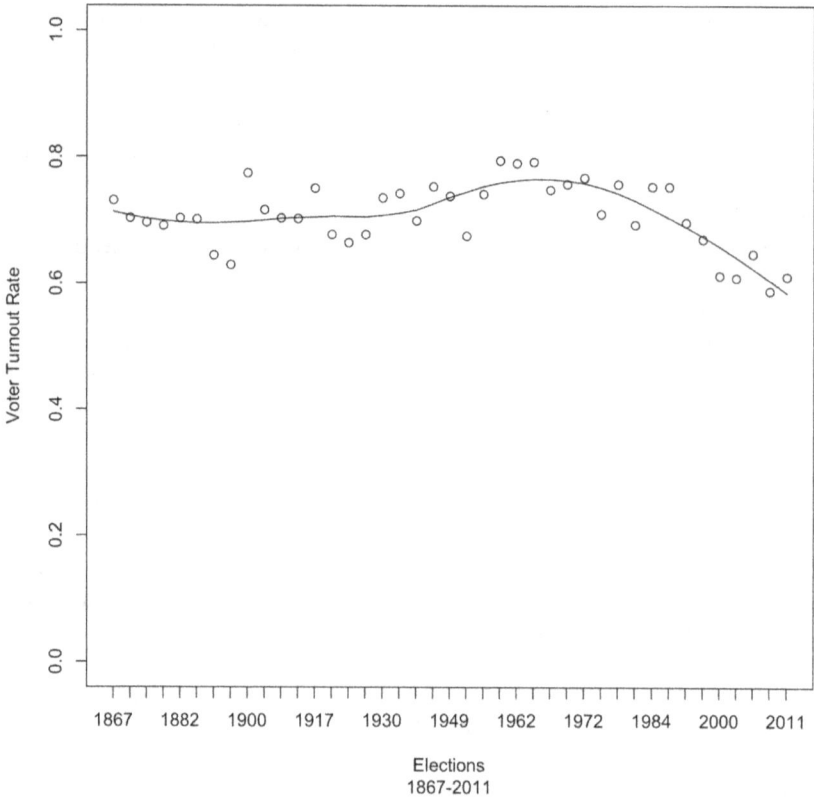

In the remainder of this chapter, we evaluate whether there are systematic patterns of differences between voters and non-voters in several public opinion surveys. We begin by looking at the partisan preferences of voters and non-voters between 1988 and 2008 in seven Canadian Election Studies. We then proceed to extend the work done by Rubenson et al. to three additional Canadian elections (2004, 2006, and 2008). In both analyses we also correct for the known over-reporting bias found in surveys about vote participation (e.g., Silver and Anderson 1986) by using a strategy similar to that of Rubenson et al.

Comparing Partisan and Voting Intentions, 1988–2008

We start our analysis by estimating whether voters and non-voters hold different attitudes in seven Canadian elections (1988–2008). Because the content of the questions varies considerably across surveys during this period, we focus only on the partisan and voting intention questions available in all studies. In each case, we compare the proportion of voters and non-voters who identified with (or intended to vote for) a specific party. Thus we have for the party identification categories: identified with the Liberal party, the Conservative party, the NDP, or as an independent. For the voting categories we have: intended to vote for the Liberal party, the Conservative party, the NDP, or undecided. The party identification and vote intention variables are collected from the pre-election wave of the surveys, while the turnout variable is from the post-election wave of the panel.[2]

As we mentioned above, the empirical strategy used by Rubenson et al. proposed to correct for the oversampling of voters in their analysis of the 2000 Canadian Election Study by weighting the respondents according to the official turnout rate. Around 83% of the 2000 CES reported voting while the official turnout rate in that election was a little over 61%. The weighting scheme adopted by Rubenson et al. is a sensible fix, because it simply aims to reflect the official turnout rate where the proportion of voters is much lower than in the sample. This procedure implies weighting self-reported non-voters/voters to correct for the under/over-representation of both groups in the sample. Specifically, self-reported non-voters are to be over-represented by a factor equal to the official proportion of non-voters in the election over the proportion of non-voters in the sample. Thus, for the 2000 federal election, one would have to weight self-reported non-voters by a factor of 2.29 (.39/.17). As for voters, one has to correct for their over-representation by a factor equal to the official proportion of voters divided, this time, by the proportion of voters in the sample (.61/.83 = .73). We adopt this weighting scheme and apply it to all seven elections under consideration.

Figure 5.2 reports the differences in party identification and vote intention between voters and non-voters in each of the seven election studies (1988–2008). Note that this value is obtained by subtracting the proportion of non-voters in one category from the proportion of voters in this same category (e.g., percentage Liberal identifiers that are voters – percentage Liberal identifiers that are non-voters). A negative value on the y axis implies that there are more non-voters in this category than voters. This bias ranges from –30% to 30%. The individual plots contain two types of points. Filled circles indicate that the mean difference is statistically significant at $p < .05$ (two-tailed), whereas empty circles indicate that the difference between voters and non-voters is not statistically significant.

The eight plots of figure 5.2 contain three interesting findings. First, as we can see with the Conservatives, significantly more voters identify with this party when compared to non-voters. This is a very important finding because it indicates that there are more Conservative supporters among voters than non-voters. This distinction holds, although less strongly, if we look at the vote intention question. We find more voters who indicate that they would support the Conservative party in the pre-election survey, especially after the 2003 election (and after the

Figures 5.2a–h Difference between Partisan Identification and Voting Intentions of Voters and Non-Voters in Seven Elections
Black filled points indicate significant difference ($p < .05$, t-test). Data are weighted according to the official turnout rate. Source: Canadian Election Studies, 1988–2008.

Party ID: Liberal

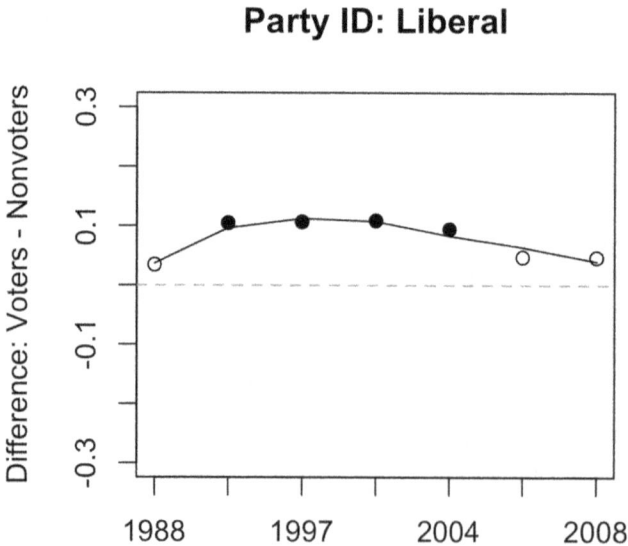

Vote Intention: Liberal

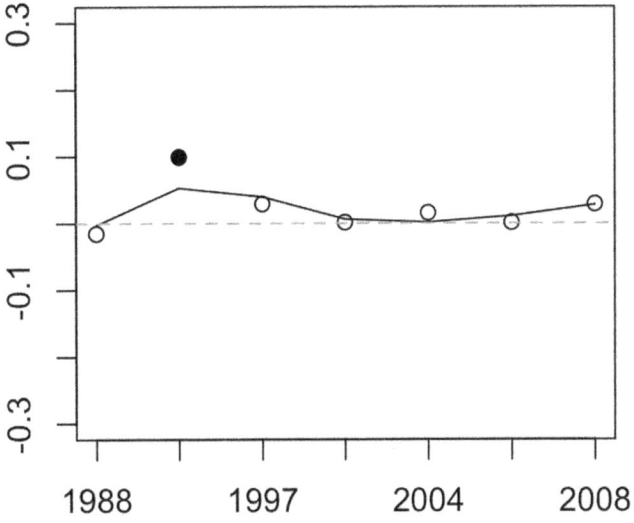

Party ID: Conservative

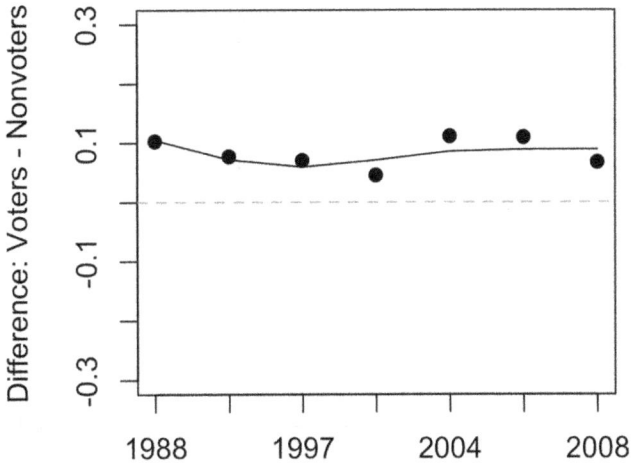

Figures 5.2a–h (Continued)

Vote Intention: Conservative

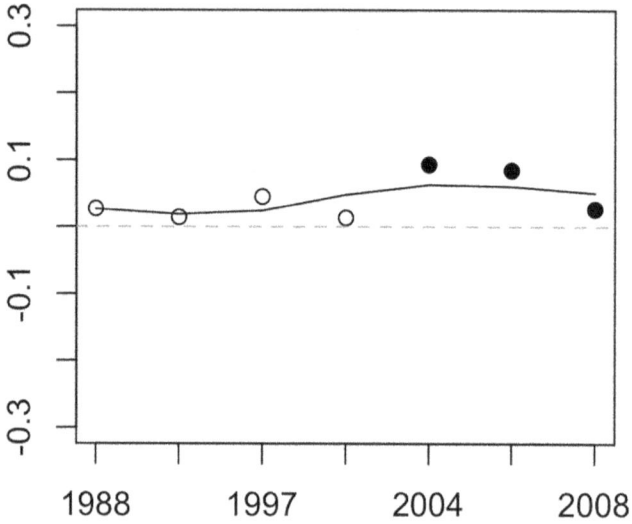

Party ID: NDP

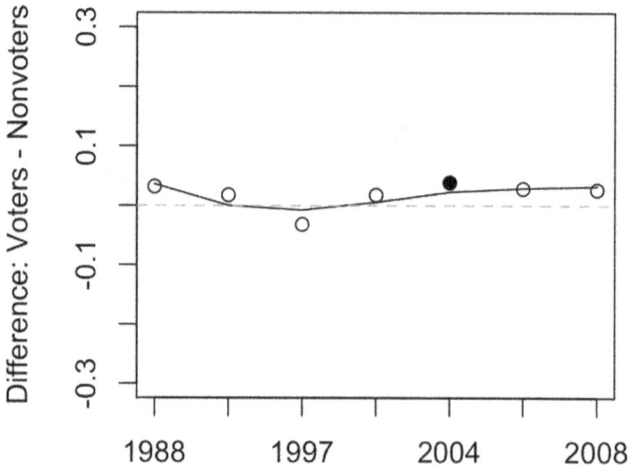

Vote Intention: NDP

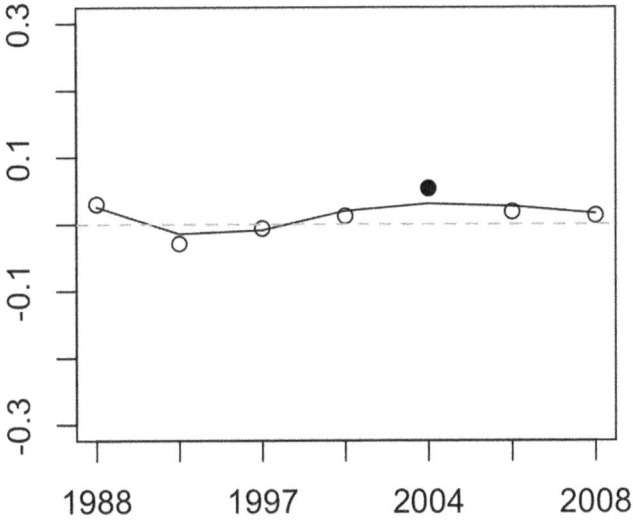

Party ID: Independent

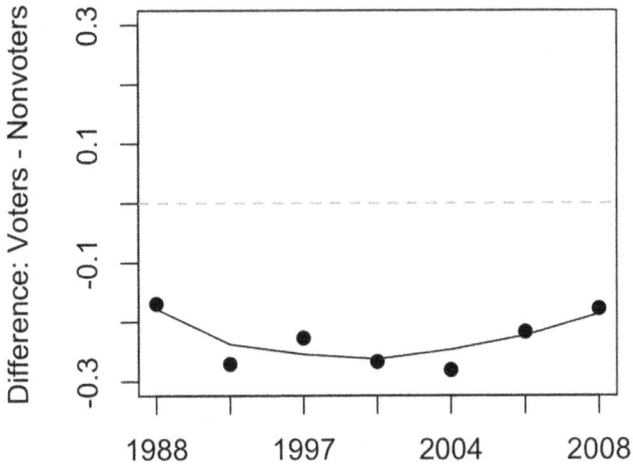

Figures 5.2a–h (Continued)

Vote Intention: Undecided

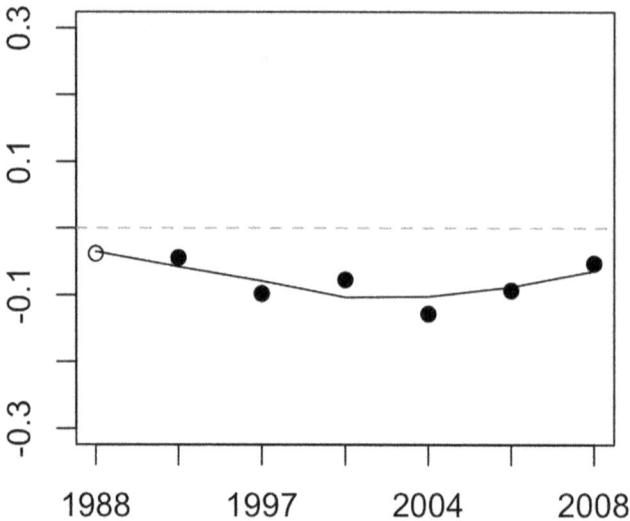

Progressive-Conservative and Canadian Alliance party merger). Incidentally, we do not find this bias in the 1988 survey when the Bloc and the Reform parties did not compete in the election.

Not surprisingly, the second most important finding is that non-voters are more likely to be undecided about their voting choice, and more likely to refuse to identify with a political party. Both relationships appear to be consistent across the whole period. They demonstrate that a much greater proportion of undecided and non-partisan respondents choose not to vote.

Finally, we find that there is a larger proportion of Liberal identifiers who participated in the 1993, 1997, 2000, and 2004 elections. In each of these elections, we always find more Liberals in the group of voters. It is interesting to note that for these four elections, the Liberal party formed the government.[3] That being said, we note that contrary to expectation, the NDP does not suffer from a turnout partisan bias. We basically find as many supporters of this party in the voting and non-voting categories of the sample.

It is important here, however, to take these time trend analyses in context. Indeed, the proportion of Liberal identifiers (or supporters) can fluctuate from one election to the next. The same is true for any other party or for independent or undecided voters. For example, in one election, the proportion of independents could be greater than the proportion of Liberals in the sample (like in 1988, 33% versus 25%). The reverse can also be true. We could find more Liberals than Independents in the sample, like in the 1997 election (31% Liberal versus 28 Independent). Thus, some of the differences in party identification or voting intentions reported above might simply reflect the changing nature of the distribution of these two variables across elections.

We can conclude that there are systematic differences between the proportion of voters and non-voters, especially with those who identify with the Conservative party. Indeed, there is a significant over-representation of this group in all post-election samples. In the next section, we turn to the task of evaluating whether self-reported voters and non-voters have different policy preferences.

The Preferences of Voters and Non-Voters, 2004–2008

In this section we continue our analysis of the preferences of voters and non-voters by extending the work of Rubenson et al. to three additional Canadian elections (2004, 2006, and 2008). Again we use a similar weighting scheme but, instead of relying uniquely on the distribution of voters/non-voters at the national level, we use information about voter participation rates disaggregated by age categories and region of residence. The construction of these different weights was done with data provided by Elections Canada for the 2004, 2006, and 2008 federal elections (Elections Canada 2004, 2006, and 2008).[4] Note that with this approach we are able to provide for a more precise turnout weight than what we used in the previous analysis. Precisely, we consider five regions (Maritimes, Quebec, Ontario, Western provinces, and British Columbia) and seven age groups (18–24, 25–34, 35–44, 45–54, 55–64, 65–74, 75+) and calculate the voter turnout rate in each of these categories. Given that age plays an important role in explaining turnout in Canada (Blais and Loewen 2011), but also that we observe varying participation rates across the different provinces, we believe that our weighting procedure is more accurate than the one used by Rubenson et al. What is important to understand here is that by using this information, our analysis allows for a greater discrimination between groups of eligible voters.

We constructed the weights by using the same variables available in the Canadian Election Studies and the Estimation of Voter Turnout by

Age Group Study of Elections Canada. With this information we calculated the frequency distribution of voters and non-voters in each age category and in the five geographic regions (i.e., 18–24 from Quebec, 18–24 from Ontario, and so on). Obtaining the individual respondent weight was purely a matter of computing the ratio of the frequency cell of the voting population in one specific age/region over the sample proportion of the same frequency cell in the CES. Therefore the distribution of preferences for voters and non-voters in the population is equal to the distribution of voter preferences in the CES sample appropriately weighted. Given the capability of obtaining a fairly accurate estimation of the individual voting and non-voting groups in each region and age group, estimating the counterfactuals becomes a simple question of correctly weighting each case in the CES. In this context, the weighting adjustment technique compensates for non-response by applying more than 35 weights (regions × age groups) across each specific class of respondents (i.e., the individual weight being applied in proportion to the inverse of their representation in the sample). This is basically the same approach used in the previous section; however, now we have more detailed information about the proportion of voters and non-voters in each region and age categories. In other words, we can correct for the over-representation of voters in the surveys by using a more precise weight than before.

Tables 5.1, 5.2, and 5.3 present the differences we obtain when comparing voters and non-voters using this weighting scheme over several different questions taken from the 2004, 2006, and 2008 CES, respectively. These questions concern different political issues and their salience, the evaluations of the economy and personal finances, and the evaluations of leaders and parties. As before, we also report party identification and voting intentions, because these estimates are now calculated with different weights. The tables compare values for voters and non-voters, but also report the differences between the two groups (last column). Statistically significant differences at .05 or .10 (two-tailed) are indicated in the tables. Like before, negative values indicate that there are more non-voters in this category than voters. Note that we include only items that were measured in pre-election surveys (except for the reported voter turnout, which is taken from the post-election wave of the surveys).

Tables 5.1, 5.2, and 5.3 present some notable differences between voters and non-voters. Let's treat each series of items in turn. The entries in the *Issues* series of the tables are percentages of the sub-populations

Table 5.1 Political Opinions and Preferences of Voters and Non-Voters, 2004 (%)

	Voters	Non-voters	Difference (voters – non-voters)
Issues			
More should be done for Quebec	23.5	25.4	−1.9
Oppose same-sex marriage	35.9	34.0	+1.9
Favour having private hospitals	42.8	46.5	−3.7
Federal government treats own province worse	35.8	31.1	+4.7**
Political parties hardly ever keep promises	49.5	59.6	−10.1*
Tough sentences for young offenders	50.4	52.4	−2.0
Canada should admit fewer immigrants	26.2	38.9	−12.6*
Favour death penalty	37.9	46.5	−8.6*
Leave it to private sector to create jobs	42.0	44.4	−2.4
Not only police and military should use guns	40.2	36.7	+3.5
People should move where jobs are	67.1	62.1	+5.0**
Women's place is at home	39.7	42.9	−3.2
The gun registry should be scrapped	57.5	54.9	+2.4
Citizen's duty to vote	96.3	73.7	+22.6*
Satisfied with how democracy works	57.2	45.0	+12.2*
More should be done to reduce gap between poor and rich	74.0	77.5	−3.5
Issue salience: among top 2 most important			
Health care	73.0	71.4	+1.6
Taxes	35.5	39.3	−3.8
Social welfare programs	26.5	20.7	+5.8*
Environment	16.4	15.1	+1.3
Corruption	41.8	43.6	−1.8
Evaluations of the economy			
Retrospective personal finance: better	19.2	21.7	−2.5
Prospective personal finance: better	22.8	29.5	−6.7*
Retrospective national economy: better	23.8	17.3	+6.4*

(Continued)

Table 5.1 (Continued)

	Voters	Non-voters	Difference (voters – non-voters)
Prospective national economy: better	25.3	17.7	+7.6*
Leader evaluations[a]			
Martin (Liberals)	49.0	41.4	+7.6*
Harper (Conservatives)	48.7	43.1	+5.6*
Layton (NDP)	45.4	39.4	+6.0*
Party evaluations[a]			
Liberals	47.2	38.7	+8.5*
Conservatives	47.6	41.3	+6.3*
NDP	43.0	38.4	+4.6*
Party identification			
Liberals	32.0	22.4	+9.6*
Conservatives	21.0	10.0	+11.0*
NDP	7.9	4.2	+3.7*
Independents	23.8	52.4	−28.6*
Vote intentions			
Liberals	28.4	25.7	+2.7
Conservatives	30.0	20.8	+9.2*
NDP	14.6	9.2	+5.4*
Undecided	9.2	21.1	−11.9*

[a] Average scores on a thermometer scale from 0 to 100

* Statistically significant differences at .05 (two-tailed); ** Statistically significant differences at .10 (two-tailed)

(voters and non-voters) that agree with the statement. Examining only the statistically significant differences for 2004, we find that:

1 fewer non-voters agree that the federal government treats their own province worse;
2 more non-voters believe that political parties never keep their promises;
3 more non-voters believe Canada should admit fewer immigrants;

Table 5.2 Political Opinions and Preferences of Voters and Non-Voters, 2006 (%)

	Voters	Non-voters	Difference (voters – non-voters)
Issues			
More should be done for Quebec	26.6	33.1	−6.5**
Oppose same-sex marriage	33.3	38.9	−5.6
Favour having private hospitals	47.6	46.4	+1.2
Federal government treats own province worse	34.4	22.1	+12.3*
Political parties hardly ever keep promises	31.1	45.5	−14.4*
Tough sentences for young offenders	47.9	54.9	−7.0**
Canada should admit fewer immigrants	21.9	29.6	−7.7*
Favour death penalty	38.5	38.1	+.4
Leave it to private sector to create jobs	33.1	40.1	−7.0**
Not only police and military should use guns	39.4	34.4	+5.0
People should move where jobs are	62.4	60.5	+1.9
Women's place is at home	36.7	41.3	−4.6
Gun registry should be scrapped	60.6	60.2	+.4
Citizen's duty to vote	96.9	77.0	+19.9*
Satisfied with how democracy works	61.8	52.3	+9.5*
Issue salience: among top 2 most important			
Health care	67.2	65.3	+1.9
Taxes	31.4	38.3	−6.9**
Social welfare programs	30.0	26.6	+3.4
Environment	22.4	20.7	+1.7
Corruption	43.2	38.6	+4.6
Evaluations of the economy			
Retrospective personal finance: better	23.9	21.3	+2.6
Prospective personal finance: better	21.7	21.6	+.1
Retrospective national economy: better	44.6	27.0	+17.6*
Prospective national economy: better	26.0	20.5	+5.5**

(Continued)

Table 5.2 (Continued)

	Voters	Non-voters	Difference (voters – non-voters)
Leader evaluations[a]			
Martin (Liberals)	46.0	40.5	+5.5*
Harper (Conservatives)	44.5	36.1	+8.4*
Layton (NDP)	51.1	42.2	+8.9*
Party evaluations[a]			
Liberals	44.7	41.8	+2.9
Conservatives	46.5	39.4	+7.1*
NDP	45.7	40.7	+5.0*
Party identification			
Liberals	32.7	28.3	+4.4
Conservatives	22.3	10.6	+11.7*
NDP	9.6	6.9	+2.7
Independents	19.9	41.6	−21.7*
Vote intentions			
Liberals	29.9	29.4	+.5
Conservatives	29.7	19.1	+10.6*
NDP	14.4	12.9	+1.5
Undecided	10.6	20.0	−*9.4*

[a] Average scores on a thermometer scale from 0 to 100

* Statistically significant differences at .05 (two-tailed); ** Statistically significant differences at .10 (two-tailed)

4 more non-voters favour the death penalty;
5 fewer non-voters believe people should relocate because of work;
6 fewer non-voters believe it is a citizen's duty to vote; and
7 fewer non-voters are satisfied with the way democracy works in Canada.

Of these sixteen issues, fifteen were also measured in the 2006 Election Study, and of these, eight showed statistically significant differences. We note five similar differences between voters and non-voters in the 2004 and 2006 surveys (i.e., treatment by federal government;

Table 5.3 Political Opinions and Preferences of Voters and Non-Voters, 2008 (%)

	Voters	Non-voters	Difference (voters − non-voters)
Issues			
Citizen's duty to vote	97.3	82.0	+15.3*
Satisfied with how democracy works	71.8	56.3	+15.5*
No point in voting for small parties	21.1	19.4	+1.7
Not feeling guilty for not voting	19.8	52.9	−33.1*
Evaluations of the economy			
Retrospective personal finance: better	21.1	25.3	−4.2
Retrospective national economy: better	12.5	14.2	−1.7
Leader evaluations[a]			
Dion (Liberals)	43.0	38.6	+4.4**
Harper (Conservatives)	51.0	46.3	+4.7**
Layton (NDP)	53.9	50.3	+3.6**
Party identification			
Liberals	24.7	22.5	+2.2
Conservatives	26.3	19.6	+6.7*
NDP	10.3	9.1	+1.2
Independents	24.3	40.0	−15.7*
Vote Intentions			
Liberals	20.3	16.6	+3.7
Conservatives	33.6	30.7	+2.9
NDP	15.7	14.4	+1.3
Undecided	12.1	19.0	−6.9*

[a] Average scores on a thermometer scale from 0 to 100

* Statistically significant differences at .05 (two-tailed); ** Statistically significant differences at .10 (two-tailed)

promises by political parties; admission of immigrants; citizen's duty to vote; and satisfaction with democracy). As compared to voters, non-voters believe that more should be done for Quebec, that young offenders should receive tougher sentences, and that it should be left to the private sector to create jobs. Unfortunately, the 2008 pre-election survey does not allow for many comparisons on issues because these questions are not included in the survey. Still, we were able to identify four issue questions, two of which also appear in the 2004 and 2006 surveys. The differences between voters and non-voters were significant in three of the four items. Again, citizen's duty to vote and satisfaction with democracy count among the statistically significant differences, just like in 2004 and 2008. The third difference indicates that more non-voters, as compared to voters, do not feel guilty for not voting.

Overall, while examining only political issues, we find great differences between voters and non-voters (and many more than what Rubenson et al. found for the 2000 election). Moreover, there appears to be a "logic" in the differences uncovered. First, and not surprisingly, non-voters are more sceptical of political parties and of the electoral process.

Indeed, fewer believe parties keep their electoral promises and that it is their duty to vote. A majority of them feel no guilt for not participating in elections. In addition, they are unsatisfied about how democracy works. But it also seems that, contrary to common wisdom, non-voters are generally more *conservative* than voters, at least on some specific issues. For instance, they are less favourable to immigration and more favourable to the death penalty and tougher sentences for young offenders. They also believe more strongly that the private sector should be left responsible for creating jobs.

The second series of items deals with *Issue salience*. In the 2004 and 2006 pre-election surveys, respondents were asked to indicate, from a list of five issues, what they considered to be the most and second most important problem facing the nation. The entries in tables 5.1 and 5.2 report the percentages of the subgroups who indicated the issue as most or second most important. The results show that voters and non-voters do not differ by much. In 2004 non-voters cared somewhat less about social welfare programs, and in 2006 non-voters were more concerned with taxation. These two differences are consistent with the findings presented above in that, if anything, non-voters lean to the right of the ideological spectrum, as they are more concerned about the taxes they pay and less about social welfare programs.

Next we look at a series of questions about the state of the economy and personal finances. The results indicate that non-voters had better prospective evaluations of their personal finances in the 2004 election, and worse retrospective and prospective evaluation of the national economy in the 2004 and 2006 surveys. Again, not much can be said about these differences beyond the fact that voters and non-voters differ on their evaluations of the national economy and their personal finances. These differences suggest, however, that individual economic conditions could also influence the decision to vote on election day.

Respondents were also asked to rate parties and leaders on a 0–100 thermometer scale. The entries for these two series of items are the average scores for voters and non-voters. Here the differences are strong and consistent across all three elections. Non-voters systematically show lower party and leader evaluations than voters. All differences but one reach statistical significance. These findings are also mostly consistent with the ones reported above about parties and the electoral process. The views of non-voters about parties and leaders – both fundamental democratic actors – are much more negative than those held by voters.

Finally, the results for party identification and vote intentions are very similar to the ones presented in the first part of the analysis. Non-voters tend to identify less with political parties and are more likely to be independent. They are also more likely to be undecided about which party to support in the upcoming election. Again most differences reach conventional statistical significance.

Discussion

Many believe that since voters and non-voters have different socio-economic characteristics, they must necessarily have different attitudes about politics in general (Lijphart 1997). Since educated, wealthier, and older citizens are more likely to vote, many assume that the gap in political participation would favour the more privileged segment of the electorate.

The preceding analysis has only partially validated this claim. Indeed, we find that voters and non-voters have different partisan preferences, but, contrary to common wisdom, we do not find that non-voters are more likely to hold progressive views or favour greater economic redistribution. To the contrary, non-voters appear to be more supportive of conservative policies.

We also find that non-voters hold more cynical views about politics and politicians; they do not appear to care much about the democratic process in general.

Our results also contradict some findings by Rubenson et al. about the Canadian electorate. While Rubenson et al. do not find much difference between the opinions and preferences of voters and non-voters, our results offer a different perspective. Indeed, we find that voters and non-voters differ on several political issues. Precisely, non-voters in the sample systematically evaluate parties and their leaders more negatively, fewer identify with political parties and show electoral support for them, and a majority of non-voters believe that parties hardly ever keep their promises. They do not believe that citizens have the duty to vote in elections, and their satisfaction with the way democracy works is decidedly lower. Non-voters have a more pessimistic and cynical view of democracy, its actors and institutions. It is not surprising they do not participate in elections.

But there is more. Non-voters, contrary to common wisdom, are also generally more conservative on some important issues of Canadian politics. They approve more strongly of the death penalty and believe that Canada should allow fewer immigrants and apply tougher sentences to young offenders. They also believe more strongly that the creation of jobs should be left to the private sector. Finally, they are more concerned about the taxes they pay and less concerned about social welfare programs. These differences are substantively large and significant when we compare them to the preferences of voters.

In our view, this constitutes a very interesting paradox. Non-voters are systematically *less* likely to identify with the Conservative party. Yet their views on many issues – such as crime, taxes, and welfare programs – match the positions of this party. Should we conclude then that the turn-out bias is actually hurting the Conservatives in Canada? Although we find that there are, on average, more Conservative party identifiers who vote than abstain, perhaps this party could find a source of additional support by mobilizing more of these alienated voters. It is perhaps ironic that Conservatives have been recently involved in a voter suppression scandal.

A final word of caution is that we should be particularly careful about generalizing the results of these analyses, because we do not have a *representative* sample of non-voters in the CES. The problem of panel attrition does not go away, even after using post-stratification weights based on the respondent's age or region of residence to correct for the under-representation of non-voters in the panel. As we show in figure 5.3, the gap between the average turnout rate as reported by the CES and the official voter turnout rate of Election Canada has greatly increased over the years. This raises the question of whether self-reported non-voters who make it into the post-election survey are representative of their pre-election survey counterparts. Clearly, more work needs

Figure 5.3 Official and Canadian Election Survey Turnout

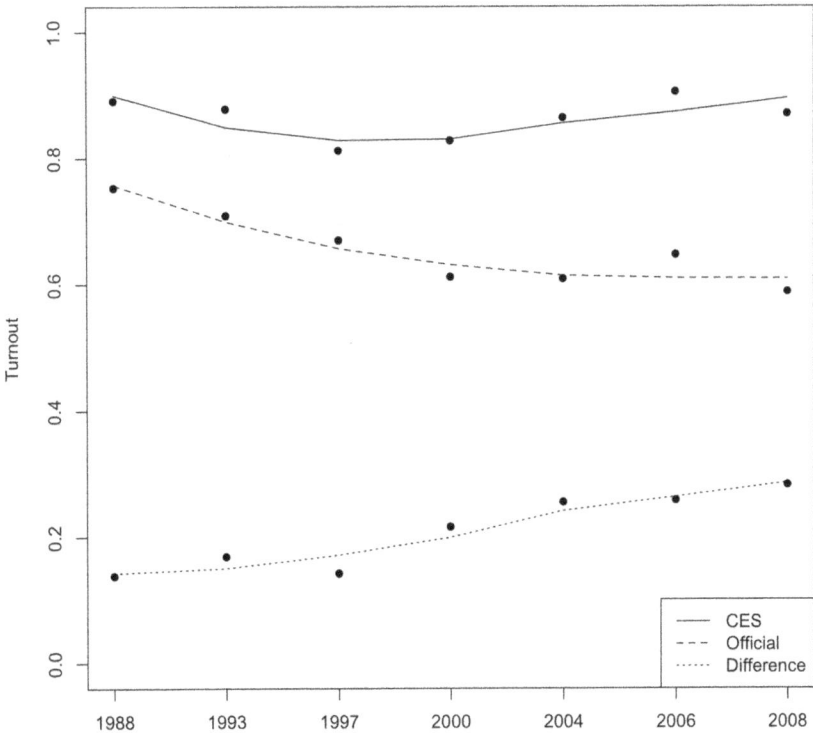

to be done here, but this seems highly unlikely. As Burden (2000) and Brehm (1993) explain, up-weighting non-voters in the panel may only make estimations worse.[5]

Researchers might use at least two strategies to better answer these questions. The first involves more careful and comprehensive sampling of non-voters in election studies and more effective maintenance of non-voters within panels. Such an approach is, however, both expensive and difficult. Traditional survey sampling is getting more difficult, not easier, and so such a strategy could prove an expensive option. Another approach is to randomly induce individuals to vote – see chapter 4 for a review of several methods – and then ascertain whether non-voters who are induced to vote change their views on politics. Such an approach would at least tell us whether the differences between non-voters and voters are due to the act of political engagement itself. This would go some way to reducing uncertainty about the nature and sources of differences between voters and non-voters.

One thing is certain, self-reported non-voters have much more negative views of politics and politicians, in general. They are more likely not to consider voting as a duty or to feel guilty about abstaining from voting. Their views of politicians and parties are much more negative on average, especially when we consider the two main political parties, the Conservative and Liberal parties.

NOTES

1 Paper prepared for a conference in honour of André Blais, Montreal, 20–1 January.
2 Note that for partisan identification, we excluded respondents who gave an answer to the follow up party identification question (e.g., Is there a party that you are leaning toward?). These respondents were coded as independent.
3 Readers should look to chapter 6 for further explanation of the (apparently temporary) demise of the Liberal Party of Canada.
4 The Elections Canada (2004, 2006, and 2008) studies use administrative data from the electoral process to verify in a sample of eligible voters who voted or abstained on the day of the election. Elections Canada also collects information about age, gender, and residence from the National Register of Electors. Therefore, we are provided with a sample of validated turnout rate by region and age group in each of these elections.
5 The concluding chapter of this volume extends this discussion by considering some of the innovations that might be made in election studies. Such innovations might, with proper attention, solve some of the problems of the under-representation of non-voters in election studies.

References

Blais, André. 2000. *To Vote or Not to Vote? The Merits and Limits of Rational Choice Theory*. Pittsburgh, PA: University of Pittsburgh Press.
Blais, A., E. Gidengil, N. Nevitte, and R. Nadeau. 2004. "Where Does Turnout Decline Come From?" *European Journal of Political Research* 43 (2): 221–36.

Blais, A., and P. Loewen. 2011. *Youth Electoral Engagement in Canada*. Ottawa: Elections Canada.

Brehm, John. 1993. *The Phantom Respondents: Opinion Surveys and Political Representation*. Ann Arbor: University of Michigan Press.

Brunell, T.L., and J. DiNardo. 2004. "A Propensity Score Reweighting Approach to Estimating the Partisan Effects of Full Turnout in American Presidential Elections." *Political Analysis* 12 (1): 28–45.

Burden, Barry C. 2000. "Voter Turnout and the National Election Studies." *Political Analysis* 8 (4): 389–98.

DeNardo, James. 1980. "Turnout and the Vote: The Joke's on the Democrats." *American Political Science Review* 74 (2): 406–20.

Elections Canada. 2004. "Estimation of Voter Turnout by Age Group." Elections Canada. http://www.elections.ca/content.aspx?section=res&dir=rec/part/estim/38ge&document=index&lang=e.

– 2006. "Estimation of Voter Turnout by Age Group." Elections Canada. http://www.elections.ca/content.aspx?section=res&dir=rec/part/estim/39ge&document=index&lang=e.

– 2008. "Estimation of Voter Turnout by Age Group." Elections Canada. http://www.elections.ca/content.aspx?section=res&dir=rec/part/estim/40ge&document=index&lang=e.

Gray, M., and M. Caul. 2000. "Declining Voter Turnout in Advanced Industrial Democracies, 1950 to 1997: The Effects of Declining Group Mobilisation." *Comparative Political Studies* 33 (9): 1091–122.

Highton, Benjamin, and Raymond E. Wolfinger. 2001. "The Political Implications of Higher Turnout." *British Journal of Political Science* 31 (1): 179–92.

Lijphart, Arend. 1997. "Unequal Participation: Democracy's Unresolved Dilemma." *American Political Science Review* 91 (1): 1–14.

Lutz, Georg, and Michael Marsh. 2007. "Introduction: Consequences of Low Turnout." *Electoral Studies* 26 (3): 539–47.

Pacek, A., and B. Radcliff. 1995. "Turnout and the Vote for Left-of-Centre Parties: A Cross-National Analysis." *British Journal of Political Science* 25 (1): 137–43. https://www.cambridge.org/core/journals/british-journal-of-political-science/article/turnout-and-the-vote-for-leftofcentre-parties-a-crossnational-analysis/64A2331A162E37352D551465F312CB81.

Pammett, J.H., and L. LeDuc. 2003. *Explaining the Turnout Decline in Canadian Federal Elections: A New Survey of Non-Voters*. Ottawa: Elections Canada.

Sides, John, Eric Schickler, and Jack Citrin. 2008. "If Everyone Had Voted, Would Bubba and Dubya Have Won." *Presidential Studies Quarterly* 38 (3): 521–39.

Silver, B.D., and B.A. Anderson. 1986. "Who Over Reports Voting?" *American Political Science Review* 80 (2): 613–24.

Rosenstone, Steven J., and John Mark Hansen. 1993. *Mobilization, Participation, and Democracy in America: New Topics in Politics.* New York: Maxwell Macmillan International.

Rubenson, D., A. Blais, P. Fournier, E. Gidengil, and N. Nevitte. 2007. "Does Low Turnout Matter? Evidence from the 2000 Canadian Federal Election." *Electoral Studies* 26:589–97.

Wolfinger, Raymond E., and Steven J. Rosenstone. 1980. *Who Votes?* New Haven, CT: Yale University Press.

PART II

Vote Choice

6 The Economy and Federal Election Outcomes in Canada: Taking Provincial Economic Conditions into Account

RICHARD NADEAU, ÉRIC BÉLANGER, AND BRUNO JÉRÔME

How does the economy matter for incumbent politicians? Empirical work showing the impact of the economy on vote choice is now commonplace (for comparative studies, see Lewis-Beck 1988; Lewis-Beck and Stegmaier 2007; Duch and Stevenson 2008; Nadeau, Lewis-Beck and Bélanger 2013; for Canada, see Nadeau and Blais 1993, 1995; Anderson 2010). These studies have mainly taken three forms. The first two, which are the oldest, make use of aggregate-level political and economic data. "Vote functions" seek to explain the result of national elections, while "popularity functions" seek to model either vote intention or satisfaction towards government (for a review of these two types, see Nannestad and Paldam 1994; Lewis-Beck and Stegmaier 2013). The third type of study relies on individual-level data and seeks to establish links between individual voters' economic perceptions and vote choice in a given election (Kiewiet 1983).

This chapter fits within the body of work looking to establish the fundamentals of a vote function for Canadian federal elections. These studies developed in two stages. Researchers first examined the link between national economic conditions and the results of federal elections (see Happy 1986, 1989, 1992; Carmichael 1990). The work of Nadeau and Blais (1993, 1995) can be seen as the final outcome of this first phase. They showed that two main factors weigh upon Canadians' vote choice: the unemployment rate and leader image. A second wave of vote function work later set upon making use of data disaggregated to the level of Canadian provinces (Gélineau and Bélanger 2005; Bélanger and Gélineau 2010). These studies mainly conclude that vote choice in the provinces during federal elections is explained by one local-level factor, that of regional partisan traditions in Canada, and by two national-level factors, the longevity of the incumbent government and the national unemployment rate.

The current study will examine more specifically this last conclusion by looking at Canadian federal elections between 1953 and 2011. The motivations behind this study are fourfold. First, there is the fact that a small amount of work has been conducted on this question in Canada. Before concluding that local or regional conditions have no influence on the result of national elections in Canada, one must examine this question in more detail.

Second, there are theoretical motivations. Certainly, it is normal that national economic conditions play a leading role during national-level elections, notably due to substantial media coverage given to statistics on national conditions and the importance that political parties give to these statistics to either defend their policies or criticize their opponents (Nadeau et al. 2000; Blais et al. 2002). However, many studies have also shown (see notably Weatherford 1983; Mondak, Mutz, and Huckfeldt 1996) that certain voters rely on local-level economic conditions to draw conclusions about how the economy has fared nationally. Using individual-level data, Cutler (2002) confirmed this phenomenon in the Canadian context. We might expect therefore that provincial-level economic conditions colour certain voters' national-level perceptions and consequently have an impact on vote choice either for or against the incumbent government.

Another theoretical argument touches upon the importance of regional economic development in political parties' discourse. During electoral campaigns, political parties send explicit messages to voters in different provinces by presenting themselves as being in a better position than their opponents to bring prosperity to the province. As a result, party discourse tends to make provincial-level economic realities more salient in the eyes of voters (Cutler 2002). In addition, many federal policy programs, as well as fiscal transfers from the federal government to the provinces, aim to improve the economy of specific regions, thus trying to level economic prosperity across the country (Savoie 1992; Brown 2007). Consequently, we should expect this dynamic to lead a certain number of voters to express a national-level economic vote based on provincial-level indicators.

A fourth and final reason for this study is the need for a re-examination of the Canadian case. It can be expected that the effect of provincial-level indicators on national-level vote choice should be more important when an election is carried out in a country where the sub-national entities exercise important powers, such as Canada.[1] In this context, regional economic statistics are largely diffused and commented on by provincial political actors. For example, these same actors may sometimes remind voters during national election campaigns that the policies of the national government have disadvantaged their province in favour of others. Work on the effects of regional-level factors on vote choice in other countries suggest that this is the case. In a pioneering study, Rosenstone (1983) proposed a model that would predict the level of support received by American presidential candidates at the state level in order to determine the number of Electoral College votes received by each candidate, thereby predicting the result of the election (see also Holbrook 1991). From this, a more parsimonious model developed by Campbell (1992) leads to an interesting conclusion. He observes that, all other things being equal, the score that a presidential candidate receives in a given state depends mainly on national economic growth but also, to a smaller extent, on growth observed at the state level, with the effect of national economic conditions being about six times more important than those of the state (see Campbell 1992, table 2, 399; for similar conclusions, see Strumpf and Phillippe 1999; Orth 2001; Eisenberg and Ketcham 2004).

These results differ from those obtained by Jérôme and Jérôme-Speziari (2005, 2010b, 2011), who studied the determinants of electoral results in France with the help of vote functions disaggregated to the level of French *départements* and *régions*. The models used by these authors include a single economic indicator that measures the unemployment rate in the *région* during the presidential mandates. The use of just this particular variable does not allow one to determine if local-level economic conditions add to explaining the vote beyond national-level economic conditions. Jérôme and Jérôme-Speziari implicitly admit this shortcoming when they say that this economic indicator "must be considered like a (dominant) national economic trend adjusted to local economic situation" (2011, 10).

Do voters take account of local as well as national economic conditions when deciding to vote? The present study will allow us to see if there is a link between regional entities' political and economic importance and the magnitude of the impact of regional economic conditions on the result of national elections. The political weight of regions appears greater in Canada, especially given the importance of the province of Quebec in the country's history. Available data indicate that the economic weight of regions is very important in the case of Canadian

Figure 6.1 Economic and Fiscal Weight of U.S. States, Canadian Provinces, and French Regions versus Decentralization of Local Upper-Level Expenditures

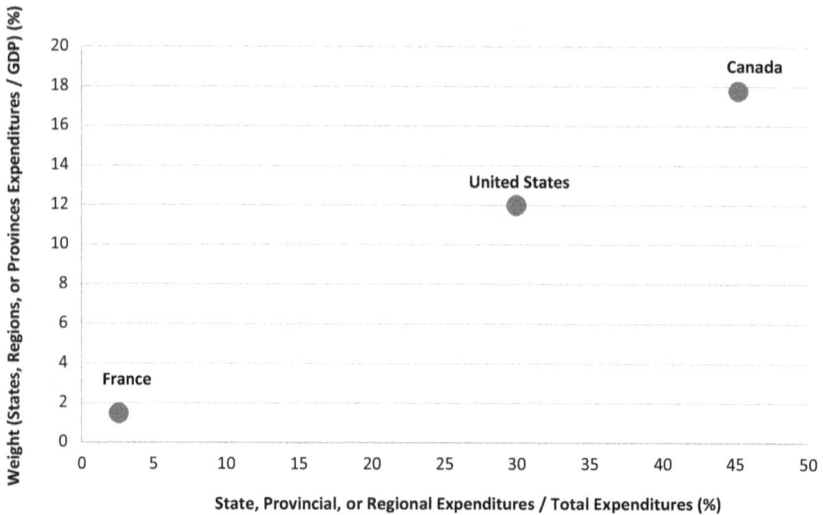

Sources: Organisation for Economic Cooperation and Development, and Direction générale des collectivités locales de France (2008 data; authors' calculus)

provinces and not very important for French *régions*, with American states occupying a position somewhere in the middle. Figure 6.1 compares the regions' economic and fiscal weight (i.e., expenditures of Canadian provinces, French regions, and American states in terms of the national GDP) with the degree of decentralization of their expenditures (i.e., as a function of total national expenditures). The figure clearly shows that Canada and France are two polar cases flanking the United States.[2] Our expectation is thus that local economic conditions will have greater impact in Canada than has been observed in the United States or in France.

The preceding remarks suggest that the work on economic voting in Canada is interesting in its own right. But the empirical conclusions based on the Canadian case also carry larger implications. As a relatively decentralized federation, Canada offers an interesting setting to test whether local economic conditions also matter to voters' judgments about incumbents. A positive conclusion would carry important implications not only about the link between the nature of political institutions and the strength of economic voting (Powell and Whitten 1993; Nadeau, Niemi, and Yoshinaka 2002) but also about voters' decision-making process in their evaluations of the economic performance of sitting governments.

The Vote Function

The theoretical foundations of vote and popularity functions are well-established (Nannestad and Paldam 1994; Lewis-Beck and Stegmaier 2013). It is generally accepted that the result of an election can be explained by a combination of political and economic factors. Therefore, the general model of a vote function for a given country is the following:

(1)   Vote = f (ECN, POL).

A majority of studies on vote functions use data aggregated at the national level. For example, a typical vote function study in Canada for elections held between 1953 and 2011 would be based on a sample of twenty cases. The model used would then try to link the results of these federal elections – in a majority of cases, the dependent variable is the percentage of popular support received by the incumbent government – to a limited number of political and economic variables such as leader popularity, longevity of the incumbent government, or the unemployment rate at the time of the election.

This approach has a number of limitations, mainly due to the small number of cases upon which it rests. To resolve this, some authors have proposed that we study the results of national-level elections by breaking them down into subdivisions of significant regions, such as American states, Canadian provinces, or French *régions* or *départements*. This method has a number of advantages. Increasing the number of degrees of freedom allows us to arrive at a more finely tuned vote model and to obtain more statistically reliable results. Conceptually, this approach allows us to conceive of national elections as the result of a series of regional-level elections. The case of American presidential elections is the clearest example of this point, where the outcome depends on the result of fifty local elections that determine the number of Electoral College votes that candidates will receive, and therefore the winner.

A disaggregated approach to the use of vote functions therefore allows one to account for both local and national dynamics at work when elections are being carried out on the national level. This type of vote function remains understudied in general, and even more so in the Canadian case. What is more, the conclusion that comes out of the rare studies using this type of vote function in Canada stipulates that only national-level economic conditions, notably the unemployment rate, have a significant impact on federal election outcomes (Gélineau and Bélanger 2005; Bélanger and Gélineau 2010).

As mentioned earlier, a re-examination of this conclusion is at the heart of the present study. The argument proposed is relatively simple. In a federal regime, voters can be conceived of as participating in a single election, but also as participating in a series of regional elections. Consequently, the result of a federal election in Canada will depend upon both national- and provincial-level political and economic factors. In this case, the vote function will take the following form:

(2) $\text{Vote} = f\ (\text{ECN}_{\text{Nat}},\ \text{ECN}_{\text{Prov}},\ \text{POL}_{\text{Nat}},\ \text{POL}_{\text{Prov}})$.

This equation simply states that the result of Canadian federal elections will depend on both local and national factors. These factors, as well as the hypotheses that concern them, are presented in the next section.

A Vote Function for Canada

The first decision to be made in a vote function study for Canada concerns the definition of the dependent variable. The usual choice at this point is to use the percentage of the vote going to the incumbent party, be it the Liberal Party or the Conservative Party. We have nonetheless opted for another way of defining the dependent variable, which is the percentage of the vote going to the Liberal Party (with appropriate adjustments made to the independent variables so as to maintain the consistency of the signs of their regression coefficients; see below). This choice is easily explained. The Liberal Party has been in power during thirty-eight of the fifty-eight years under study, which is about 66% of the time between 1953 and 2011, and thus has been the country's dominant party for most of that period (Blais 2005). This political organization, unlike the Conservative Party, has not seen any schisms or major divisions over the period under study. Its support, with perhaps the exception of the last two elections, has fluctuated within a stable margin. It can therefore be believed that the variations in support for the Liberal Party are a more accurate reflection of the fluctuations in short-term variables, such as the unemployment rate, than anything else. Finally, using the Liberal vote as the dependent variable marks a return to Nadeau and Blais's (1993, 1995) original model specification.

Vote function studies in Canada (Nadeau and Blais 1993, 1995; Gélineau and Bélanger 2005; Bélanger and Gélineau 2010) generally conclude that unemployment is the economic indicator most directly and systematically linked to federal electoral outcomes. A preliminary analysis of our data confirms this assertion. Therefore, the first independent variable that will be included in our vote function model is the unemployment rate. Keeping in mind the objectives of the present study, both the national and provincial unemployment rates will be included in the model. However, there still remains the matter of establishing the most appropriate lag between the economic measure chosen and the date of the election. The decision about the exact lag structure to be used is both a conceptual and an empirical one. In order to take into account the fact that it may take some time for unemployment data to be published, reach voters, and possibly influence their vote decision, we need our unemployment rate variables to be measured a few weeks or months prior to the election actually taking place (i.e., the unemployment variables must be time-lagged relative to our dependent variable). The search for a more systematic empirical link between unemployment data and vote choice should also guide our decision. Different tests have been carried out, and a lag of three months between unemployment data and the election seems to be the best choice from both a theoretical and empirical point of view.[3]

In addition to the unemployment rate,[4] political variables need to be included in the model. The first among them is the lagged dependent variable, which captures the effect of all the factors explaining inertia or stability of the Liberal vote over time. The inclusion of this variable in the vote function offers several theoretical and empirical advantages. On the theoretical side, the lagged variable allows us to capture electoral adjustments due to the political parties' "captive" voter base being more or less loyal to them over time. Also the lagged variable registers the residual memory effect associated with past economic and political shocks. If such dynamic effects are plausible, then it is essential from a statistical point of view to include an endogenous, autoregressive-type variable on the right-hand side of the vote equation. The quality of the model is even higher when the autoregressive trend sustains itself over time.

Other political variables should also be included. The disaggregated models must take into account political parties' regional strongholds (see Campbell 1992; Jérôme and Jérôme-Speziari 2010b; Bélanger and Gélineau 2010). We keep this factor in mind and include in the model a series of dichotomous variables that allow us to take into account the regional bases of Liberal Party support in Canada (the omitted province is Alberta; the regression coefficients in this case will measure the difference between support for the Liberal Party in Alberta and in the other provinces). These strongholds have remained rather consistent across the period under study – with the exception of Quebec, a Liberal bastion until the 1984 election, when it deserted this party following the repatriation of the Canadian Constitution without Quebec's consent. A special dichotomous variable will take account of this historic break between Quebec and the Liberal Party.

One last national-level political variable that is likely to influence vote choice is the popularity of the party leader. Unfortunately, there is no satisfactory series of opinion data measuring this variable over time in Canada. The strategy used for this study is to introduce dichotomous variables for each of the Liberal Party leaders, with the most recent (i.e., Michael Ignatieff in 2011) being the omitted category. The inclusion of the leader variable responds to an imperative to be prudent in this sort of aggregate-level study. Its inclusion should allow us to significantly increase the percentage of explained variance and avoid overestimating the impact of unemployment on electoral results. Thus, the vote function that will be estimated takes the following form:

$$(3) \quad \text{VLIB}(PR/E_t) = b_0 + b_1 \text{VLIB}(PR/E_{t-1}) + b_2 \text{LEADERS} + b_3 \text{PROVS} + b_4 \text{UNR}(NAT/t-3) + b_5 \text{UNR}(PR/t-3) + e$$

'VLIB(PR/E_t)' is the percentage of the vote received by the Liberal Party in the ten Canadian provinces during the twenty federal elections that took place in Canada between 1953 and 2011 ($N = 200$); 'VLIB(PR/E_{t-1})' is the percentage of votes received by the Liberal Party in the ten Canadian provinces during the previous election (1949 to 2008); 'LEADERS' is a series of dichotomous variables that take the value of 1 for elections where the Liberal Party was led by Louis St-Laurent (1957), Lester Pearson (1958, 1962, 1963, 1965), Pierre Elliott Trudeau (1968, 1972, 1974, 1979, 1980), John Turner (1984, 1988), Jean Chrétien (1993, 1997, 2000), Paul Martin (2004, 2006) and Stéphane Dion (2008) (omitted category = Michael Ignatieff in 2011); 'PROVS' are dichotomous variables that take the value of 1 for each province (with the exception of Alberta) and 0 otherwise; 'UNR(NAT/t–3)' is the national unemployment rate measured three months before the election; 'UNR(PR/t–3)' is the unemployment rate in each of the ten Canadian provinces measured three months before the election; finally, 'e' is the error term.

The components of equation 3 that interest us in particular are the national and provincial unemployment rates. Provincial unemployment rates are often absent from studies of national vote functions in Canada. The implicit hypothesis in this case would therefore be that $b_5 = 0$. For reasons mentioned in the previous sections, we believe that the impact of provincial unemployment rates could be significant, without being as important as that of the national unemployment rate. Therefore, the two hypotheses that we will test in the next section can be formalized as follows:

(H1) $b_4, b_5 \neq 0$

(H2) $|b_4| > |b_5|$

Findings

The vote function results are presented in table 6.1. The statistical analysis relies on ordinary least-squares regression with panel-corrected standard errors to address potential problems of heteroskedasticity. This specification is introduced because of the cross-sectional nature of the data set, for which residuals cannot be assumed to be independent across provinces (the inclusion of dichotomous provincial variables also allows control for possible heterogeneity across units). An additional variable is introduced into the model. This variable, called "incumbency," takes the value of 1 when the Liberal Party was the incumbent government during an election and –1 otherwise. The national and provincial unemployment rates have been multiplied by this variable, thus ensuring the consistency of their signs (negative), whether or not the Liberal Party was in power.

The results of column 1 correspond to the model based on the hypothesis that the unemployment rate in a province would not influence the vote in that province during a federal election (i.e., $b_5 = 0$). The overall performance of the model is very good, since 80% of the variation both in a province's vote and from one election to another is explained by the model. The coefficients of the different variables are of the expected sign and statistically significant. The coefficient of the lagged dependent variable accounts for the stability of the Liberal vote across space and time. The size and sign of the "incumbency" variable's coefficient show the advantage of having formed the incumbent government when an election is called. It also reflects the fact that periods of Liberal Party rule culminate in large amounts of support for this political organization.

The dichotomous provincial variables reflect the presence of regional strongholds for the Liberal Party. The positive and similar coefficients in the Atlantic (Newfoundland and Labrador, Prince Edward Island, Nova Scotia, New Brunswick) and central (Quebec and Ontario) provinces clearly show that the electoral strength of the Liberal Party has been more important in eastern Canada. However, this supremacy has not been immutable, as shown by the variable "Quebec break," which very clearly demonstrates the drop in Liberal Party support in Quebec after 1980. Furthermore, two periods of LPC domination stand out. Between 1953 and 1984, this party held onto power almost continuously (from 1953 to 1957, and from 1963 to 1984, with the only exception of Joe Clark's brief mandate for nine months in 1979). The Liberal Party then was in power for nearly thirteen years, between 1993 and 2006, thanks to the support of the Atlantic provinces and huge support in Ontario, which allowed the Liberals to compensate for losses in Quebec due to the rise of the Bloc Québécois.

The effect of unemployment on vote choice is at the heart of the present study. The results of the first model are unequivocal. The effect of unemployment on Liberal Party support is of the expected sign, statistically significant, and of an important magnitude. The coefficient of 1.44 associated with this variable shows that the provincial vote share for the Liberal Party is nearly 1.5 percentage points lower in a province when unemployment is 1 point higher while the Liberals are in power; it also shows that the inverse effect is seen when the LPC is in opposition. Separate regressions corresponding to the Liberals' periods in power and in opposition demonstrate the relative stability of this effect.[5] The results presented in column 1 show that the model used to explain the outcome of Canadian federal elections from 1953 to 2011 performs on a level that is comparable to similar vote functions used in both Canada and elsewhere. Thus, the significant effect of the provincial unemployment rate, to be shown in the next part of the analysis, is not due to a model under-specification.

The regression including provincial unemployment is presented in column 2 of table 6.1. From this, two findings stand out. The first is

Table 6.1 OLS Regressions of Liberal Party Vote Share in Canadian Federal Elections, 1953–2011

	Model 1	Model 2	Model 3
Liberal vote t–1	0.42***	0.40***	0.37***
	(0.07)	(0.06)	(0.07)
Incumbency	9.76***	10.07***	10.21***
	(1.31)	(1.29)	(1.52)
UNR national t–3	−1.44***	−1.05***	−1.22***
	(0.17)	(0.22)	(0.23)
UNR provincial t–3	–	−0.38***	−0.39***
		(0.14)	(0.12)
Newfoundland	16.45***	17.57***	18.37***
	(2.74)	(2.63)	(2.54)
Nova Scotia	10.54***	11.00***	11.49***
	(1.93)	(1.84)	(1.76)
New Brunswick	12.45***	13.10***	13.70***
	(2.19)	(2.14)	(1.91)
Prince Edward Island	14.81***	15.48***	16.14***
	(2.12)	(2.07)	(2.00)
Quebec	18.05***	18.93***	19.59***
	(2.99)	(2.99)	(2.89)
Quebec break	−13.54***	−13.85***	−13.97***
	(3.24)	(3.30)	(3.16)
Ontario	11.61***	12.09***	12.62***
	(2.07)	(2.06)	(1.80)
Manitoba	4.94***	5.16***	5.40***
	(1.70)	(1.69)	(1.45)
Saskatchewan	1.22	1.22	1.30
	(1.38)	(1.31)	(1.09)
British Columbia	2.70	2.94*	3.06**
	(1.67)	(1.62)	(1.44)
St-Laurent	–	–	10.44***
			(2.37)

(Continued)

Table 6.1 (Continued)

	Model 1	Model 2	Model 3
Pearson	–	–	12.76***
			(1.67)
Trudeau	–	–	12.77***
			(1.78)
Turner	–	–	12.47***
			(1.84)
Chrétien	–	–	15.43***
			(1.83)
Martin	–	–	15.48***
			(1.98)
Dion	–	–	7.18***
			(2.08)
Constant	11.20***	11.54***	0.04
	(1.74)	(1.68)	(2.03)
R^2	0.80	0.81	0.87
N	200	200	200

***$p < 0.01$; **$p < 0.05$; *$p < 0.10$ (two-tailed test)

obviously the stability of our previous results. All of the aforementioned conclusions, including those regarding the national unemployment rate, are confirmed in this new specification of the model. The second finding speaks to confirming our two hypotheses. The provincial unemployment rate has an autonomous effect, independent from the national unemployment rate, in explaining the results of Canadian federal elections. This effect is, as was expected, not as pronounced as that observed for the national unemployment rate, with the relationship between the two being around 3 to 1 ($1.05/0.38 = 2.76$). That said, the impact of provincial unemployment seems far from being negligible. The coefficient indicates that an increase of one point in unemployment in a province corresponds with a decrease of close to one-half point of support for the Liberal Party when it is in power (and to an increase of similar magnitude when it is in opposition). What is more, this impact is added to that of national-level unemployment. Certainly, the two rates are correlated – the simple bivariate correlation coefficient between the two variables is 0.65 – and this is particularly true for the most populous provinces. However, this correlation is not as high as one might have expected. The economic situation of a province is strongly related to the national economic situation, but it is not uniquely determined by these national conditions. Deterioration in the economy of one province can have an autonomous influence on the outcome of an election, as was the case in British Columbia due to the forestry crisis or in Ontario when the automobile industry was severely affected during the last recession. Thus, the effect of the economy on the behaviour of Canadian voters may actually be more important than previous studies that included only national economic indicators would suggest.

There remains one more important national-level factor, leader popularity, that is absent from the first two models of table 6.1. This variable is also missing from many Canadian vote functions, notably because of the absence of satisfactory data measuring leader popularity over a long period of time (however, see Crête and Simard 1984; Nadeau and Blais 1995). The model presented in column 3 includes a series of dichotomous variables that try to take into account the effect of leader image on Liberal vote share. These variables are surely far from being ideal indicators for the leadership phenomenon. However, the substantial increase in the percentage of variance explained, which goes from 81% to 87%, shows that these dichotomous variables partially capture this effect. The variables also probably capture the decline in Liberal Party support since the mid–2000s, which can be seen as an advantage since we are interested in the effect of the economic situation beyond structural variables believed to influence the outcome of an election. For example, it seems clear from our regression results in column 3 that the last two Liberal leaders (Dion and Ignatieff) have been the least popular ones, and that this situation might help explain in part why the incumbent Conservatives were re-elected in both the 2008 and 2011 elections, in spite of relatively difficult economic conditions. In short, it is obvious from our results that vote shares change with leaders in sensible ways, as reflected in earlier findings on leader image effects in Canada (e.g., Clarke et al. 1991; Mendelsohn and Nadeau 1999; Gidengil and Blais 2007; Fournier et al. 2013).

That said, the most notable result of the model shown in column 3 is that the inclusion of a variable measuring a national-level political effect does not reduce the influence of the national unemployment variable, whose coefficient grows in absolute value by 15% (from 1.05 to 1.22). The coefficient of the provincial unemployment variable stays practically the same (it goes from −0.38 to −0.39), and the t-statistic associated with it increases considerably (from 2.71 to 3.25). The relative effect of national unemployment in relation to provincial unemployment remains roughly the same, that is to say 3 to 1 (1.22/0.39 = 3.12), which constitutes a perfectly plausible result, taking into account the visibility of national-level economic indicators during federal election campaigns. Finally, it is interesting to note that the inclusion of new variables that help push the percentage of explained variance up to nearly 90% does not diminish the effect of political and economic variables in the vote model. It can be believed that the results showing a relationship between vote shares and both national and provincial unemployment rates rests on solid grounds. An examination of observed and predicted values (using the technique of "out-of-sample forecasts") confirms the good explanatory power of the model. As table 6.2 shows, the mean absolute prediction error is 2.2 percentage points, which is a level similar to that observed in the United States (Nadeau and Lewis-Beck 2012) and in Great Britain (Nadeau, Lewis-Beck, and Bélanger 2009).

Table 6.2 Observed and Predicted Values of Liberal Party Vote Share at the National Level

Election	Actual share	Predicted share (weighted) *	Difference (error)
1953	48.6	48.4	−0.2
1957	40.9	45.1	4.2
1958	33.5	37.9	4.4
1962	37.2	38.2	1.0
1963	41.7	38.1	−3.6
1965	40.2	44.0	3.8
1968	45.5	43.9	−1.6
1972	38.4	42.3	3.9
1974	43.2	40.8	−2.4
1979	40.1	36.9	−3.2

Election	Actual share	Predicted share (weighted) *	Difference (error)
1980	44.4	42.0	−2.4
1984	28.0	27.8	−0.2
1988	31.9	32.3	0.4
1993	41.2	41.6	0.4
1997	38.5	33.5	−5.0
2000	40.9	36.3	−4.6
2004	36.7	36.6	−0.1
2006	30.2	33.2	3.0
2008	26.2	25.8	−0.4
2011	18.9	19.9	1.0
Mean absolute error			2.2

* The predicted national vote share is calculated as the weighted average of predicted provincial-level vote shares. The weighting is based on the size of each province's population. Note, however, that computing an unweighted average of predicted provincial scores provides very similar results.

Conclusion

The use of regional units of analysis in the study of vote functions is a fruitful approach, but still not very widespread. First used in the United States (Rosenstone 1983; Holbrook 1991; Campbell 1992) and then in France (Jérôme and Lewis-Beck 1999), this approach has been recently used to study the Canadian case (Gélineau and Bélanger 2005; Bélanger and Gélineau 2010).

The small number of studies focused on Canada and the main conclusion drawn from them, that local economic conditions have no effect on federal-level voting in Canadian provinces, has led us to re-examine this question with the help of more complete data and a different model. The results of these efforts have been clear; they show that regional economic conditions, namely the provincial unemployment rate, have an impact on vote choice, which is combined with the more important factor of national economic conditions.

The results of the study show that the effect of national unemployment is about three times larger than that of provincial unemployment. This result is not surprising, given the nationwide character of federal elections and the visibility of national-level economic indicators during this time. The most surprising aspect was the absence of provincial economic conditions in previous studies. This conclusion could seem surprising for two reasons. First, it can be surprising given the economic and political importance of Canadian provinces. For example, in terms of economic importance, provincial government expenditures are a large part of Canada's entire public sector spending; in terms of political importance, Quebec seems to be the clearest example of provinces affecting national politics. Second, it is surprising in light of work done in the United States showing the significant effect of both national- and state-level economic conditions in presidential elections. In fact, given the importance of regional governments in the three countries where disaggregated vote functions have been used – very important for Canadian provinces, not very important for French *régions*, and somewhere in between for American states – it is in Canada that the effect of regional economic conditions on vote choice should have been more commonly observed.

Our study confirms not only that regional economic conditions weigh upon the result of national-level elections in Canada, but also that the effect appears to be the most pronounced in Canada. For example, in Campbell's (1992) study of American elections, the effect of national economic conditions is about six times more important than that of local conditions. For Canada, the impact of national-level conditions is about three times higher, while the results for France suggest that local-level conditions play only a marginal role in French presidential elections. The hierarchy of the impact of local economies during national elections, stronger in Canada than in the United States and in France, thus seems to reflect the political and economic importance of regional governments in these three countries. In the future, it would be interesting to extend the study of disaggregated vote functions to other countries in order to see if this relationship between political importance of regional entities and the impact of local-level economic conditions on the outcome of national-level elections can be observed beyond the three cases examined until now.

Our findings carry larger implications for the economic voting literature. Previous works have shown that institutional arrangements have an impact on the nature and strength of economic voting (Powell and Whitten 1993; Nadeau, Niemi, and Yoshinaka 2002; Duch and Stevenson 2008). Our results confirm this conclusion but add an interesting twist to it, which is the notion that institutional factors combine themselves to strengthen or weaken economic voting. The first-past-the-post (FPTP) voting system in Canada usually leads to the formation of one-party governments, an outcome that makes things easier for voters to blame (or praise) the incumbent politicians for current economic conditions. This should lead us to expect that economic voting will be stronger in Canada than in other democracies with proportional representation voting systems and multi-party governments. Besides, as a decentralized federation, Canada offers voters two well-publicized sources of information for assessing the economic situation: the local and the national economic conditions. The combination of these two conditions could produce two outcomes. It could strengthen economic voting by combining the benefits of the clarity of responsibility for economic conditions and the multiplicity of the sources of information (local and national) about these conditions. Or it could, to the contrary, dampen economic voting by blurring the responsibility for the economic situation between the provincial and federal governments. Our results tend to suggest that the first scenario characterizes the Canadian case, which means that economic voting in Canada appears to be stronger, not lesser, than in other democracies. That conclusion may not be a definitive one, but it nevertheless underlines the richness and the interest of the Canadian case for the economic voting literature.

The findings for Canada are also useful in that they help to understand when and why local conditions might matter. Several studies have shown that some voters rely on local-level conditions as a shortcut to evaluate how the economy has fared nationally (see Cutler 2002). These voters are usually less sophisticated and less attentive to politics; they usually base their political judgment on shortcuts taken from their direct experience (Krause 1997) such as the local level of unemployment. This argument is "micro" in the sense that it explains why different voters use different sources of information by referring to their personal characteristics (level of attention, sophistication, etc.). The Canadian case suggests that the reality is more complex and that a macro-micro process might be driving the use of local information by voters. In a decentralized federation, with well-publicized local-level information, even inattentive voters can grasp some evidence about the national economic situation. This suggests that local economic conditions should play a greater role for less informed voters when local-level economic information (e.g., the provincial level of unemployment) is easily available, a key condition that seems to be met in the Canadian case. Future research combining individual-level data (voters' characteristics) and institutional characteristics (level of decentralization) will help to disentangle and clarify the various components of this macro-micro interaction process. But the results in this chapter already suggest that this path of investigation appears promising.

NOTES

1 The last third of this book is dedicated to understanding how electoral systems condition the behaviour and attitudes of voters. This observation suggests another relevant feature, namely federalism, a factor also considered in chapter 10.

2 The economic and fiscal weight of Canadian provinces represents 18% of the GDP while that of French regions represents only 1.4% of the GDP (for the United States the ratio is 12%). Also Canadian expenditures are more decentralized (ratio of 45%) than American (30%) and French (2.6%) expenditures. The Canadian model thus corresponds to the canon of fiscal federalism as theorized by Oates (1972). Note, however, that the French case appears less extreme when one looks at the economic and fiscal weight of the "local state" (*lato sensu*), that is when one takes into account lower territorial strata – like the French *départements* and *communes* – in the calculus (see Gilbert 1996). Even though French regions remain "economic midgets," they are sufficiently large – both demographically and geographically – for voters to perceive the local consequences of macroeconomic policies (see Jérôme and Jérôme-Speziari 2010a, 227). Still, the relatively light economic and fiscal weight of regions can affect only the national-level vote under exceptional circumstances.

3 The unemployment data come from Statistics Canada. In order to go as far back as 1953, annual unemployment data had to be used (see Gélineau and Bélanger 2005, 412). These annual measures were weighted for the month in which the specific federal election occurred, on the basis of the following formula: $\rho = [\rho_{(t-1)} * (12-\sigma_{(t)})/12] + [\rho_{(t)} * (\sigma_{(t)}/12)]$, whereas "$\rho$" is the annual unemployment measure, "σ" the month of the election, and "t" the election year. For example, if an election was held in March 2007, we would multiply the 2006 annual indicator by 9/12 and add it to the 2007 annual indicator multiplied by 3/12.

4 No other economic indicator has proven to be statistically significant when included in our analyses.

5 The coefficient is -1.36^{**} (0.17) when the Liberal Party is in power and -2.24^{**} (0.33) when it is in opposition. This slight asymmetry in effects is consistent

with the findings of Bélanger and Gélineau (2010), who show that, when in power, the Liberal vote share is slightly less affected by the national unemployment rate than the Conservative vote share, for reasons having to do with the Liberals being generally perceived as more competent economic managers (for a micro-level examination of this economic competence effect, see Bélanger and Nadeau 2014, 2015). The difference between the two coefficients is smaller when the provincial unemployment rate is added to the model (−1.10** when in power versus −1.23** when in opposition).

References

Anderson, Cameron D. 2010. "Economic Voting in Canada." In *Voting Behaviour in Canada*, edited by Cameron D. Anderson and Laura B. Stephenson, 139–62. Vancouver: University of British Columbia Press.

Bélanger, Éric, and François Gélineau. 2010. "Does Perceived Competence Matter? Political Parties and Economic Voting in Canadian Federal Elections." *Journal of Elections, Public Opinion, and Parties* 20:83–101.

Bélanger, Éric, and Richard Nadeau. 2014. "Economic Crisis, Party Competence and the Economic Vote." *Acta Politica* 49:462–85.

– 2015. "Issue Ownership of the Economy: Cross-Time Effects on Vote Choice." *West European Politics* 38:909–32.

Blais, André. 2005. "Accounting for the Electoral Success of the Liberal Party in Canada." *Canadian Journal of Political Science* 38:821–40.

Blais, André, Elisabeth Gidengil, Richard Nadeau, and Neil Nevitte. 2002. *Anatomy of a Liberal Victory: Making Sense of the Vote in the 2000 Canadian Election.* Peterborough, ON: Broadview.

Brown, Douglas. 2007. "Fiscal Federalism: Searching for Balance." In *Canadian Federalism: Performance, Effectiveness, and Legitimacy*, 2nd ed., edited by Herman Bakvis and Grace Skogstad, 63–88. Toronto: Oxford University Press.

Campbell, James E. 1992. "Forecasting the Presidential Vote." *American Journal of Political Science* 36:386–407.

Carmichael, Calum M. 1990. "Economic Conditions and the Popularity of the Incumbent Party in Canada." *Canadian Journal of Political Science* 23:713–26.

Clarke, Harold D., Jane Jenson, Lawrence LeDuc, and Jon H. Pammett. 1991. *Absent Mandate: Interpreting Change in Canadian Elections.* Toronto: Gage.

Crête, Jean, and Johanne Simard. 1984. "Conjoncture économique et élections: une étude des élections au Québec." In *Comportement électoral au Québec*, edited by Jean Crête, 165–97. Quebec: Gaëtan Morin.

Cutler, Fred. 2002. "Local Economies, Local Policy Impacts and Federal Electoral Behaviour in Canada." *Canadian Journal of Political Science* 35:347–82.

Duch, Raymond, and Randy Stevenson. 2008. *The Economic Vote: How Political and Economic Institutions Condition Election Results*. Cambridge: Cambridge University Press.

Eisenberg, Daniel, and Jonathan Ketcham. 2004. "Economic Voting in U.S. Presidential Elections: Who Blames Whom for What?" *B.E. Journal of Economic Analysis & Policy* 4:497–521.

Fournier, Patrick, Fred Cutler, Stuart Soroka, Dietlind Stolle, and Éric Bélanger. 2013. "Riding the Orange Wave: Leadership, Values, Issues, and the 2011 Canadian Election." *Canadian Journal of Political Science* 46:863–97.

Gélineau, François, and Éric Bélanger. 2005. "Electoral Accountability in a Federal System: National and Provincial Economic Voting in Canada." *Publius* 35:407–24.

Gidengil, Elisabeth, and André Blais. 2007. "Are Party Leaders Becoming More Important to Vote Choice in Canada?" In *Political Leadership and Representation in Canada*, edited by Hans Michelmann, Donald Story, and Jeffrey Steeves, 39–59. Toronto: University of Toronto Press.

Gilbert, Guy. 1996. "Le fédéralisme financier: perspectives de microéconomie spatiale." *Revista de Economia (Curitiba)* 47:311–63.

Happy, J.R. 1986. "Voter Sensitivity to Economic Conditions: A Canadian-American Comparison." *Comparative Politics* 19:45–56.

– 1989. "Economic Performance and Retrospective Voting in Canadian Federal Elections." *Canadian Journal of Political Science* 22:377–87.

– 1992. "The Effect of Economic and Fiscal Performance on Incumbency Voting: The Canadian Case." *British Journal of Political Science* 22:117–30.

Holbrook, Thomas M. 1991. "Presidential Elections in Space and Time." *American Journal of Political Science* 35:91–109.

Jérôme, Bruno, and Véronique Jérôme-Speziari. 2005. "The 2004 French Regional Elections: Politico-Economic Factors of a *Nationalized* Local Ballot." *French Politics* 3:142–63.

– 2010a. *Analyse économique des élections*. Paris: Economica.

– 2010b. "Fonctions de vote et prévisions électorales: une application à la présidentielle française de 2007." *Canadian Journal of Political Science* 43:163–86.

– 2011. "Modeling and Forecasting the 2010 French Regional Elections: A Political Economy Approach" (unpublished).

Jérôme, Bruno, and Michael S. Lewis-Beck. 1999. "Is Local Politics Local? French Evidence." *European Journal of Political Research* 35:181–97.

Kiewiet, D. Roderick. 1983. *Macroeconomics and Micropolitics: The Electoral Effects of Economic Issues*. Chicago: University of Chicago Press.

Krause, George A. 1997. "Voters, Information Heterogeneity, and the Dynamics of Aggregate Economic Expectations." *American Journal of Political Science* 41:1170–200.

Lewis-Beck, Michael S. 1988. *Economics and Elections: The Major Western Democracies.* Ann Arbor: University of Michigan Press.

Lewis-Beck, Michael S., and Mary Stegmaier. 2007. "Economic Models of Voting." In *The Oxford Handbook of Political Behavior,* edited by Russell J. Dalton and Hans-Dieter Klingemann, 518–37. Oxford: Oxford University Press.

– 2013. "The VP-Function Revisited: A Survey of the Literature on Vote and Popularity Functions after over 40 Years." *Public Choice* 157:367–85.

Mendelsohn, Matthew, and Richard Nadeau. 1999. "The Rise and Fall of Candidates in Canadian Election Campaigns." *International Journal of Press/ Politics* 4:63–76.

Mondak, Jeffery J., Diana C. Mutz, and Robert Huckfeldt. 1996. "Persuasion in Context: The Multilevel Structure of Economic Evaluations." In *Political Persuasion and Attitude Change,* edited by Diana C. Mutz, Paul M. Sniderman, and Richard A. Brody, 249–66. Ann Arbor: University of Michigan Press.

Nadeau, Richard, and André Blais. 1993. "Explaining Election Outcomes in Canada: Economy and Politics." *Canadian Journal of Political Science* 26:775–90.

– 1995. "Economic Conditions, Leader Evaluations and Election Outcomes in Canada." *Canadian Public Policy* 21:212–18.

Nadeau, Richard, André Blais, Elisabeth Gidengil, and Neil Nevitte. 2000. "It's Unemployment, Stupid! Why Perceptions about the Job Situation Hurt the Liberals in the 1997 Election." *Canadian Public Policy* 26:78–93.

Nadeau, Richard, and Michael S. Lewis-Beck. 2012. "Campaigns Effects and Forecasting." *Foresight* 24:15–18.

Nadeau, Richard, Michael S. Lewis-Beck, and Éric Bélanger. 2009. "Election Forecasting in the United Kingdom: A Two-Step Model." *Journal of Elections, Public Opinion, and Parties* 19:333–58.

– 2013. "Economics and Elections Revisited." *Comparative Political Studies* 46:551–73.

Nadeau, Richard, Richard G. Niemi, and Antoine Yoshinaka. 2002. "A Cross-National Analysis of Economic Voting: Taking Account of the Political Context across Time and Nations." *Electoral Studies* 21:403–23.

Nannestad, Peter, and Martin Paldam. 1994. "The VP-Function: A Survey of the Literature on Vote and Popularity Functions after 25 Years." *Public Choice* 79:213–45.

Oates, Wallace E. 1972. *Fiscal Federalism.* New York: Harcourt Brace Jovanovich.

Orth, Deborah A. 2001. "Accountability in a Federal System: The Governor, the President, and Economic Expectations." *State Politics & Policy Quarterly* 1:412–32.

Powell, Bingham, and Guy Whitten. 1993. "A Cross-National Analysis of Economic Voting: Taking Account of the Political Context." *American Journal of Political Science* 37:391–414.

Rosenstone, Steven J. 1983. *Forecasting Presidential Elections*. New Haven, CT: Yale University Press.

Savoie, Donald J. 1992. *Regional Economic Development*. 2nd ed. Toronto: University of Toronto Press.

Strumpf, Koleman S., and John R. Phillippe. 1999. "Estimating Presidential Elections: The Importance of State Fixed Effects and the Role of National versus Local Information." *Economics and Politics* 11:33–50.

Weatherford, M. Stephen. 1983. "Evaluating Economic Policy: A Contextual Model of the Opinion Formation Process." *Journal of Politics* 45:866–88.

7 Who Responds to Election Campaigns? The Two-Moderator Model Revisited

PATRICK FOURNIER, FRED CUTLER,
AND STUART SOROKA

Campaign events affect election outcomes. This claim, once unpopular, is now virtually undisputed (e.g., Johnston et al. 1992; Johnston, Hagen, and Jamieson 2004; Holbrook 1996; Blais et al. 1999, 2003; Blais and Perrella 2008; Farrell and Schmitt-Beck 2002; Brady and Johnston 2006). But which voters are influenced by campaign events and the information they generate? Scholars and campaign operatives alike have assumed that some voters are too set in their ways to be open to conversion and some voters pay too little attention to be swayed by campaign information; this likely leaves only a minority susceptible to changing their minds on the basis of the news of the campaign. In spite of this widely recognized argument, however, most research on campaign effects demonstrates only the total effect of campaign events.[1]

Finding the subset of voters susceptible to campaign influence should provide a more satisfying portrayal of the campaign processes that can drive election outcomes (Hillygus and Shields 2008). Indeed, some campaign effects that are important to outcomes but statistically undetectable among all voters might be visible if we know where to look.

To do so, we deploy and revise the dominant model of persuasion by new information, elaborated by Zaller (1992, 1996), and based in earlier work by Converse (1962) and McGuire (1968, 1969). It conceives of attitude change as resulting from a pair of cognitive psychological mechanisms: (1) reception of persuasive information and (2) acceptance of that information. This two-moderator model of attitude change has received much theoretical attention, but its empirical implementation has been sporadic and unconvincing. Only Zaller himself – in an early article (1989) and an infrequently referenced chapter towards the end of *The Nature and Origins of Mass Opinion* (1992) – has used the two-moderator model to account for opinion change in an election campaign. Some applied work has simplified the model by operationally combining reception and acceptance into a non-monotonic one-moderator model, namely media use or political information (Converse 1962; Dreyer 1971; Macaluso 1977; Zukin 1977; Nadeau and Guay 1990; Nadeau et al. 2008). However, Zaller argued forcefully that this one-moderator model is inappropriate in the context of elections (1992). That said, his own statistical approach was not thoroughly convincing, as it involved multiple functions using the same variables in each. Nor did Zaller use dynamic data that directly measured the potentially persuasive information. It is regrettable indeed that the statistical model derived by Zaller from this theory has been all but ignored in the nearly three decades since its appearance.

Our goal is to clarify, simplify, and refine the Converse-McGuire-Zaller (CMZ) model for use in election campaigns by drawing particularly on recent work on ambivalence and cross-pressured voters (Hillygus and Shields 2008). We test this revised model on three prominent campaign effects: advertisements, debates, and media coverage. Our data are drawn from two Canadian election surveys conducted with the rolling cross-section design: the 2003 Ontario Election Study (OES) and the 2011 Canadian Election Study (CES), allowing us to measure information flow and voting behaviour daily over a one-month election campaign.[2]

The results fall squarely in line with recent work on campaigns by showing that the campaign did matter in these elections, which is to say that information conveyed during the campaigns had an effect on individuals' voting choices. But we use the two-moderator model to show that the more complete story is that campaign information has strong effects on only a subset of voters: those with both relatively high levels of information and ambivalence about their vote choice. Before moving to analysis, the following section reviews the literature on campaign effects and the two-moderator model.

Campaigns and the Cognitive Two-Moderator Model

The significance of election campaigns for voting behaviour has a chequered past. In a literature that began with an emphasis on the stability of partisan preferences and on voter inattentiveness and ignorance, it has taken a long time for researchers to answer affirmatively to the question, "Do campaigns matter?"

While campaign effects have been detected regularly over the past two decades, and they are sometimes quite large (e.g., Johnston et al. 1992, 1994, 1996; Johnston, Hagen, and Jamieson 2004; Nevitte et al. 2000; Blais et al. 2002; Hillygus and Jackman 2003; Holbrook 1996), it is reasonable to expect their impact to be strong for some voters while other voters are immune. We infer this from the many reports of interpersonal heterogeneity in political behaviour and political attentiveness (e.g., Rivers 1988; Sniderman, Brody, and Tetlock 1991; Krosnick 1988, 1990; Zaller 1992; Bartels 1996; Miller and Krosnick 2000). With respect to campaigns in particular, both Fournier (2005) and Hillygus and her colleagues (Hillygus and Jackman 2003; Hillygus and Shields 2008) provide evidence of interpersonal variation in the propensity for attitude change. Yet pointed analyses of individual differences in response to campaign forces are limited.[3] Attempts to identify groups more and less susceptible to campaign effects have argued that partisanship and attention moderate the impact of campaign information (Geer 1988; Gwiasda 2001; Hillygus and Jackman 2003; Johnston 1992 et al.; Johnston, Hagen, and Jamieson 2004; Zaller 1992). Only very recently, Hillygus and Shields have returned to an earlier theory of cross-pressured voters to find *The Persuadable Voter*, arguing that "individuals conflicted by the considerations underlying their vote decision should be open to campaign persuasion" (2008, 85). As in that study, we use theories of attitude change to propose a more general way to identify voters susceptible to the campaign.

The Existing Two-Moderator Model

The two-moderator model of attitude change is rooted in the study of social cognition (Fiske and Taylor 1991). For a communication to register and thereby affect judgment, several cognitive events must take place: exposure, attention, comprehension, yielding, memorizing, retrieval, and activation (McGuire 1999). In most of the relevant theory, this process is boiled down to two key cognitive processes: reception and acceptance.

These processes are unfortunately not directly measurable outside of the laboratory. And separating the moderating effects of two processes is difficult, since many individual characteristics have cross-cutting effects on the probability of receiving and of accepting new information (Converse 1962; McGuire 1968, 1969). In the context of modern mass politics, the most important moderators, political attention and sophistication, increase the likelihood of receiving a message but also decrease the likelihood of accepting it (see McGuire 1968; Zaller 1992; Miller and Krosnick 2000).[4] For the most part, rather than try to disentangle the two processes, researchers have relied on theory and assumptions about the intensity of campaign information to specify a non-monotonic moderating relationship using one variable, usually some measure of political attention and sophistication (Converse 1962; McGuire 1969; Dreyer 1971; Macaluso 1977; Zukin 1977; Nadeau and Guay 1990; Zaller 1996). The standard approach is to argue that citizens with moderate levels of sophistication or attention should be the most susceptible to influence – they are more likely to both receive and accept persuasive communications.

One can hardly criticize the use of political sophistication as a source of individual differences in political attitude change.[5] But there are clear dangers in taking a theory constructed with two independent moderators and reducing it in practice to a one-moderator, albeit non-monotonic, model. Zaller's landmark research (1989, 1992, 1996) highlighted the potential perils of this approach, attempting to faithfully operationalize the two-step process. Zaller's empirical models specify a separate function for reception and acceptance. The problem is that his approach, as Zaller himself acknowledges, leads to complex and unwieldy empirical models. Consider, for instance, his model of two-sided information flows as applied to support for the Vietnam war (1992, 199). It includes political awareness (reception) entered three times directly and three times in an interaction term. Even after a constrained form is estimated, few of the conditional effects are significant. While more manageable, Zaller's electoral choice models clearly have low statistical power to detect effects (1992, chapter 10). This is perhaps why Zaller's empirical model, while highly regarded and widely cited, is rarely replicated.

Zaller's work is best remembered for its demonstrations of sophistication moderating persuasion over relatively long periods – typically over two-year intervals between ANES panel waves. Less well-remembered is his very clear argument that a one-measure, non-monotonic moderator is inappropriate and even misleading for the analysis of election campaigns (1992, chapter 10). In campaigns the partisan content of messages is so obvious that acceptance should not be moderated by attentiveness or sophistication. In the model of general opinion change on issues, the theory is that the less sophisticated lack the ability to connect new, potentially persuasive information with their predispositions, and so they are more likely than the more sophisticated to yield to that information. But in elections, the ubiquity of partisan cues means that even the less aware are able to distinguish between comfortable and uncomfortable information on the basis of its source; there is no group of moderately aware individuals who are open to information contrary to their partisan disposition, because all information is so clearly partisan.[6] As a consequence, in a campaign context, awareness/attentiveness measures *only* the probability of reception of campaign messages. There is, however, another moderating variable that captures acceptance, namely, resistance to new information, made up of both (1) partisan resistance, where opponents' messages are discounted or rejected, and (2) inertial resistance, where new information is integrated into a "pre-existing mass of stored partisan considerations" (1992, 237). The former is measured by strength of partisanship; the latter by the balance of party likes and dislikes. Zaller (1992) finds that both individually, as well as in combination, lower the probability that new information will be accepted, given that it is received.[7]

A number of studies have sought to test Zaller's theory of the influence of information in election campaigns (e.g., Dobrzynska and Blais 2008; Goren 2004; Kriesi 2002; Krosnick and Brannon 1993; Dalton, Beck and Huckfeldt 1998), and most appear to cast doubt on the accuracy or applicability of Zaller's theory. But this body of work has sought to apply Zaller's general theory of opinion change on political issues to voter choice in election campaigns – rather, that is, than apply the theory specific to election campaigns discussed above. In short, tests of Zaller's theory do not use Zaller's own critical modification of his theory for the campaign context (see also Claassen 2011).

Here we seek to add to this body of research, but we use the election-specific theory introduced later in Zaller's book. In short, our innovation is to re-specify what is in fact a more straightforward and important element of the Zaller-Converse-McGuire theory: the clarity and bulk of predispositions themselves. Simply put, the influence of new messages is moderated by predispositions. Without clear predispositions that point towards a particular attitude or behaviour, citizens have no motivation to resist new information, and no one-sided store of considerations into which that information might sink. For these voters, new information has much greater persuasive potential. The weight of voters' predispositions, then, is the second of the two moderators of campaign information, entirely separate from the first moderator measuring the likelihood of reception of that information.[8]

Hillygus and Shields (2008), without much acknowledging Zaller-Converse-McGuire, use very similar theory and find that "persuadable" voters, defined as having at least two important policy opinions at odds with their party, are indeed far more likely to defect from their partisanship in presidential elections. They find that rates of defection are much higher among persuadable voters when they: (1) experience more campaign activity (in battleground states), (2) are habitually interested in and attentive to politics (91), or (3) are interviewed shortly after campaign events like conventions and debates (99). Our operationalization of ambivalence, below, bears a strong resemblance to their operationalization of cross-pressured, persuadable voters. Our study, conceived independently, ultimately complements theirs by using different data, from a very different electoral context, with a more explicit specification of the two moderators as jointly necessary for influence by campaign information, and with more direct measurement of persuasive information. We turn to that specification now.

The Two-Moderator Model: Towards a New Specification

Part of the complexity in Zaller's models of campaign opinion change is a function of data availability: he does not use measurements of campaign information as a cause of change but rather infers its effect by demonstrating that the link between partisanship and vote choice is moderated by determinants of reception and acceptance, including contextual measures of campaign intensity (1992, chapter 10; see also Hillygus and Shields 2008). A more direct test of the model for campaign effects is the focus of this chapter. We radically simplify the operationalization and test it on data better suited to detecting the influence of changing information over an election campaign.

The first moderator – probability of reception – is operationalized simply as a voter's level of political information. Information is a better measure than indicators of news consumption, because reception is more than a question of exposure and attention (Price and Zaller 1993; Zaller 1996; Luskin 1987; but see Krosnick and Brannon 1993). As we have argued, political awareness should enter the model exclusively in the reception function.

For the second moderator – probability of acceptance – we agree with Hillygus and Shields (2008) that a simpler direct measure is readily available: ambivalence. Ambivalence refers to the extent to which the elements people take into account when making a decision push towards opposing positions simultaneously, in contrast to elements entirely consistent with a single position (Zaller 1992; Zaller and Feldman 1992; Alvarez and Brehm 1995, 1997, 2002; Lavine 2001; Basinger and Lavine 2005).[9] Even many well-informed, attentive voters have conflicts among the attitudes that contribute to their decision. To use a now-dated term revived by Hillygus and Shields (2008) they are "cross-pressured," closer to indifference among choices and therefore more likely to be pushed one way or another by new information (Lazarsfeld, Berelson, and Gaudet 1944; Berelson, Lazarsfeld, and McPhee 1954; A. Campbell et al. 1960; J. Campbell 2000; Glasgow 2004).

Hillygus and Shields sum up the psychological research on persuasion that provides a foundation for this theory: "When the underlying structure of an attitude is less consistent, that attitude is more responsive to new information" (2008, 84; see also Eagly and Chaiken 1995). Research in political psychology confirms that ambivalence is related to political attitude change. Ambivalent voters tend to exhibit greater variability in policy preferences (Alvarez and Brehm 1995), to change their issue positions more frequently over time (Zaller 1992; Zaller and Feldman 1992) or in response to counterarguments (Fournier 2003), and to exhibit instability in their vote choice during campaigns (Lavine 2001; Fournier 2005; Hillygus and Shields 2008).

The least ambivalent voters have one-sided prior considerations and are more likely to recognize messages that are at odds with their initial position and reject them. And the new information, even if accepted, will probably not tip the balance to the other candidate or party. Ambivalent, cross-pressured voters, by contrast, have a mixed set of relevant attitudes and are (1) more likely to accept persuasive messages from various sides and, (2) if integrated, the messages will be more decisive. Ambivalence, then, subsumes under a more general rubric other potential moderators such as strength of partisanship and levels of opinion, which have sometimes been used in a relatively ad hoc way as moderators of attitude change in campaigns (Hillygus and Jackman 2003). In truth, ambivalence is effectively a reduced form of the partisan and inertial resistance processes identified by Zaller: it measures the volume and strength of partisan and other considerations that would blunt or dilute the impact of new information.

Together, information and ambivalence yield a simple and straightforward operationalization of the model's reception and acceptance functions. Combining the two moderators in this way allows us to directly test a theory of campaign effects derived from Converse, McGuire, and

Zaller. Response to campaign information should be greatest when information and ambivalence are jointly found at high levels.

Data

We examine campaign effects using surveys from two relatively vola-
tile elections in Canada where campaign movement was pronounced.
The first is the 2003 provincial election in Ontario. Provincial elections
in Canada are among the most intensely followed, objectively important sub-national elections in the world – they are by no means the
poor cousins of national elections (Cutler 2008). The second is the 2011
Canadian federal election, and we focus on Quebec, where massive
movement over the campaign produced a truly shocking result. Both
surveys were conducted using a rolling cross-section methodology
(Johnston and Brady 2002).[10] The rolling cross-sectional design is the
appropriate instrument to capture public reactions to campaign events,
as each day's sample is a nearly independent one. Figure 7.1 shows the

Figure 7.1a Vote Intentions over the Campaign, Ontario 2003 (3-Day
Averages)

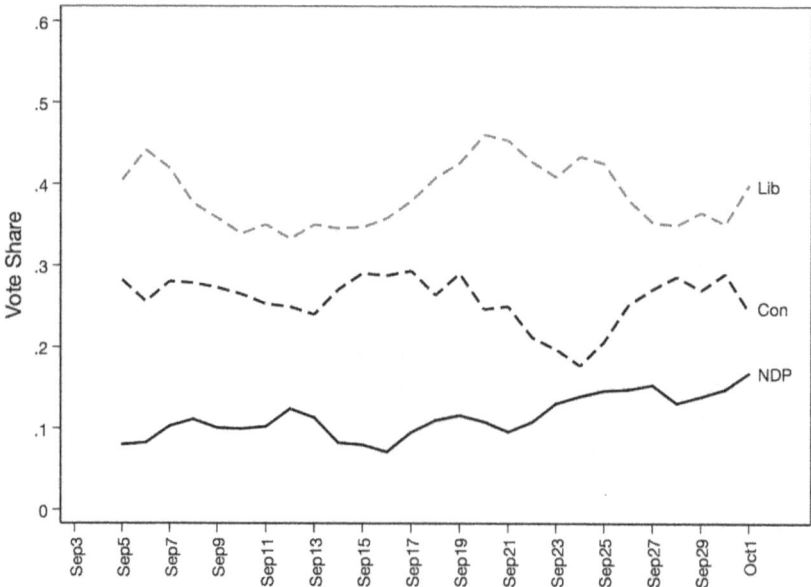

Figure 7.1b Vote Intentions over the Campaign, Quebec 2011 (3-Day Averages)

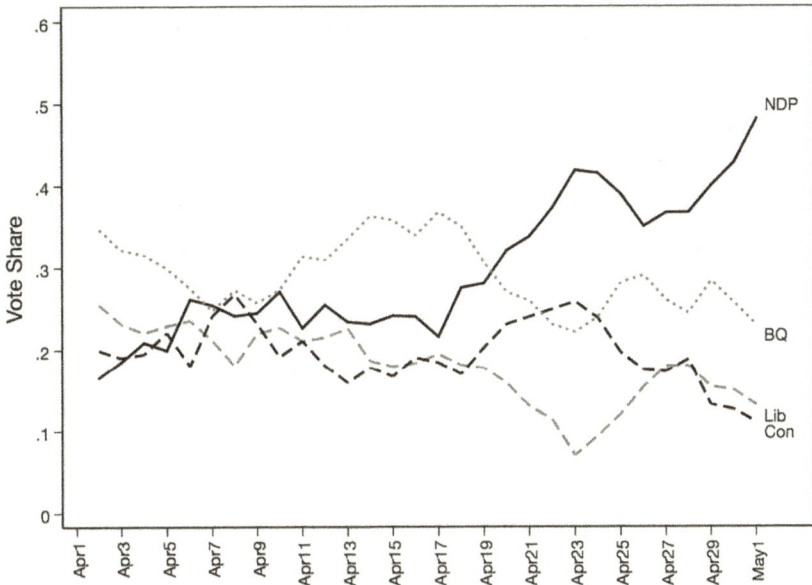

campaign tracking of vote intentions for Ontario 2003 and Quebec 2011 respectively. These elections are, to be fair, atypical in the size of the campaign movement. But we do not think they are atypical with respect to our research question: in the way the strength of these effects are distributed through the electorate. These are simply "most-likely" cases where we have greater statistical power to detect the effects we expect.

Campaign Effects

Campaign effects are usually defined as changes in the balance of party/candidate preferences due to new information provided in the campaign. That information may result from events like debates and candidate appearances, from parties' and candidates' statements, or from media coverage. The dependent variable, therefore, is the voter's intended choice from among the major parties, measured during the campaign. The estimates of effects presented here are derived from a multinomial logit model of choice among the major parties. In Ontario these are the centre-right Progressive Conservative (PC) party, centrist Liberal party, and democratic socialist New Democratic Party (NDP).[11] In Quebec in 2011 these are the Conservative Party of Canada (CPC), the Liberal party, the New Democratic Party, and the nationalist Bloc Québécois (BQ). Decided voters and leaners are included, undecided voters are excluded.[12]

Key to establishing campaign effects, in our view, is careful identification and measurement of exactly the information that might be influential in a given campaign. Independent variables operationalizing campaign information are necessarily identified after a campaign and are specific to a particular campaign. In Ontario we examine three important forms of campaign information: advertisements (e.g., Freedman, Franz, and Goldstein 2004; West 1997; Shaw 1999; Johnston et al. 2004), debates (e.g., Geer 1988; Johnston, Jamieson, and Hagen 1992; Blais and Boyer 1996; Blais et al. 1999; Holbrook 1996), and the balance of media coverage of different issues (e.g., Johnston et al. 1992; Mendelsohn 1996; Miller and Krosnick 2000).[13] For the 2011 election in Quebec we examine the impact of media coverage of the party leaders and of the issue of Quebec's sovereignty.

Ontario 2003

Advertisements

Advertisements are a prime suspect for campaign effects in Ontario in 2003. First, a series of highly negative PC television ads may have driven that party's support down by prompting voters to characterize the PC leader, Ernie Eves, as "too negative." Their extreme negativity brought widespread critical coverage, with the media reporting criticism of the ads even by PC candidates and partisans. The independent variable capturing the ad effect is a dummy variable indicating whether the respondent reported seeing TV election ads about the Liberals. (Unfortunately, the sample for this analysis is limited to the twelve days on which the question about ad reception was asked, though this covers the crucial period of the introduction and withdrawal of the negative PC ads.)

Our first hypothesis is therefore that seeing TV ads in this period drove voters away from the PC party and to the Liberals – they should

have left the NDP unaffected – but only among those generally attentive (information) and with a high level of ambivalence.

Debate

The party leaders' debate appeared to stem the Liberal tide in the 2003
Ontario election, if only temporarily, preventing a runaway victory. The
debate is treated as a campaign event, measured for each respondent as
the number of days since the debate took place (see also Geer 1988; Hillygus and Jackman 2003; Hillygus and Shields 2008; Johnston et al. 1992).
(Also included is a quadratic term to allow for the influence of the debate
to decay or strengthen over time.) We prefer this measurement of the
influence of the debate to other approaches, such as using debate viewership, since previous work has shown that debate effects extend through
media coverage and word-of-mouth to non-viewers (Johnston et al. 1992;
Blais and Boyer 1996; Blais et al. 1999). We include all respondents interviewed prior to the debate with values of zero on the debate variables.
To corroborate this representation of the debate we also estimate a model
using respondents' report of having seen the debate themselves.

We hypothesize that only attentive and ambivalent voters move
away from the Liberals in the days immediately following the debate,
but that these voters come back to the Liberals as the influence of the
debate and the Liberal-positive media interpretation of the debate
kicks in, or the short-term effect of the debate simply recedes in voters'
consciousness.

Issue Coverage

Throughout the 2003 campaign, a considerable majority of voters
(regardless of partisanship) preferred the PC party on taxes and the
economy while a majority preferred the Liberals on health care and
education. There is little change over the campaign in responses to the
question "What party do you think will do a better job dealing with
…" Issues that began as Liberal issues remained so, and vice versa; and
this is true even though vote intentions change considerably over the
campaign (see figure 7.1).

This "issue ownership" would not bear notice, but for the fact that
media coverage of "Liberal issues" versus "PC issues" was variable over the campaign. Indeed, shifts in the coverage of these issues

quite nicely capture the dynamics in vote intention we have seen in figure 7.1. Our third independent variable measuring campaign information is thus drawn from a daily content analysis of all election stories (not opinion or editorials) in the *Toronto Star* and the *Ottawa Citizen*, broadly typical of election coverage province-wide across newspapers, TV, and radio. Only news stories were included (not opinions and editorials). The measure is the relative weight given to Liberal versus PC issues:

(% Education articles + % Health articles) / (%Taxes articles + % Economy articles).

Figure 7.2 tracks both Liberal and PC issues over the campaign. The balance in coverage tells an important story about the 2003 contest: coverage of Liberal issues was relatively steady over the campaign, while coverage of PC issues rose and fell considerably. The figure shows these data as rolling three-day prior averages, and it is in this form that they are included in the individual-level data set. Each individual at day *t* is assigned a value equivalent to the three-day average of the proportion

Figure 7.2 The Media Issue Agenda over the Campaign (3-Day Averages)

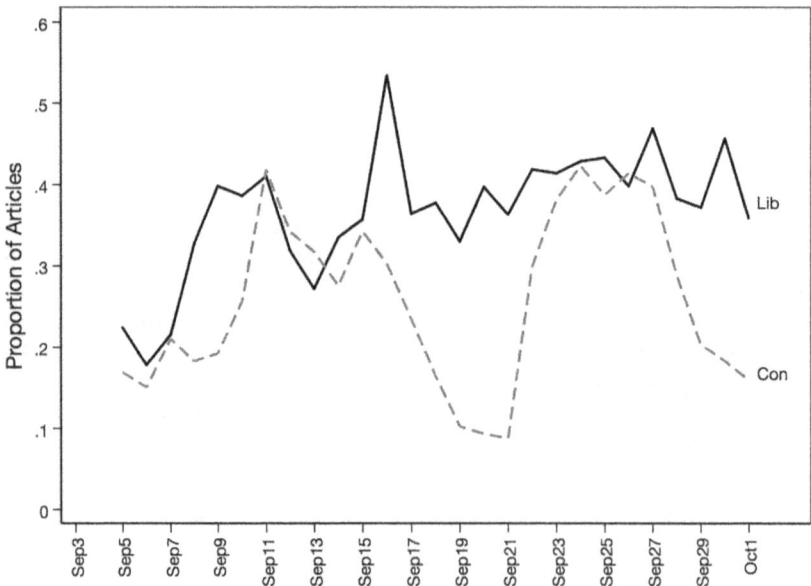

of stories about Liberal-owned issues from $t-3$ to $t-1$. This media content measure is our best measure of campaign information, as it covers the whole campaign period and has considerable variation. And our expectation is that coverage pushed voters to the Liberals (and possibly the NDP) by inducing voters of Liberal-owned issues to place greater importance on the Liberal strengths. We hypothesize that variations in media coverage of the issues will affect the vote intentions of only voters who are both attentive (informed) and ambivalent.

Quebec 2011 (Federal Election)

Media Coverage of Jack Layton, Volume and Tone

Canada's 2011 federal election featured a barnstorming run from third place into the opposition benches by the NDP and its leader, Jack Layton. Most of the action occurred, or occurred first, in Quebec. Certainly that province was the object of most analysis of the astonishing result, so we examine campaign effects in Quebec exclusively. We have shown elsewhere that most of the story is about Jack Layton's favourability advantage growing in phases over the campaign, and that voters also came to weigh leadership more heavily in their decisions by voting day (Fournier et al. 2013). Here we use two separate measures of media coverage of Layton in Quebec. The first is the volume of coverage of Layton. This allows us to assess the priming hypothesis that as Layton occupied more media space, voters based their decisions more heavily on assessments of him. The second variable is the tone of coverage of the NDP in Quebec.[14] We look for a direct impact of NDP tone from the previous three days on the voter's intention. For both volume and tone, the expectation is that only attentive and ambivalent voters will be affected.

Issue Coverage: Sovereignty

It was widely suggested that the decisive moment leading many former Bloc Québécois voters to jump ship was its leader Gilles Duceppe appearing at a (provincial) Parti Québécois convention with its leader Pauline Marois, reinforcing the Bloc's commitment to a referendum on Quebec's sovereignty. This moment signalled a shift of the Bloc's main campaign message. We operationalize the campaign information as the volume of media mentions of sovereignty, including references to referendum, independence, and the like. Our hypothesis is that as mentions of sovereignty increased, all but the hard sovereigntists moved away from the Bloc and into the arms of the suitor with momentum, the NDP; but as we have argued, the effect should be strongest among the high information / high ambivalence group.

Moderators: Information and Ambivalence

As hypothesized, these campaign effects should be moderated by a combination of information and ambivalence.

Information

We employ a measure of political information to capture attention to the news of the campaign. We simply follow standard practice in using a measure of general factual knowledge about politics (Luskin 1987; Fiske, Lau, and Smith 1990; Zaller 1990; Delli Carpini and Keeter 1993). The index is formed from questions asking respondents to identify the three main party leaders or three other political figures. It ranges from zero to three correct answers.[15]

We point out that we do not specify variation in the intensity of the campaign "messages," as Zaller would call them: ads, the debate, leader and issue coverage. Variation in intensity would imply different patterns of mediation by information, and thus our information measure would be expected to have different effects on the three kinds of campaign event. Since these three forms of campaign communication are all familiar and prominent elements of modern election campaigns, we assume that there is a roughly linear relationship between political information and reception of these forms of campaign information.

Ambivalence

Drawing from existing research (Zaller and Feldman 1992; Lavine 2001; Basinger and Lavine 2005; Hillygus and Shields 2008), we consider that internal conflict may emerge from the various types of reasons that can motivate an individual to vote for one party or candidate over another. To capture relevant considerations, we use correlates of the decision.[16] All items that were found to be associated with vote intentions were considered candidates for relevant considerations. The strongest were retained for construction of an ambivalence index. In

Ontario: party identification, party leader evaluations, local candidate preference, and issue position on cutting taxes. In Quebec: party identification, leader evaluations, support for Quebec sovereignty, personal taxes, corporate taxes, spending on the environment, spending on defence, and satisfaction with democracy.[17] Responses to each of these items were coded as being consistent with the respondent's vote intention, neutral (discrete or moderate or a don't know on the vote determinant), or inconsistent.[18]

The ambivalence index is the number of inconsistent considerations. Thus, a person scores low on ambivalence in Ontario if he likes his chosen party's leader more than any other leader, identifies with the party he voted for, prefers that party's local candidate, and shares that party's position on cutting taxes. A high score results from liking another leader more than one's preferred party's leader, identifying with a party other than one's vote intention, preferring another party's local candidate, and being at odds with one's party on taxes. This operationalization of ambivalence has been found to surpass subjective measures based on open-ended and closed-ended survey questions in predicting instability of opinion (Fournier 2005).[19] It must be noted, however, that this measure is taken not before the campaign, but rather at the same time as the measurement of vote choice and its determinants. We believe this will only produce conservative estimates of the moderating effect of ambivalence. We provide an extended justification of this assumption in the appendix.

This operationalization produces a five-point scale, with a fairly uniform distribution. We dichotomize the variable so that the top two points on the scale fall into the High Ambivalence category – three or four determinants inconsistent with the voter's preference – which amounts to 40% of the decided voters from whom we have the vote choice measurement.

Four group dummies are created for the combination of information and ambivalence. A dummy variable was then computed for each of four possible pairings:

– Low Information / Low Ambivalence (LILA, 31% [ON] and 15% [QC]),
– Low Information / High Ambivalence (LIHA, 24% [ON] and 15% [QC]),
– High Information / Low Ambivalence (HILA, 30% [ON] and 41% [QC]), and

– High Information / High Ambivalence (HIHA, 15% [ON] and 30% [QC]).

We note that there is a strong negative relationship between information and ambivalence. In Ontario, for example, the mean number of facts correct for those with zero ambivalence is 2.52, while for those with all four considerations at odds with their choice, factual information averages 1.77.

In the models below, these ambivalence/information group dummy variables interact with campaign information measures to determine the magnitude of the campaign effects within each group.[20]

Results

At the risk of setting up a straw man, tables 7.1 (ON) and 7.2 (QC) present homogeneous models against which to compare our subsequent dissection of the electorate.[21] Alongside the campaign effects variables and moderators, we include party identification, education, income, gender, and age as controls. We do not walk the reader through these coefficients.

Campaign effects in the expected direction are detected for issue coverage, but not for ads or the debate in Ontario 2003. In Quebec 2011, we find that coverage of Layton primed feelings about him in voters' calculus and that the tone of coverage of the NDP moved voters in that party's direction. But we find no effect in the full sample for coverage of sovereignty. We show below that these conclusions, lumping all voters together, would be seriously incomplete.

Information, Ambivalence, and Campaign Effects

Now to the main event: Are there campaign information effects hidden in tables 7.1 (ON) and 7.2 (QC), limited to those we predict will receive, accept, and be open to influence by the information contained in ads, debates, and media content? Tables 7.3 and 7.4 present our evidence for each campaign effect. Analyses are patterned after those in the first two tables, but with group dummy variable interactions for all four of the groups defined by the information/ambivalence measure (as suggested by Brambor, Clark, and Golder 2006, 69–70).[22] That is, we show the effect of each campaign effect for each of the four groups, in marginal probability changes.[23]

Table 7.1 A Model of Homogeneous Campaign Effects, Ontario 2003

		Lib support	PC support
Campaign Effects	Saw ads about Liberals	.00	.00
		(.03)	(.03)
	Days since debate	−.01	.00
		(.02)	(.02)
	Days^2 since debate	.00	.00
		(.00)	(.00)
	Issue coverage	.02***	−.02*
		(.01)	(.01)
Controls	PID PC	−.25***	.36***
		(.05)	(.03)
	PID Liberal	.46***	−.26***
		(.04)	(.03)
	PID NDP	.05	−.32***
		(.06)	(.07)
	Education	.03***	−.03***
		(.01)	(.01)
	Female	.03*	−.02
		(.02)	(.02)
	Under 30	−.02	−.05**
		(.03)	(.03)
	Over 60	−.01	.01
		(.02)	(.02)
	Low income	−.03	−.03
		(.02)	(.02)
	High income	.02	.01
		(.02)	(.02)
	Missing income	−.06**	.02
		(.03)	(.03)
N		1569	
Pseudo R^2		.41	

Note: Cells contain average marginal effects, based on a multinomial logit model. Standard errors (corrected for clustering by day) are in parentheses.

* $p < .10$; ** $p < .05$; *** $p < .01$

Table 7.2 A Model of Homogeneous Campaign Effects, Quebec 2011

		NDP support
Campaign Effects	Layton coverage x Layton feeling	.80**
		(.33)
	Sovereignty coverage	.0007
		(.0005)
	Tone of NDP coverage	.03**
		(.01)
Controls	Feeling towards Layton	.17**
		(.07)
	PID Bloc	−.11***
		(.04)
	PID Conservative	−.20***
		(.06)
	PID Liberal	−.10**
		(.04)
	PID NDP	.43***
		(.07)
	Rural resident	.01
		(.03)
	Under 35	−.03
		(.04)
	Over 55	.01
		(.03)
	Female	−.05
		(.03)
	Visible minority	.01
		(.09)
	Non-francophone	.00
		(.05)
	High school dropout	−.02
		(.04)
	University graduate	.00
		(.03)
N		809
Pseudo R^2		.43

Note: Cells contain average marginal effects, based on a multinomial logit model. Standard errors (corrected for clustering by day) are in parentheses.

* $p < .10$; ** $p < .05$; *** $p < .01$

Table 7.3 Campaign Effects, Ontario 2003, Moderated by Information and Ambivalence

	Saw ads about Liberals		Debate & debate[2]		Issue coverage	
	Lib support	PC support	Lib support	PC support	Lib support	PC support
Low Information / Low Ambivalence	−.03	.00	−.02	.02**	.01	−.02*
	(.03)	(.02)	(.02)	(.01)	(.01)	(.01)
			.00	−.004***		
			(.00)	(.002)		
High Information / Low Ambivalence	−.01	.06**	−.01	.00	.02*	−.02
	(.03)	(.03)	(.03)	(.03)	(.01)	(.01)
			.00	.00		
			(.00)	(.00)		
Low Information / High Ambivalence	−.05	.05	.00	−.01	.01	−.01
	(.06)	(.05)	(.02)	(.04)	(.02)	(.02)
			.00	.00		
			(.00)	(.01)		
High Information / High Ambivalence	.14***	−.19***	−.12***	.07***	.08***	−.06*
	(.04)	(.06)	(.03)	(.02)	(.02)	(.03)
			.02***	−.01***		
			(.00)	(.00)		
N	726		1683		1548	
Pseudo R^2	.46		.44		.43	

Note: Cells contain average marginal effects, based on a multinomial logit model. Control variables not shown: PID, socio-demographics. Standard errors corrected for clustering by day) are in parentheses.

* $p < .10$; ** $p < .05$; *** $p < .01$

Table 7.4 Campaign Effects, Quebec 2011, Moderated by Information and Ambivalence

	Layton coverage x Layton feeling	Sovereignty coverage	Tone of NDP coverage
	NDP support	NDP support	NDP support
Low Information / Low Ambivalence	1.42*	.0019	−.03
	(.76)	(.0014)	(.06)
High Information / Low Ambivalence	.47	.0017**	−.04
	(.40)	(.0008)	(.03)
Low Information / High Ambivalence	.29	.0026	.04
	(.72)	(.0023)	(.07)
High Information / High Ambivalence	1.35***	.0032***	.08***
	(.41)	(.0010)	(.02)
N	807	652	807
Pseudo R^2	.46	.39	.41

Cells contain average marginal effects, based on a multinomial logit model. Control variables not shown: PID, socio-demographics. Standard errors (corrected for clustering by day) are in parentheses.

* $p < .10$; ** $p < .05$; *** $p < .01$

Note: Hard sovereigntists excluded in middle column

Ontario, 2003

Looking at table 7.3 for Ontario first, the pattern of coefficients for ads, the debate, and media coverage in the four groups lends strong support to the two-moderator theory as applied to campaign effects: campaign effects sway only the minority of voters that pay close attention and have some ambivalence about their choice. In fact, these three forms of campaign information have a stunning influence on voters who are attentive and yet ambivalent (HIHA – High Information / High Ambivalence). There are only weak, inconsistent, or non-existent effects for the other three groups. And as we note in the subsection below, all three effects operate through sensible intermediate attitudes or perceptions.

The effects are illustrated graphically in figures 7.3A–7.3C. These graphs show predicted Liberal vote probabilities based on results in table 7.3 when we set the campaign effect variable at its high and low value and leave all other variables at their real values (displayed on the

Figure 7.3 Campaign Effects by Group, Ontario 2003

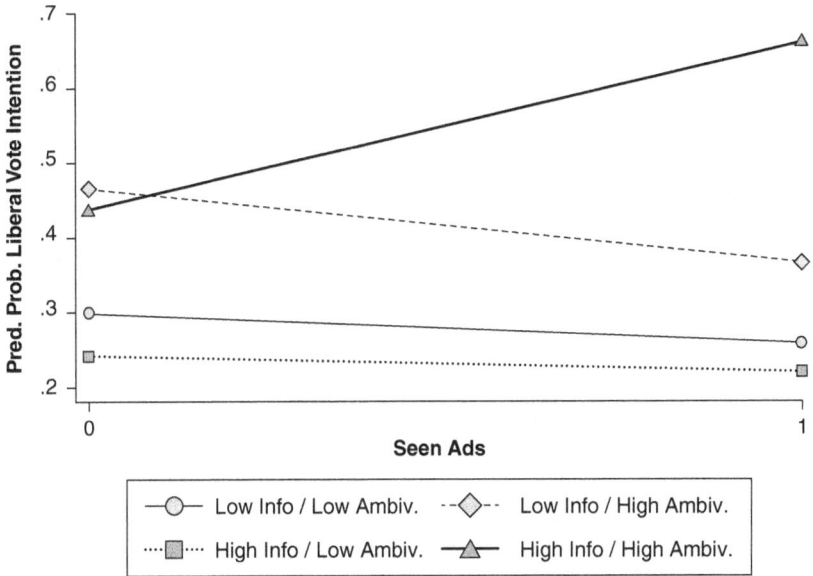

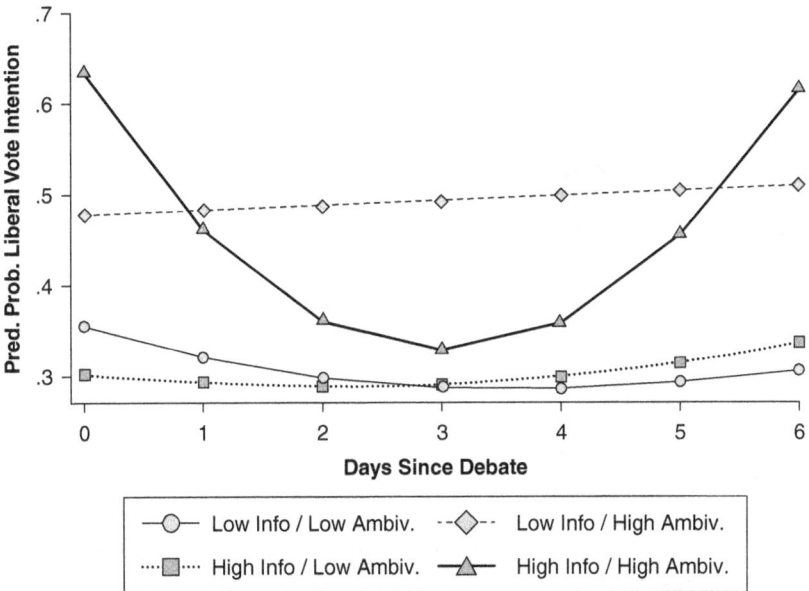

Figure 7.3 (Continued)

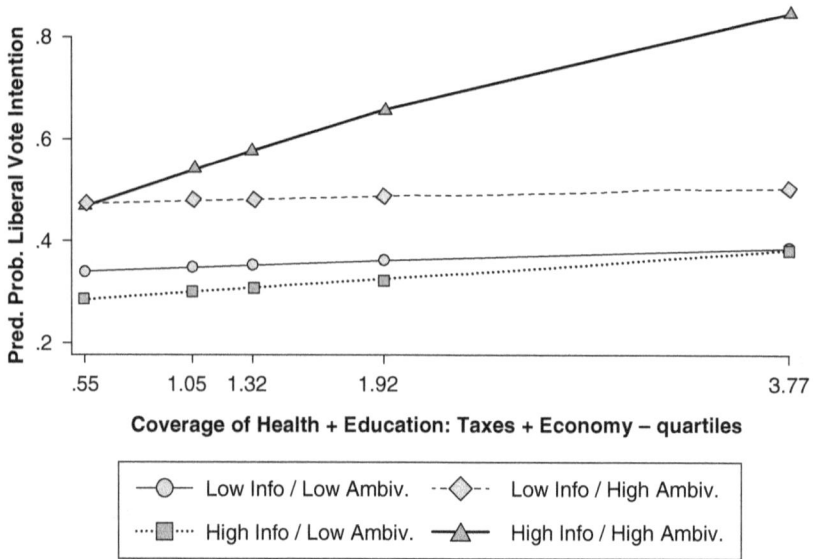

x-axis). The graphs show four lines, one for each of the four informa-tion/ambivalence groups.[24] We choose not to include error bars, be-cause with four lines they would overlap so much as to make the figure unreadable. We note simply that the p-values for all three campaign effects for the HIHA group are less than .01 (even the nonlinear effect for the debate), and for the other three groups, most of the p-values are well above .05.[25] These effects burn through even with a relatively small number of cases in the HIHA category.

Figure 7.3A shows that the gratingly negative PC ads and positive Lib-eral ones pushed viewers of TV advertisements towards the Liberals by nearly twenty points, but only in the HIHA group. That is, for these atten-tive, ambivalent voters, viewers of the ads were fifteen percentage points more likely to say they would vote Liberal, all else equal. No signifi-cant ad influence is found among the other groups. The two-moderator model is, therefore, strongly supported for the effect of advertising.

It bears noting, however, that our ad-viewership variable is differ-ent from the other two campaign variables in that it is a direct report of information reception. The information part of our High Informa-tion / High Ambivalence category is therefore working to facilitate the connection between information in the ad content and vote choice. We interpret this as the information effect representing two things: first, political sophistication in the sense of skills and knowledge that allows better-informed voters to put the raw information to use; and second, consumption of media reports about the ads, which provided interpretation and strongly reinforced viewers' perceptions that the ads were too negative and in bad taste (see also Freedman, Franz, and Goldstein 2004, 726).

Turning to the effect of the debate, figure 7.3B shows clearly that again the effect is limited to the HIHA group. These voters swing away from the Liberals for a few days following the debate, but this impulse fades within a week and this group returns to pre-debate levels of Liberal support.[26] The other groups simply do not move over this period. Estimates using self-reported debate viewership tell the same story: viewers in the HIHA group were nineteen points more likely to report a Conservative vote intention in the days immediately following the debate (not shown). Whether the effect is direct or is reinforced by media commentary on the debate, these results again provide strong evidence that campaign effects are governed by the two-moderator model.

Finally, we turn to the most striking effect in this campaign: the media agenda. Media issue coverage – the balance of "Liberal issues" to "PC issues" in the preceding three days' coverage – had a powerful effect on voters, but only some voters. Again, the effect was limited to the HIHA group (see figure 7.3C).[27] Comparing a High Information / High Ambivalence voter who heard three times as many references to Liberal issues with an otherwise identical voter who heard perfectly balanced coverage of issues, the model predicts the former voter to be seventeen points more likely to vote Liberal. As with advertisements and the debate, the other groups simply do not exhibit any susceptibility to influence from this campaign information.

Figure 7.4 shows the results for our 2011 data from Quebec. Our original analysis of the 2003 Ontario election was conducted shortly after that election and so the 2011 data act as something of a "testing" data set after seeing evidence consistent with the two-moderator model in our "training" data set from 2003. Figures 7.4A through 7.4C show the effects graphically.

First, we measured media content and assess how it affects vote intention over the campaign. Since the meteoric rise of the NDP is in need of explanation, we present only marginal effects on the probability of an NDP vote intention in the tables and graphs. In the first column of

Figure 7.4 Campaign Effects by Group, Quebec 2011

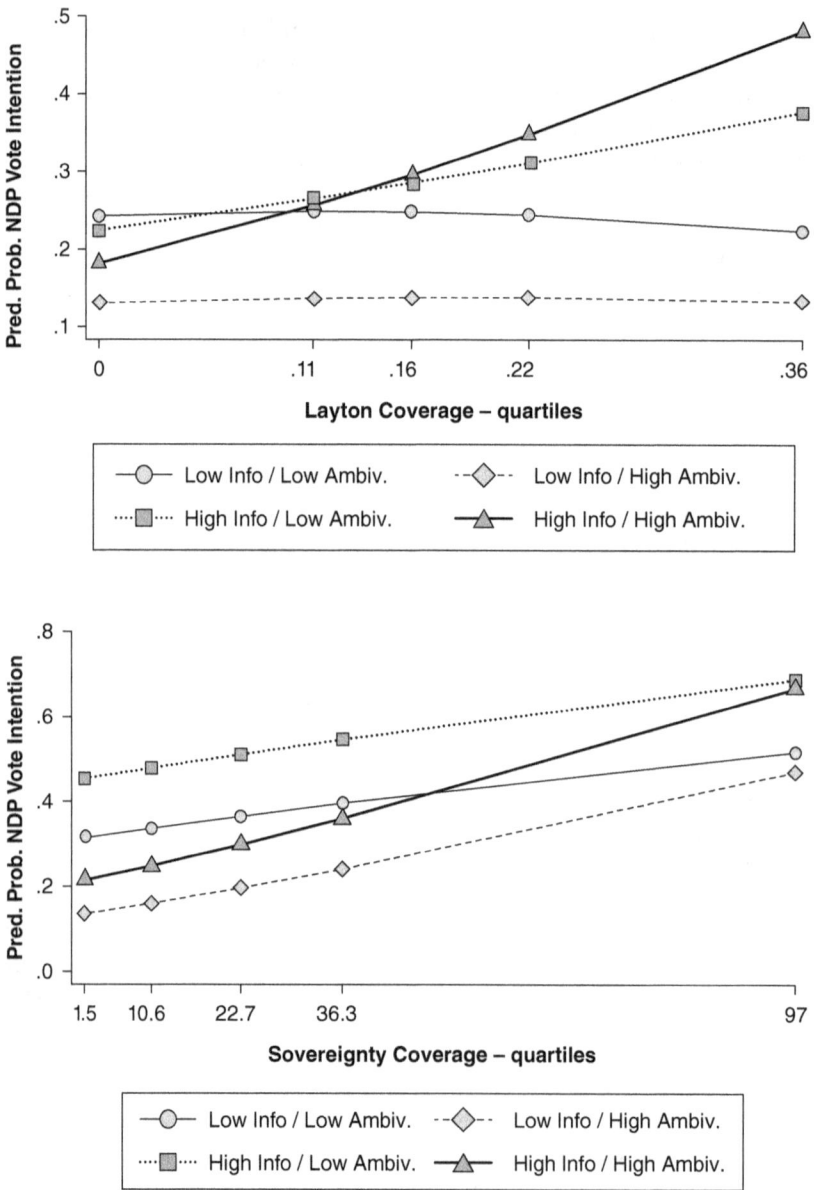

Low Info / Low Ambiv.   Low Info / High Ambiv.

High Info / Low Ambiv.   High Info / High Ambiv.

Low Info / Low Ambiv.   Low Info / High Ambiv.

High Info / Low Ambiv.   High Info / High Ambiv.

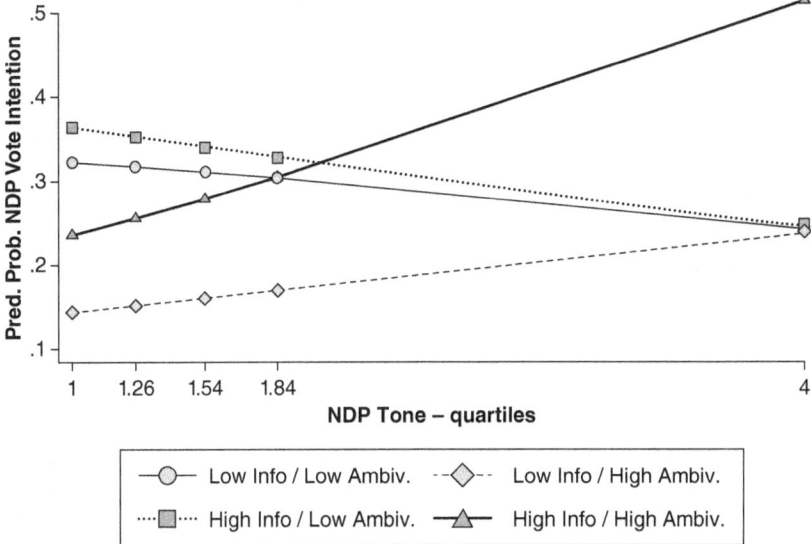

the table and in figure 7.4A, we show the interactive effect of the volume of coverage of Jack Layton and feelings about Layton on the vote. Substantively, when Layton received more coverage, voters who paid attention (highly informed) weighed their feelings about Layton more heavily in their voting decisions. Although the effect is visible in the High Information / Low Ambivalence group, we note that it is significant only in the HIHA group. For the most part, the effect was that for these voters, Layton became a more important determinant of the decision as the campaign went on.

Second, we examine the effect of coverage of sovereignty, with the expectation that increasing coverage of sovereignty in the wake of Gilles Duceppe's appearance at the PQ convention would have spooked all but the hard sovereigntists. Our model specification reflects this expectation, in that we exclude hard sovereigntists. The results in figure 7.4B show an effect of sovereignty coverage on NDP vote, but it is apparent across the board, in all groups. It is, however, steepest and most reliably estimated (three times the standard error) in the HIHA group. This could simply be a campaign effect that is not well-measured. Sovereignty coverage is a very tight linear function of time and as such is highly correlated with all of the campaign forces that may have pushed voters towards the NDP.

Finally, we look at the tone of NDP coverage for a direct media influence. In figure 7.4C, we see clearly a strong and significant effect limited to the HIHA group. In table 7.2, the full sample undifferentiated by the two moderators, this effect is invisible. In figure 7.4C, the difference in the predicted probability of an NDP vote across the full range of NDP tone is nearly twenty-five percentage points for the HIHA group, while it is less than half that for the Low Information / High Ambivalence group and negative for the Low Ambivalence groups.

Discussion and Conclusion

Studies of campaign effects have begun to take seriously the notion that voting decisions by a minority of voters can be influenced by the flow of information in a typical campaign (Fournier 2005; Hillygus and Jackman 2003; Hillygus and Shields 2008). In doing so, scholars can better understand how campaigns work and detect a much wider array of campaign effects. Here, for instance, we have added the media policy agenda and advertisements to the usual campaign suspects: conventions and debates. The results in this chapter complement studies by Hillygus and her colleagues in showing that the events and information of election campaigns can have powerful effects on vote choice among only a particular set of voters: the roughly one-in-five voters in these campaigns that our method classifies as attentive and ambivalent. Vote intentions in this group are powerfully affected by advertising, debates, and media issue coverage. Now that we have provided this corroborating evidence from a different electoral context and with a different research design, scholars can be more confident about the implications for the study of election campaigns with surveys and, more broadly, for the study of short-term attitude change.

On one hand, the findings amplify the importance of properly theorizing and modelling heterogeneity in voters' susceptibility to campaign effects. Specifically, using two separately measured moderators to model susceptibility to campaign effects is fundamental to understanding how, when, and for whom campaigns matter. Reception of, and resistance to information – both "partisan resistance" and "inertial resistance" – clearly moderate campaign effects. Even though informed and ambivalent persons constitute a minority of voters, this group's response to the campaign has the potential to tip the balance in favour of the candidate or party who has a better campaign. These are indeed cross-pressured, "persuadable" (Hillygus and Shields 2008), "swing voters" (Mayer 2007). And the influence of events on the outcome might even be much larger if there is a kind of campaign multiplier effect through polls and a two-step flow of information (Cukierman 1991; Katz and Lazarsfeld 1955). Our findings are one more nail in the coffin of the view that campaigns are mere sound and fury, signifying nothing (e.g., Berelson, Lazarsfeld, and McPhee 1954; Gelman and King 1993).

If analysts of campaigns are interested primarily in the response of these persuadable voters to information, they must design survey instruments appropriately. Obviously, the rolling cross-section (Johnston and Brady 2002) and multi-wave campaign panels (Hillygus and Jackman 2003) are indispensable. Survey designers must also collect, in parallel, the time-varying data that measure the information produced by the campaign. Moreover, because the group is relatively small, in light of issues of statistical power (Zaller 2002) it may also be worth considering oversampling those voters who can easily be identified early in a survey as cross-pressured.

On the other hand, our analyses bolster support for the theory of attitude change developed by Converse, McGuire, and Zaller as applied to election campaigns. A number of recent studies have cast doubt on the applicability of the theory to elections, but they have all used the wrong theory (Dobrzynska and Blais 2008; see also Goren 2004; Kriesi 2002; Krosnick and Brannon 1993; Dalton, Beck, and Huckfeldt 1998). Following Zaller's *specifically electoral theory of persuasion*, we show that the theory is indeed a powerful theoretical tool to find those voters who respond to election campaigns and more often than not determine the outcome. However, the tool is useful only when it is used properly: that is, researchers implement it as a two-moderator model, with reception and acceptance measured and included in the model separately.

The theory is even more robust in light of the fact that our study presents a different type of empirical evidence in favour of the two-moderator model. Rather than relying on indirect inferences where opinion change is measured imperfectly as defection from partisanship (but see Hillygus and Jackman 2003), we successfully apply the reception-resistance model to dynamic evidence that links daily movements in campaign information to individuals' vote intentions.

More generally, we have proposed a new empirical specification of the theory that is both simple and straightforward (see also Hillygus and Shields 2008). Instead of a single moderator – usually information – that confounds reception and resistance, or a complex setup that tries to disentangle these two dimensions statistically, we use information and ambivalence to capture each of the two moderators separately. In particular, the perpetual dilemma about which predispositions should matter for resistance (Claassen 2011) is resolved: ambivalence enables us to jump straight to the relevant concept. Furthermore, this implementation can easily be exported to topics other than vote choice. General political sophistication and internal conflict about an issue are operationalized with items regularly found in public opinion surveys. These two variables provide the means to identify attentive and ambivalent citizens, the individuals who should be – and are – most susceptible to opinion change in response to political communication.

Appendix: Measuring Ambivalence During the Campaign

Our discussion of the effect of ambivalence on susceptibility to new information conceives of ambivalence as existing prior to the reception of the new information. But without a pre-campaign wave of the survey, this ambivalence (call it A) remains an unmeasured variable. Thus, the measure of ambivalence we use (A*) is better characterized as indicating how many considerations the voter has that ought to be pushing her towards a party other than the one she gives as her current vote intention. This measure of ambivalence, generated from the same interview as the vote choice, is therefore only a proxy, and one that could be so poor a proxy as to hide the moderating effect of ambivalence completely. It therefore warrants an extended discussion.

When the sample is divided into High and Low Ambivalence groups on the basis of A* (A^*_{lo} and A^*_{hi}), those two groups will each contain voters high and low on A.

$$A^*_{lo} = \theta(A_{lo}) + (1-\theta)A_{hi}, \ 0 < \theta < 1$$
$$A^*_{hi} = \lambda(A_{hi}) + (1-\lambda)A_{lo}, \ 0 < \lambda < 1$$

Consider the Low Ambivalence group first. It contains both voters who have had their ambivalence resolved by the time of the interview (A_{hi}, A^*_{lo}), perhaps by the same events we identify, as well as those who have had one-sided considerations all along, such as strong partisans (A_{lo}, A^*_{lo}). Our High Ambivalence group, by the same logic, will consist of those who have been ambivalent all along (A_{hi}, A^*_{hi}), and those who were not ambivalent but who have become ambivalent, probably in response to the events of the campaign (A_{lo}, A^*_{hi}). Importantly, the distribution of A and A* may not be identical. That is, the campaign might systematically reduce or increase ambivalence (though in practice we find no change during the campaign wave).

The true moderating effect of A will therefore be expressed in our models through coefficients on variables that include interactions with both A^*_{lo} and A^*_{hi}. The relative shares will be determined by the proportions of A_{lo} and A_{hi} in A^*_{lo} and A^*_{hi}.

If real campaign effects on vote choice are limited to those who were a priori ambivalent (A_{hi}), our coefficient estimates on the interaction of ambivalence (A*) with a campaign event would never be biased upward. They would be biased downward, roughly by a factor of 1-λ, the proportion of initially Low Ambivalence voters who have become ambivalent over the campaign. Of course, there will turn out to be some among the Low Ambivalence group (A_{lo}) who become ambivalent (A^*_{hi}) and who change their vote intention. In that case, part of the campaign effect that really belonged in the Low Ambivalence group ends up in the High Ambivalence group. Yet this upward bias is justified in some sense as a campaign effect among those who were not so low on ambivalence that they were inoculated against campaign information.[28]

In practice, however, we believe that our estimates of the moderating effect of ambivalence will remain conservative, because we believe that campaign events are more likely to resolve ambivalence than create it. Fundamentally, we assume that all of the ambivalent are in some sense available to have their ambivalence resolved, whereas many of the Low Ambivalence group are strong partisans who are highly resistant to changing the attitudes that affect their vote choice, as Zaller argued (1992, chapter 10). In the Ontario campaign, for example, ambivalence appears to have risen slightly through the middle of the campaign and then dropped slightly at the end, though no linear or quadratic trend is statistically significant.

NOTES

1 Studies of campaign effects accurately reflect the net impact of campaigns but largely ignore the potential for different responses to campaign events by different kinds of voters. There are some exceptions, including Zaller

(1989, 1992, 1996), Johnston et al. (1996), Hillygus and Jackman (2003), Fournier et al. (2004), and Hillygus and Shields (2008).

2   We point the reader to the concluding chapter in this volume for a longer discussion of both the history and merits of this electoral study design.

3   See note 1 for exceptions.

4   Research on social influence has, as a result, repeatedly encountered the conundrum of contrary findings when using one moderator at a time.

5   Sophistication has proven to be an important discriminator of political cognition and behaviour: notably agenda-setting and framing effects (Iyengar and Kinder 1987; Nelson, Oxley, and Clawson 1997; Miller and Krosnick 2000), information processing (Fiske, Lau, and Smith 1990; McGraw, Lodge, and Stroh 1990; McGraw and Pinney 1990; McGraw and Steenbergen 1995), interpersonal heterogeneity in decision-making (Stimson 1975; Sniderman, Brody, and Tetlock 1991; Johnston et al. 1996; Fournier 2006), and deviations from enlightened opinions (Bartels 1996; Althaus 1998, 2003; Luskin, Fishkin, and Jowell 2002).

6   In chapter 10, Zaller (1992) finds no solid negative relationship between awareness and acceptance. He infers that "what is different for candidate [i.e., election] considerations, in comparison with issue-relevant considerations, is that the least politically aware people exhibit nearly as much partisan discrimination as the most aware ... this can only be because the cueing information necessary to achieve partisan resistance is much more widely available in election campaigns" (242).

7   Zaller finds that only at high levels of awareness is there a difference by partisan strength/inertia in the acceptance of messages. The group he measures as "disaffected partisans" (weak partisans with little inertia) accept the messages at all levels of political information while the "strong partisans" (strong partisans with high inertia) do not (Zaller 1992, 225, figure 10.1).

8   Zaller points out that "political awareness is associated with resistance to persuasion in part because it is a proxy for inertial resistance" (1992, 221). Proxies, of course, should be replaced with direct measures if they are available, and in the case of election campaigns, we almost always have the direct measure. Thus Zaller says that "in adding the inertia variable [party likes and dislikes] to the acceptance function, I am able, for the first time, to make a direct test for inertial resistance." Having done so, he can conclude, "Insofar as attentiveness affects the acquisition of campaign information, it appears therefore to be mainly via its effect on reception" (Zaller 1992, 243).

9   Readers may recall that Zaller (1992) himself treats ambivalence. However, he does so only in the context of his survey response framework. It is not considered as an indicator for the acceptance axiom.

10 In Ontario 2003, each night of the campaign – from 3 September through 1 October – a unique sample replicate was telephoned. Each number was called twice a day for the first four days and once a day for the final three. A target of eighty completed interviews per night was established, and this target was reached and maintained after five days. Unreached sample from earlier replicates were re-released for the last three days as response rates declined near the end of the campaign. Fieldwork was conducted by Opinion Search, Inc. using CATI interviewing. A core survey was established and run throughout the election. Additional questions were added to the core survey at various points in the campaign.

  For Canada 2011, a similar methodology was employed, conforming to the normal practice of Canadian Election Studies conducted by the Institute for Social Research at York University.

11 This specification allows for the possibility that campaign effects can push voters toward one party and away from another but leave some parties unaffected. Effectively, the model estimates binary comparisons among the three parties (Alvarez, Nagler, and Bowler 2000; Dow and Endersby 2004). This makes for a more difficult test for the model, since sample sizes for the estimates of standard errors involved only those voters who chose two of the three options. In what follows, if the effect is in the same direction for one party in its two comparisons with the other two parties (meaning the campaign effect pushes voters from both other parties toward the party in question), we note that fact and present the total effect with appropriate standard errors.

12 It is worth pointing out that conditional on attention to the campaign, the undecided are the most susceptible to campaign effects through their high level of ambivalence. Our findings are, then, probably conservative estimates of the true effects.

13 We also considered as campaign effects what are called "poll effects" (e.g., Bartels 1988; Johnston et al. 1992; Mutz 1998; Mebane 2000) but do not include them here for two reasons. First, we could not convince ourselves that the simple estimation strategy of including prior polls as independent variables is unbiased and consistent, since any unmeasured determinants of the vote choice are also determinants of poll numbers, so the latter will be correlated with vote choice, even if there is no causal effect. Second, we are not convinced that polls are "messages" like other campaign information and thus fit the two-moderator theory.

14 Tone is based on automated content analysis using the Lexicoder Sentiment Dictionary (LSD). We do not discuss that dictionary in detail here, but see Young and Soroka (2012) and Soroka et al. (2015) for details.

15 Two separate measures were used during the Ontario campaign as a result of other researchers' priorities. One, asked for the first nineteen days of the campaign, involved three questions about the leaders of the three main political parties in Ontario. The other, asked over the last ten days, asked respondents to identify "the last NDP premier of Ontario," the "federal minister of finance," and "Last year, former Saskatchewan Premier Roy Romanow headed a royal commission. Can you recall what was the subject of that royal commission?" The first measure turned out to be easier. In the dichotomized measure used below, we classified two correct answers as low information on the party leaders measure and as high information on the more difficult second measure. Alternative operationalizations, such as adjusting to equalize the means, produced results with identical substantive implications.

In 2011 the questions asked about the respondent's premier, the federal minister of finance, and the recently replaced governor general.

16 Note that Hillygus and Shields (2008) use only policy attitudes, and the congruence or incongruence is relative to party identification rather than the vote decision.

17 In Quebec we use four items for each voter-party ambivalence calculation, with different issues being used for different parties, but with that variation constant across respondents.

18 We admit that strategic voters will be classified by this method as ambivalent. We are not overly concerned about this for two reasons. First, rates of strategic voting are very low (Blais 2002). Second, we would overestimate campaign effects only among the ambivalent if non-ambivalent NDP voters were voting strategically Liberal and were deciding to do so in response to the campaign events we measure in this chapter. We think this impossible by definition, since if they are non-ambivalent NDP voters choosing the Liberals strategically, the campaign information we measure here (ads, media coverage, and the debate) should not affect that decision. That is, they may respond to polls giving them relevant information, but not to substantive information, since, by definition, they are not being persuaded to choose the Liberals sincerely.

19 Glasgow (2004) has shown that existing measures of ambivalence are virtually indistinguishable from measures of indifference or neutrality. However, when indifference is controlled, ambivalence still dominates models of attitude change (Fournier 2003). We exclude indifference from our analyses in order not to overtax our interactive models.

20 In theory, we ought to use all the information in the information and ambivalence variables by using continuous interactions rather than these

dichotomizations. We did estimate models using interaction terms built from the raw measures of information and ambivalence. The results were substantively similar but plagued by large standard errors because of the inherent multi-collinearity and the small measurement scales for these variables. Presenting those results would require numerous, imprecisely estimated fitted values. Our dichotomization of the two variables gives cleaner estimates, is true to the theory, and is common practice in similar studies (e.g., Erikson 1979; Sniderman, Glaser, and Griffin 1990; Lupia 1994; Johnston et al. 1996; Miller and Krosnick 2000; Holbrook et al. 2001; Hillygus and Shields 2008).

21 We use Stata 11's margins command to produce the mean effect of the variable across respondents, given their real values of the other variables.

22 Note that we still include only three of the group dummy variables themselves, since there is a constant in the model. The presentation of marginal effects omits the constant. The raw multinomial estimates are available upon request (or online).

23 Standard practice would be to include one general estimate of the campaign effect variable and three of the four possible group interactions, where the omitted interaction would be for one group and the coefficients for the other groups, calculated by adding their coefficients to the general one. We aim to make the table easier to use by reporting mathematically equivalent but more easily interpretable estimates with all four group dummy interactions. This specification gives us built-in t-tests of the difference of each group's coefficient (the estimate of the campaign effect for that group) from zero, rather than the typical test for the difference of each group from the arbitrary baseline group's coefficient. Of course, t-tests can easily be calculated for differences between the groups' effects.

24 These predicted values are estimated using Stata 11's margins command.

25 The clear exception is the debate effect in the High Information / Low Ambivalence group. See below for our interpretation of this result.

26 We do not make very much of the upward trend in days six and seven – this may be a consequence of other trends in the last two days of the campaign, but is likely also to be because of the rather quick decay in effects from day three to five.

27 Granted, the effect for the Low Information / Low Ambivalence group is more than twice its standard error, but it is a weak effect indeed, nearly four times smaller than the effect in the High Information / High Ambivalence group.

28 We also investigated an instrumental variables approach to mitigate the endogeneity of the ambivalence measure. We would need an instrument

correlated with A but not with A*, which would be hard to find. And in fact, suitable instruments could not be found: even a "kitchen sink" model of ambivalence could produce an R^2 of only .05.

References

Althaus, Scott L. 1998. "Information Effects in Collective Preferences." *American Political Science Review* 92:545–58.

– 2003. *Collective Preferences in Democratic Politics*. Cambridge: Cambridge University Press.

Alvarez, R. Michael, and John Brehm. 1995. "American Ambivalence towards Abortion Policy: Development of a Heteroskedastic Probit Model of Competing Values." *American Journal of Political Science* 39:1055–89.

– 1997. "Are Americans Ambivalent about Racial Policies?" *American Journal of Political Science* 41:345–75.

– 2002. *Hard Choices, Easy Answers*. Princeton: Princeton University Press.

Alvarez, R. Michael, Jonathan Nagler, and Shaun Bowler. 2000. "Issues, Economics, and the Dynamics of Multiparty Elections: The British 1987 General Election." *American Political Science Review* 94:131–49.

Bartels, Larry M. 1988. *Presidential Primaries and the Dynamics of Vote Choice*. Princeton: Princeton University Press.

– 1996. "Uninformed Votes: Information Effects in Presidential Elections." *American Journal of Political Science* 40:194–230.

Basinger, Scott, and Howard Lavine. 2005. "Ambivalence, Information, and Electoral Choice." *American Political Science Review* 99:169–84.

Berelson, Bernard R., Paul F. Lazarsfeld, and William N. McPhee. 1954. *Voting*. Chicago: University of Chicago Press.

Blais, André. 2002. "Why Is There so Little Strategic Voting in Canadian Plurality Rule Elections?" *Political Studies* 50:445–54.

Blais, André, and Martin Boyer. 1996. "Assessing the Impact of Televised Debates." *British Journal of Political Science* 26:143–64.

Blais, André, Elisabeth Gidengil, Richard Nadeau, and Neil Nevitte. 2002. *Anatomy of a Liberal Victory: Making Sense of the Vote in the 2000 Canadian Election*. Peterborough, ON: Broadview.

– 2003. "Campaign Dynamics in the 2000 Canadian Election: How the Leader Debates Salvaged the Conservative Party." *PS, Political Science & Politics* 36:45–50.

Blais, André, Richard Nadeau, Elisabeth Gidengil, and Neil Nevitte. 1999. "Campaign Dynamics in the 1997 Canadian Election." *Canadian Public Policy* 25:197–205.

Blais, André, and Andrea Perrella. 2008. "Systemic Effects of Televised Leaders' Debates." *International Journal of Press/Politics* 13:451–64.

Brady, Henry E., and Richard Johnston. 2006. *Capturing Campaign Effects*. Ann Arbor: University of Michigan Press.

Brambor, Thomas, William Roberts Clark, and Matt Golder. 2006. "Understanding Interaction Models: Improving Empirical Analyses." *Political Analysis* 14:63–82.

Campbell, Angus, Philip E. Converse, Warren E. Miller, and Donald E. Stokes. 1960. *The American Voter*. New York: John Wiley.

Campbell, James. 2000. "The Science of Forecasting Presidential Elections." In *Before the Vote: Forecasting American National Elections*, edited by James Campbell and James Garand, 169–87. Thousand Oaks, CA: Sage Publications.

Claassen, Ryan L. 2011. "Political Awareness and Electoral Campaigns: Maximum Effects for Minimum Citizens?" *Political Behavior* 33:203–23.

Converse, Philip E. 1962. "Information Flow and the Stability of Partisan Attitudes." *Public Opinion Quarterly* 26:578–99.

Cukierman, Alex. 1991. "Asymmetric Information and the Electoral Momentum of Public Opinion Polls." *Public Choice* 70:181–213.

Cutler, Fred. 2008. "One Voter, Two First-Order Elections?" *Electoral Studies* 27:492–504.

Dalton, Russell J., Paul A. Beck, and Robert Huckfeldt. 1998. "Partisan Cues and the Media: Information Flows in the 1992 Presidential Election." *American Political Science Review* 92:111–26.

Delli Carpini, Michael X., and Scott Keeter. 1993. "Measuring Political Knowledge: Putting First Things First." *American Journal of Political Science* 37:1179–206.

Dobrzynska, Agnieszka, and André Blais. 2008. "Testing Zaller's Reception and Acceptance Model in an Intense Election Campaign." *Political Behavior* 30:259–76.

Dow, Jay K., and James W. Endersby. 2004. "Multinomial Probit and Multinomial Logit: A Comparison of Choice Models for Voting Research." *Electoral Studies* 23:107–22.

Dreyer, Edward C. 1971. "Media Use and Electoral Choices." *Public Opinion Quarterly* 35:544–53.

Eagly, Alice H., and Shelly Chaiken. 1995. "Attitude Strength, Attitude Structure, and Resistance to Change." In *Attitude Strength: Antecedents and Consequences*, edited by R.E. Petty and J.A. Krosnick, 413–32. Mahwah, NJ: Erlbaum.

Erikson, Robert. 1979. "The SRC Panel Data and Mass Political Attitudes." *British Journal of Political Science* 9:89–114.

Farrell, David, and Rudiger Schmitt-Beck. 2002. *Do Political Campaigns Matter?: Campaign Effects in Elections and Referendums*. New York: Routledge.

Fiske, Susan T., Richard R. Lau, and Richard A. Smith. 1990. "On the Varieties and Utilities of Political Experience." *Social Cognition* 8:31–48.

Fiske, Susan T., and Shelley E. Taylor. 1991. *Social Cognition*. New York: McGraw-Hill.

Fournier, Patrick. 2003. "The Individual Determinants of Political Persuasion." Paper presented at the Annual Meeting of the American Association for Public Opinion Research, Nashville, 15–18 May.

– 2005. "Ambivalence and Attitude Change in Vote Choice: Do Campaign Switchers Experience Internal Conflict?" In *Ambivalence, Politics, and Public Policy*, edited by Stephen C. Craig and Michael D. Martinez, 27–46. New York: Palgrave Macmillan.

– 2006. "The Impact of Campaigns on Discrepancies, Errors, and Biases in Voting Behavior." In *Capturing Campaign Effects*, edited by Henry Brady and Richard Johnston, 45–77. Ann Arbor: University of Michigan Press.

Fournier, Patrick, Fred Cutler, Stuart Soroka, Dietlind Stolle, and Éric Bélanger. 2013. "Riding the Orange Wave: Leadership, Values, Issues, and the 2011 Canadian Election." *Canadian Journal of Political Science* 46 (4): 863–97.

Fournier, Patrick, Richard Nadeau, André Blais, Elisabeth Gidengil, and Neil Nevitte. 2004. "Time-of-Voting Decision and Susceptibility to Campaigns." *Electoral Studies* 23:661–81.

Freedman, Paul, Michael Franz, and Kenneth Goldstein. 2004. "Campaign Advertising and Democratic Citizenship." *American Journal of Political Science* 48: 723–41.

Geer, John. 1988. "The Effects of Presidential Debates on the Electorate's Preferences for Candidates." *American Politics Research* 16:486–501.

Gelman, Andrew, and Gary King. 1993. "Why Are American Presidential Election Campaign Polls so Variable When Votes Are so Predictable?" *British Journal of Political Science* 23:409–51.

Glasgow, Garrett. 2004. "Reconsidering Tests for Ambivalence in Political Choice Survey Data." Working paper, University of California Santa Barbara.

Goren, Paul. 2004. "Political Sophistication and Policy Reasoning: A Reconsideration." *American Journal of Political Science* 48:462–78.

Gwiasda, Gregory W. 2001. "Network News Coverage of Campaign Advertisements: Media's Ability to Reinforce Campaign Messages." *American Politics Research* 29:461–82.

Hillygus, D. Sunshine, and Simon Jackman. 2003. "Voter Decision Making in Election 2000: Campaign Effects, Partisan Activation, and the Clinton Legacy." *American Journal of Political Science* 47: 583–96.

Hillygus, D. Sunshine, and Todd G. Shields. 2008. *The Persuadable Voter: Wedge Issues in Presidential Campaigns*. Princeton: Princeton University Press.

Holbrook, Allyson L., Jon A. Krosnick, Penny S. Visser, Wendi L. Gardner, and John T. Cacioppo. 2001. "Attitudes toward Presidential Candidates and Political Parties." *American Journal of Political Science* 45:930–50.

Holbrook, Thomas M. 1996. *Do Campaigns Matter?* Thousand Oaks, CA: Sage.

Iyengar, Shanto, and Donald R. Kinder. 1987. *News That Matters*. Chicago: University of Chicago Press.

Johnston, Richard, André Blais, Henry Brady, and Jean Crête. 1992. *Letting the People Decide: The Dynamics of a Canadian Election*. Montreal and Kingston: McGill-Queen's University Press.

Johnston, Richard, André Blais, Henry E. Brady, Elisabeth Gidengil, and Neil Nevitte. 1996. *The Challenge of Direct Democracy: The 1992 Canadian Referendum*. Montreal and Kingston: McGill-Queen's University Press.

Johnston, Richard, André Blais, Elisabeth Gidengil, Neil Nevitte, and Henry E. Brady. 1994. "The Collapse of a Party System? The 1993 Canadian General Election." Paper presented at the Annual Meeting of the American Political Science Association, New York, 1–4 September.

Johnston, Richard, and Henry E. Brady. 2002. "The Rolling Cross-Section Design." *Electoral Studies* 21:283–95.

Johnston, Richard, Michael Hagen, and Kathleen Hall Jamieson. 2004. *The 2000 Presidential Election and the Foundations of Party Politics*. New York: Cambridge University Press.

Katz, Elihu, and Paul Lazarsfeld. 1955. *Personal Influence*. New York: Free Press.

Kriesi, Hanspeter. 2002. "Individual Opinion Formation in a Direct Democratic Campaign." *British Journal of Political Science* 32:171–85.

Krosnick, Jon A. 1988. "The Role of Attitude Importance in Social Evaluation: A Study of Policy Preferences, Presidential Candidate Evaluations, and Voting Behaviour." *Journal of Personality and Social Psychology* 55:196–210.

– 1990. "Government Policy and Citizen Passion: A Study of Issue Publics in Contemporary America." *Political Behavior* 12:59–92.

Krosnick, Jon A., and Laura A. Brannon. 1993. "The Impact of the Gulf War on the Ingredients of Presidential Evaluations: Multidimensional Effects of Political Involvement." *American Political Science Review* 87:963–75.

Lavine, Howard. 2001. "The Electoral Consequences of Ambivalence toward Presidential Candidates." *American Journal of Political Science* 45:915–29.

Lazarsfeld, Paul F., Bernard R. Berelson, and Hazel Gaudet. 1944. *The People's Choice: How the Voter Makes Up His Mind in a Presidential Campaign*. New York: Duell, Sloan and Pearce.

Lupia, Arthur. 1994. "Shortcuts versus Encyclopedias: Information and Voting Behavior in California Insurance Reform Elections." *American Political Science Review* 88:63–76.

Luskin, Robert C. 1987. "Measuring Political Sophistication." *American Journal of Political Science* 31:856–99.

Luskin, Robert C., James S. Fishkin, and Roger Jowell. 2002. "Considered Opinions: Deliberative Polling in Britain." *British Journal of Political Science* 32:455–87.

Macaluso, Theodore. 1977. "Political Information, Party Identification and Voting Defection." *Public Opinion Quarterly* 41:255–60.

Mayer, William G. 2007. "The Swing Voter in American Presidential Elections." *American Politics Research* 35 (3): 358–88.

McGraw, Kathleen M., Milton Lodge, and Patrick Stroh. 1990. "On-line Processing in Candidate Evaluation: The Effects of Issue Order, Issue Salience and Sophistication." *Political Behavior* 12:41–58.

McGraw, Kathleen M., and Neil Pinney. 1990. "The Effects of General and Domain-Specific Expertise on Political Memory and Judgement." *Social Cognition* 8:9–30.

McGraw, Kathleen M., and Marco Steenbergen. 1995. "Pictures in the Head: Memory Representations of Political Actors." In *Political Judgment: Structure and Process*, edited by Milton Lodge and Kathleen M. McGraw, 15–42. Ann Arbor: University of Michigan Press.

McGuire, William J. 1968. "Personality and Susceptibility to Social Influence." In *Handbook of Personality Theory and Research*, edited by E.F. Borgatta and W.W. Lambert, 1130–87. Chicago: Rand McNally.

– 1969. "The Nature of Attitudes and Attitude Change." In *Handbook of Social Psychology*, edited by G. Lindzey and E. Aronson, 3:136–314. Reading: Addison-Wesley.

– 1999. *Constructing Social Psychology*. Cambridge: Cambridge University Press.

Mebane, Walter R. 2000. "Coordination, Moderation, and Institutional Balancing in American Presidential and House Elections." *American Political Science Review* 94:35–57.

Mendelsohn, Matthew. 1996. "The Media and Interpersonal Communications: The Priming of Issues, Leaders, and Party Identification." *Journal of Politics* 58:112–25.

Miller, Johanne M., and Jon A. Krosnick. 2000. "News Media Impact on the Ingredients of Presidential Evaluations: Politically Knowledgeable Citizens Are Guided by a Trusted Source." *American Journal of Political Science* 44:301–15.

Mutz, Diana C. 1998. *Impersonal Influence*. Cambridge: Cambridge University Press.

Nadeau, Richard, and Jean-Herman Guay. 1990. "La qualité de l'information en tant que déterminant du changement de l'opinion: une étude quasi-expérimentale portant sur le libre-échange." *Canadian Journal of Political Science* 23:727–49.

Nadeau, Richard, Neil Nevitte, Elisabeth Gidengil, and André Blais. 2008. "Election Campaigns as Information Campaigns: Who Learns What and Does It Matter?" *Political Communication* 25:229–48.

Nelson, Thomas E., Zoe M. Oxley, and Rosalee A. Clawson. 1997. "Toward a Psychology of Framing Effects." *Political Behavior* 19:221–46.

Nevitte, Neil, André Blais, Elisabeth Gidengil, and Richard Nadeau. 2000. *Unsteady State: The 1997 Canadian Federal Election*. Don Mills, ON: Oxford University Press.

Price, Vincent, and John Zaller. 1993. "Who Gets the News: Alternative Measures of News Reception and Their Implications for Research." *Public Opinion Quarterly* 57:133–64.

Rivers, Douglas. 1988. "Heterogeneity in Models of Electoral Choice." *American Journal of Political Science* 32:737–57.

Shaw, Daron. 1999. "The Effect of TV Ads and Candidate Appearances on Statewide Presidential Votes, 1988–96." *American Political Science Review* 93:345–61.

Sniderman, Paul M., Richard A. Brody, and Philip E. Tetlock. 1991. *Reasoning and Choice*. Cambridge: Cambridge University Press.

Sniderman, Paul M., James M. Glaser, and Robert Griffin. 1990. "Information and Electoral Choice." In *Information and Democratic Processes*, edited by John A. Ferejohn and James H. Kuklinski, 117–35. Chicago: University of Illinois Press.

Soroka, Stuart, Dominik Stecula, and Christopher Wlezien. 2015. "It's (Change in) the (Future) Economy, Stupid: Economic Indicators, the Media, and Public Opinion." *American Journal of Political Science* 59:457–74.

Stimson, James A. 1975. "Belief Systems: Constraint, Complexity, and the 1972 Election." *American Journal of Political Science* 19:393–417.

West, Darrell M. 1997. *Air Wars: Television Advertising in Political Campaigns, 1952–1996*. Washington: Congressional Quarterly Press.

Young, Lori, and Stuart Soroka. 2012. "Affective News: The Automated Coding of Sentiment in Political Texts." *Political Communication* 29:205–31.

Zaller, John R. 1989. "Bringing Converse Back In: Modeling Information Flow in Political Campaigns." *Political Analysis* 1:181–234.

– 1990. "Political Awareness, Elite Opinion Leadership, and the Mass Survey Response." *Social Cognition* 8:125–53.

– 1992. *The Nature and Origins of Mass Opinion*. Cambridge: Cambridge University Press.
– 1996. "The Myth of Massive Media Impact Revived: New Support for a Discredited Idea." In *Political Persuasion and Attitude Change*, edited by D.C. Mutz, P.M. Sniderman, and R.A. Brody, 17–78. Ann Arbor: University of Michigan Press.
– 2002. "The Statistical Power of Election Studies to Detect Media Exposure Effects in Political Campaigns." *Electoral Studies* 21:297–329.
Zaller, John R., and Stanley Feldman. 1992. "A Simple Theory of the Survey Response: Answering Questions versus Revealing Preferences." *American Journal of Political Science* 36:579–616.
Zukin, Cliff. 1977. "A Reconsideration of the Effects of Information on Partisan Stability." *Public Opinion Quarterly* 41:244–54.

8 Bureaucrats, Policy Attitudes, and Political Behaviour: A Reappraisal

JAMES C. GARAND AND PING XU

The size of the public sector in democratic political systems has long drawn the attention of both scholars and political observers. While a wide range of theoretical arguments have been considered in explaining variation in the size of government, most explanations can be grouped into two broad categories (Lowery and Berry 1983). On one hand there are the *responsive government* explanations, which suggest that the size of the public sector is best explained by the preferences for government goods and services in the mass public. Here government size is seen as a reflection of the level of government activity (and the associated costs of that level of activity) that is preferred by some aggregation of mass preferences, often as represented in the preferences of the median voter. On the other hand, the *excessive government* explanations suggest that the growth in the size of the public sector is a function of actions by government officials to expand the size of government beyond what the mass public would prefer. Scholarly advocates of excessive government explanations paint a less benevolent view of the public sector, suggesting that government officials use a combination of political power, deception, or obfuscation to secure greater support for government programs than would normally be supported by voters.

Public-sector employees play a major role in some of the excessive government theories.[1] For instance, Niskanen (1971) proposes what has been termed the *bureau information monopoly* theory, in which he contends that government bureaucrats are motivated by self-interest to seek larger budgets for their government agencies. According to Niskanen, public-sector employees use their near-monopoly over policy-relevant information to press political decision-makers for larger budgets. In Niskanen's formulation, most of the influence exerted by bureaucrats takes place in institutional settings, such as congressional committee hearings and other legislative-bureaucratic interactions.

Alternatively, other scholars have suggested that there is an electoral mechanism for translating the relative preferences of government employees into their preferred size of the public sector. The *bureau voting* theory suggests that government bureaucrats are more liberal and pro-spending than other citizens, that they are more likely to turn out to vote, and that they show a greater propensity to cast votes for left-leaning parties and candidates who, presumably, are more supportive of an expanded public sector (Sears and Citrin 1982; Blais and Dion 1990; Blais, Blake, and Dion 1997; Garand, Parkhurst, and Seoud 1991a; Corey and Garand 2002). The implication is that government employees constitute a larger share of the electorate than of the general population, and this gives them disproportionate influence over electoral outcomes and, ultimately, over elected officials (Blair 2003). Scholars have uncovered discernible evidence to support this theoretical argument, in both the United States (Lewis 1990; Garand, Parkhurst, and Seoud 1991a; Corey and Garand 2002) and Western industrial democracies (Blais, Blake, and Dion 1991; Blake 1991; Jensen, Sum, and Flynn 2009).

In this chapter we build on previous research to provide an updated evaluation of the bureau voting theory. The lion's share of previous research on the bureau voting theory was conducted during the 1990s, and it is arguably time to revisit the empirical support for this theory using more recent survey data. Specifically, we ask whether government bureaucrats are more likely to cast votes for left-leaning political parties and candidates – i.e., those who typically favour an expanded public sector and greater government spending. Our approach here is explicitly comparative. In order to explore these research questions, we use survey data from a variety of sources in the United States, Canada, and other Western industrial democracies. These data sets include the American National Election Study (2004, 2008), the Canadian Election Study (2008), and the World Values Survey (2005). The results of our analyses provide a comparative, cross-national test of hypotheses about political attitudes and behaviour among public-sector employees that are derived from the bureau voting theory.

What Do We (Think We) Know?

The scholarly literature has generally provided fairly strong support for the bureau voting theory, though there is no consensus about the degree to which government employees differ from other citizens in their political attitudes and behaviour. Much of the early work on bureaucratic attitudes focused on senior executives, both in the United States (Aberbach and Rockman 1976; Aberbach, Putnam, and Rockman 1981; Dolan 2002) and in Western democracies (Putnam 1973). This is the very group of bureaucrats that draws the attention of Niskanen, since these bureaucrats are in positions of authority in government departments and agencies. In early research, scholars did not directly explore a full range of attitude differences between senior executives and the non-bureaucracy mass public; rather, that work tends to focus on work responsibilities, perceptions of political and bureaucratic processes, and demographic attributes. Aberbach, Putnam, and Rockman (1981) indeed find a left-leaning tendency in the political attitudes of senior executives in the United States, though in a more recent work Dolan (2002) finds that American senior executives are significantly *less* likely than the general public to support greater spending in a variety of policy areas.

Public-sector employees are a much more diverse group than senior executives, since government employment covers a wide range of occupations, salary levels, and work responsibilities. Studies that are based on large-scale surveys of the mass public and that differentiate public-sector employees and other individuals are more likely to find support for the bureau voting model. In the United States, Garand, Parkhurst, and Seoud (1991a, 1991b) find considerable support for the idea that public-sector employees differ from their civilian counterparts in their political attitudes and behaviours. Using data from the American National Election Studies (ANES) from 1982, 1984, and 1986, they find that government employees are generally more likely to hold more liberal attitudes, hold more favourable views towards Democrats and liberal political figures, and support spending in some selected policy areas. Moreover, Garand, Parkhurst, and Seoud (1991a) find that public-sector employees are substantially more likely to turn out to vote; the differences in turnout rates for government employees and other citizens range from 9% to 22% across years and races for different offices. This finding of higher turnout rates for public-sector employees is reinforced by Corey and Garand (2002), who find that public-sector employees are significantly more likely to turn out during the 1996 American national elections. Garand, Parkhurst, and Seoud (1991a) also find that bureaucrats are significantly more likely to vote for Democratic candidates, presumably as a reflection of greater willingness to support more liberal candidates. Finally, Garand, Parkhurst, and Seoud (1991b) use data from the 1982 ANES to consider differences in attitudes and behaviour among federal government employees, state and local government employees, and the mass public; they find support for the bureau voting theory among both federal and state-local government employees, though the behaviour and attitudes of state and local bureaucrats are more in line with expectations from the bureau voting model than those of federal government employees.

In cross-national research, scholars have also found support for the bureau voting theory. Perhaps the most important comparative work on the attitudes and behaviour of government bureaucrats is by Blais and Dion (1991), who collected a series of essays assessing empirical support for the budget-maximizing behaviour by public-sector bureaucrats. Blake (1991) finds support for the view that public-sector employees in Canada, Norway, Sweden, and the United States are more likely to stake out a position to the left of other citizens, though controls for union membership tend to depress the effect of government employment by a discernible amount. It is interesting to note that Blake finds the strongest effects of government employment on ideology among those in professional and managerial/technical occupations, while individuals in other occupational categories hold relatively indistinct political views based on whether or not they work for the public sector. Regarding voting behaviour, Blais, Blake, and Dion (1991) find that government employees are significantly more likely to support left-leaning political parties and candidates in Australia, Great Britain, Japan, and the Netherlands, while little support is found to support this assertion for Germany and Switzerland. For other countries (i.e., Canada, Denmark, France, and the United States), the results are somewhat ambiguous. More recently, Jensen, Sum, and Flynn (2009) explore the degree to which public-sector employment affects ideology, turnout, and vote choice in eighteen Western democracies. Their findings suggest strong evidence of government employment effects in the aggregate, though when they specify country-specific effects of government employment they find that relatively few countries simultaneously exhibit strong support for the ideology, turnout, *and* vote choice components of the bureau voting theory. Interestingly, Jensen, Sum, and Flynn find little evidence that unionized government employees differ from their non-unionized counterparts in the attitudes and behaviours.

Overall, it appears that there is moderately strong evidence that government employees differ in predictable ways from other citizens.

Although there is (1) variation in support for the three components of the bureau voting theory across countries and (2) sometimes inconsistent levels of support among the three major components of the bureau voting theory within countries, the evidence in favour of the theory is sufficiently strong to support the extension of this research program to cover a more recent time frame.

Bureaucrats and the Public Sector

Why should bureaucrats be budget maximizers, if indeed they are? More specifically, why should government employees be more likely than other citizens to hold left-leaning views, support greater government spending, exhibit higher turnout rates, and vote for left-leaning candidates?

Niskanen's Bureau Information Monopoly Theory

We begin with Niskanen's (1971) view that government bureaucrats are rational self-interested actors, and their support of expanded agency budgets is derived from their self-interest. For Niskanen, public-sector bureaucrats seek to maximize agency budgets in order to achieve any number of goals, including higher salaries, flexibility in policymaking, and ease of bureaucratic management, among other things. Simply, Niskanen suggests that higher budgets bring bureaucrats greater personal reward and greater ease and flexibility in conducting their jobs. Not only are bureaucrats more likely to increase their personal salaries and benefits when funds are readily available, their jobs are also made easier by having department or agency budgets that permit them to hire adequate personnel, purchase equipment and supplies, and administer department programs. Government bureaucrats are also often strong adherents of the policy goals of their home agencies; bureaucrats who advocate for their agency policy mission – Downs (1967) refers to these bureaucrats as zealots and, to some extent, advocates – will support increased budgets for their agencies as a means of carrying out these policy goals in the strongest possible way. Finally, in more recent work Niskanen (1991) focuses attention on government bureaucrats' efforts to secure adequate discretionary budgets, though even here public-sector employees likely express a preference for expanded agency budgets in order to create discretionary funds within the overall agency budget.

How do government bureaucrats achieve their goal of budget maximization, if indeed they do? Niskanen points to the role of informational monopolies in helping government employees to make a case for larger budgets. Public-sector bureaucrats are intimately familiar with the workings of their agencies and departments, as well as the clients with whom they are dealing, the resources necessary to fulfil agency goals, and what is necessary to satisfy personal self-interest goals. This information is far less readily available to political decision makers, most of whom must be policy generalists who cannot invest the time, energy, and resources necessary to compete with government bureaucrats over the operation of their departments and agencies. The result is that bureaucrats have a strong information advantage over elected officials when they are providing advice through legislative committee hearings and other forms of legislative-executive contact.

Bureau Voting Theory

An alternative mechanism through which government employees can affect government spending is found in the electoral arena. If government employees are more likely to (1) support more liberal, pro-spending policies, (2) cast votes for candidates who promote liberal, pro-spending policies, and (3) turn out on election day, they can shift the position of the median voter to the left and hence influence government policy related to spending in a liberal direction.[2] Hence budget maximization – or at least budget expansion – can take place through other processes and without the information monopolies in political institutions envisioned by Niskanen.

Of course, government employees are a diverse group, and by no means can one assume that all government bureaucrats behave in the manner suggested by the bureau voting theory. Clearly, public-sector employees do not comprise a single-minded monolith. Rather, there will be variation in the attitudes and behaviours of public-sector employees, just as there is variation in the attitudes and behaviours of other citizens. However, the bureau voting theory does not require a monolithic group of government bureaucrats marching in lockstep to the polls. As the attitudes and behaviours of the average government employee deviates from those of other citizens, bureaucrats become an electoral force to be reckoned with and increase their influence over elected officials by shifting them to the left (Blair 2003).

What explains the possible differences in attitudes and behaviours for public-sector employees and other citizens? Following Garand, Parkhurst, and Seoud, we suggest that there are two possible processes at work. First, attitudinal and behavioural differences can be explained by *selection*, whereby individuals who are predisposed towards an active government and liberal policies are more likely to seek a career that takes them into government employment. If someone perceives that an active government is necessary to protect the environment, alleviate poverty, teach public-school children, and direct the economy (among many other things), it is more likely that this person would seek a career in government service as a means of furthering those policy goals. Hence the selection model would predict that individuals who seek careers in government will be different in their political attitudes and behaviours from those who seek other careers. This means that differences between government employees and others would be observed early in their career cycles.

Second, attitudinal and behaviour differences can be explained by organizational *socialization*, whereby individuals enter into government service with political predispositions that are similar to those of other individuals but that over time they are socialized by their employing government agencies into pro-government, pro-spending dispositions. Socialization can occur as a result of explicit indoctrination, whereby the messages coming from agency leadership or from the general organizational culture constantly make clear the need for the agency to secure additional funds to achieve its goals. Alternatively, socialization can occur through an explicit recognition of self-interest as public-sector employees learn that their personal well-being and that of their agencies require expanding budgets over time.

It is important to note that attitudes and behaviours that are consistent with the bureau voting theory can occur as a result of both selection and socialization. Individuals may well select themselves into government service on the basis of their political propensities to support an active government and higher levels of spending, but these propensities may be developed and/or reinforced as individuals work with other, like-minded government employees who come to work for the public sector as a result of their own selection processes.

Data and Methods

In previous research, scholars have often tested the bureau voting theory using survey data collected from large samples drawn from the mass public. In this study, we also use large sample survey data to test one important aspect of the bureau voting theory, that is, whether or not bureaucrats are more likely to vote for left political parties and candidates. However, unlike previous research we revisit and reassess empirical support for the bureau voting theory using data from several sources in the United States, Canada, and other Western democracies. Our general approach is to combine bivariate and multivariate analyses to draw broad conclusions about the bureau voting theory. We begin by estimating the difference-in-means for government employees and other citizens on attitudinal and behavioural variables for which the bureau voting theory would predict differences. We begin by estimating the difference-in-means for government employees and other citizens on the likelihood that they cast votes for left-leaning political parties and candidates. We then estimate multivariate models that include government employment and various control variables as independent variables; here we explore whether differences in vote choices for government employees and other citizens are observed, even as we control for the effects of other variables expected to be related to our various dependent variables.

Data

In order to test the bureau voting model empirically, it is necessary to have data on voting behaviour as well as on respondents' employment sector (public-sector versus other) and appropriate control variables. Fortunately, appropriate data are available from several sources: (1) for the United States, the American National Election Study (ANES) surveys for 2004 and 2008; (2) for Canada, the 2008 Canadian Election Study (CES); (3) for Western industrial democracies, the 2005 World Values Survey (WVS). For the World Values Survey, we use data from the United States, Italy, Canada, Australia, Norway, Sweden, Finland, Switzerland, and Germany.[3]

Analytical Strategy

As noted, the bureau voting theory suggests that government employees are more likely than other citizens to vote for liberal candidates. At a basic level, empirical support for the bureau voting theory requires only that we find that the bivariate relationship between government employment and liberal attitudes, turnout, and voting for liberal candidates is positive and significant. Hence we present here the bivariate test of the core hypothesis developed from the bureau voting theory, and we do so comparatively by using data from the above-mentioned scholarly surveys.

Demonstrating that government employees behave as expected in comparison to other citizens is not the same thing as explaining such difference. In order to explain the differences, we also estimate multivariate models of vote choice that include government employment as the key independent variable, but that are accompanied by other variables that capture individuals' long-standing attributes. With the multivariate models, our goal is to answer a key question: is there something intrinsic about government employment per se that socializes individuals from all political stripes and transforms them (or at least some of them) into individuals who are more likely to vote for more liberal candidates, all in comparison to non-bureaucrats who have not had those same government employment experiences? Alternatively, is there selection at work, whereby individuals who tend to vote for liberal candidates are more likely to seek government employment in the first place?

The observation of a simple bivariate relationship between public-sector employment, on one hand, and liberal vote choice, on the other, tells us little about *why* government employees differ from other citizens. Answering the "why" question requires a more detailed and intentional research design than what we propose here. However, we suggest that it is possible to provide a rough, indirect test of these competing explanations of differences between public-sector employees and other individuals. Following Garand, Parkhurst, and Seoud (1991a), we contend that we can use a multivariate model to estimate indirectly the degree to which differences between government employees and others are due to government employment per se (i.e., that individuals shift their political positions or behaviours as the result of public-sector employment) or to long-term dispositions of individuals that predispose them to government employment in the first place.

Our logic is as follows. We include in our models a set of independent variables that represent individuals' attributes of long standing. This includes political attitudes (e.g., partisan identification, ideological orientation) that are developed through socialization and that tend to remain fairly stable over time, as well as fixed or relatively stable personal attributes (e.g., gender, race, education, social class) that are generally found to be associated with political attitudes and behaviour. If the effect of government employment remains intact after we control for the effects of these long-standing attributes, we suggest that government employment per se is likely affecting individuals' values on the dependent variable. In other words, if controlling for the effects of variables that should affect political attitudes and behaviour at the time that individuals choose their career path (i.e., the selection stage) does not diminish the coefficient for government employment, it would appear that government employment has an independent effect on their attitudes and behaviour. On the other hand, if the effect of government employment disappears once the effects of these long-standing attributes are taken into account, it would appear that it is these attributes that explain the observed bivariate government employment effect.

Of course, in testing the selection and socialization explanations of public-sector employment effects, there is no substitute for a longitudinal study that tracks political attitudes and behaviour for government employees and other citizens from their pre-employment period into their employment period. Yet short of having such longitudinal data, we can do the best that we can with existing data to suggest an indirect test of these explanations.

Variables and Measurement

A detailed summary of how our dependent and independent variables are measured can be found in appendices 1–3. Here we briefly describe the variables used in our analysis.

Independent Variable: Government Employment

In each survey we are able to distinguish public-sector employees from other citizens, and we do so here by creating a variable coded 1 for respondents who are government employees, and 0 for respondents who do not designate themselves as government employees. This is the traditional measurement approach in previous studies on differences in the political attitudes and behaviour of government employees and other citizens. Given the arguments that we make regarding the bureau voting model, we expect that government employees will be more likely to support candidates affiliated with liberal political parties.

We do note, however, two shortcomings with this measure. First, this variable fails to captures fully the self-interest component of government employment, primarily because the surveys on which we rely do not include data on the occupational status of respondents' spouses or other family members. Individuals married to a government employee may be affected, albeit less directly, by the same self-interest concerns that affect their government employee spouses. Second, this variable lack specificity of respondents' department or agency job assignments or, in federal systems, the level of government (federal, state, or local) for which the respondent works. A public-sector employee who is a public school teacher may have a configuration of interests that are different from other public-sector employees working for, say, the state Department of Transportation, the federal Department of the Treasury, or a local welfare agency. Unfortunately, standard survey data sets do not include specific questions to measure either (1) whether the employees works for the federal, state, or local level, or (2) which agency or department employs the respondent.

Dependent Variable: Vote Choice

One of the core hypotheses for the bureau voting theory is that public-sector employees should be more likely than other citizens to vote for candidates and political parties that are on the liberal side of the ideological spectrum – i.e., parties and candidates who are likely to be more amenable to an expanded and active public sector. Hence government employment should be positively related to voting for liberal candidates or parties and negatively related to voting for conservative candidates or parties.

In a comparative project on vote choice, one must account for the variety of party and candidate choices with which voters are confronted. In the United States, this is relatively straightforward. For the 2004 and 2008 elections, we code the vote choice variable as 1 for respondents who reported that they voted for the Republican candidates, and 0 for respondents who reported that they voted for the Democratic candidates. We explore the effect of government employment on voting for president, the U.S. House, and the U.S. Senate. We hypothesize that the coefficient for public-sector employment in a logit model of vote choice will be negative, indicating that government employees are less likely to support Republican candidates.

For other countries the task of estimating a model of vote choice that compares government employees and other individuals is made more complicated by the multiple viable choices available to voters. For the CES and WVS data sets, we create a nominal variable that codes vote intentions or party voting preferences for all parties on the ballot. We then estimate a multinomial logit model to test the hypothesis that public-sector bureaucrats will be less likely to vote for conservative parties and/or candidates. We identify the most conservative major party in each country using mean self-placements on the liberal-conservative scale for those voting for each party; the most conservative party becomes the baseline (comparison) group in a multinomial logit model. Hence the coefficients for public-sector employment should be positive, particularly for comparisons involving more liberal parties. The positive coefficient would indicate that there is a greater propensity for government employees (than for other individuals) to cast their votes for more liberal parties and/or candidates in comparison to the most conservative party.

Independent (Control) Variables

As noted, we include in our basic multivariate models a variety of control variables, most of which represent long-standing political attitudes and other attributes. The variables included in our models differ across data sets (primarily as the result of data availability) and for different dependent variables (primarily as the result of theoretical considerations). Not all models are identical, but we suggest that our multivariate models permit us to estimate the effect of government employment on vote choice, our dependent variable.

In all of our vote choice models we include four common independent variables: (1) ideological self-identification, or left-right placement; (2) education; (3) income; and (4) gender. Here again, these variables are expected to be related to vote choice in a variety of electoral contexts. We also include in selected models other variables available in specific data sets, including economic evaluations, race and ethnicity, social class, church attendance and religiosity, and union membership.

Empirical Results

We now turn to our empirical tests of the vote choice component of the bureau voting theory. The bureau voting theory suggests that government employees will be more likely to lend their electoral support to liberal parties and candidates. Liberal parties and candidates are likely to adopt policy positions that favour an expanded public sector and more active government and that will, hence, be more generous to public-sector employees (Blais, Blake, and Dion 1997). Therefore, we would expect government employees to demonstrate a greater propensity to vote for (or express an intention to vote for) liberal parties and candidates.

We begin with data from the 2004 and 2008 ANES surveys. In table 8.1 we report the proportion of government employees and other citizens who voted for the Republican candidate for president, U.S. House, and U.S. Senate in the 2004 and 2008 elections. Because the dependent variable is measured in the Republican direction, we posit that the coefficients reported in this table will be negative, indicating that government employees are less likely to support Republican candidates. As one can readily see, there is strong support for this hypothesis. In 2004, only 34.4% of government employees supported George Bush for president, compared to 55.4% of other citizens; this 21% difference is highly significant ($t = -5.05$). We also find that public-sector employees are more likely than other citizens to vote for Republican House candidates ($b = -0.155$, $t = -3.48$) and Republican Senate candidates ($b = -0.114$, $t = -2.10$). For 2008, the differences in voting behaviour for government employees and other citizens are not quite as stark, though there is a

Table 8.1 Difference in Means for Government Employees and Other Respondents on Vote Choice in the United States (2004, 2008), Various Data Sets

Variable	Means				Multivariate logit results	
	Government employees	Others	Difference	T-ratio	b	t-ratio
American National Election Study (2004)						
Republican presidential vote	0.344	0.554	−0.210	−5.05***	−0.248	−0.70
Republican House vote	0.348	0.504	−0.155	−3.48***	0.470	1.34
Republican Senate vote	0.368	0.482	−0.114	−210*	0.396	1.02
American National Election Study (2008)						
Republican presidential vote	0.461	0.397	−0.064	−1.83*	0.050	0.18
Republican House vote	0.368	0.484	−0.116	−3.09***	−0.323	−1.20
Republican Senate vote	0.437	0.499	−0.062	−1.23	−0.087	0.23

***$p < 0.001$; **$p < 0.01$; *$p < 0.05$

government employment effect for both presidential voting (b = –0.064, t = –1.83) and House voting (b = –0.116, t = –3.09). We note, however, that any government employment effects disappear in a full multivariate logit model, suggesting that there is not anything intrinsic about government employment per se that creates the greater propensity of government employees to vote for Democratic candidates. Rather, the occupational voting gap appears to be due to the effects of other variables such as partisanship, ideology, and demographic and socioeconomic attributes.

For Canada, we have data from the 2008 CES, and we again find some support for the vote choice component of the bureau voting theory. Government employees are significantly less likely than other Canadians to report that they voted for the Conservative Party in 2008, and they are more likely to have voted for the New Democratic Party (NDP), Bloc Québécois, and the Green Party. The χ^2 value for voting differences is highly significant (χ^2 = 20.08, p < 0.001). We also report results from a multinomial logit model that includes government employment and other control variables as independent variables (see table 8.2). Here we find that the differences between government employees and other citizens disappear in the face of statistical controls, as is the case for the United States.

We can also test this component of the bureau voting theory using comparative cross-national survey data. The WVS includes a vote intention question:

> If there were a national election tomorrow, for which party on this list would you vote? Just call out the number on this card. If you are uncertain, which party appeals to you most?

On the basis of responses to this question in each of eight countries for which this question was asked in the WVS, we code a nominal vote intention variable. We compare the distribution of party vote preferences for government employees and other citizens in each country, and we also estimate a multinomial logit model that includes government employment and other control variables. We use the most conservative major party, as determined by mean ideological positions for individuals who state a preference for each respective party, as the baseline category in our multinomial logit model.

Table 8.2 Party Vote Preferences for Government Employees and Other Respondents in Canada, Canadian Election Study (2008)

Country / party	%		Pearson's χ^2	Government employment Multinomial logit coefficients	
	Government employees	Others		b	t-ratio
Canadian Election Study (2008)					
Liberal Party	31.40	31.80	20.08***	−0.248	−0.73
Conservative Party	30.30	38.90		–	–
New Democratic Party (NDP)	17.20	14.20		−0.767	−1.82
Bloc Québécois	15.30	11.30		−0.039	−0.09
Green Party	5.80	3.70		0.585	−0.98
Total	100	100			
Group N	(522)	(1800)			

***$p < 0.001$; **$p < 0.01$; *$p < 0.05$

The results from these analyses are presented in table 8.3. As one can see, there is considerable evidence that government employees differ from other citizens in their party vote intention preferences. For six of the eight countries, there is a significant difference in vote preferences for public-sector employees and other citizens. In Australia, government employees are much less likely to support the Liberal Party and more likely to support the Australian Labor Party and the Greens; taken as a whole, these differences are statistically significant ($\chi^2 = 32.40$, $p < 0.001$). In Canada respondents who are employed in the public sector are considerably less likely to support the Liberal and Progressive Conservative parties but are more likely to express a voting preference for the NDP and Bloc Québécois; here again, these differences are statistically significant ($\chi^2 = 19.59$, $p < 0.001$). In Finland most of the differences for particular political parties are small, but collectively these differences achieve conventional levels of statistical significance. Specifically, by a margin of 17.4% to 9.8%, public-sector employees are more likely than other citizens to lend electoral support to the Green League. In Norway there are several discernible differences in the party vote intentions of public-sector employees and others (χ^2 = 50.74, p < 0.001). The former are more likely to support the Socialist Left Party (16.2% to 6.3%) and the Labour Party (38.4% to 32.8%) and are less likely to support the Progressive Party (14.5% to 21.8%) and the Conservative Party (12.5% and 21.4%). Similarly, in Sweden government employees differ significantly in their distribution party vote intentions (χ^2 = 37.03, p < 0.001). Swedish government employees are more likely to support the Social Demokraterna (37.4% to 31.0%) and Vansterpartiet (10.3% to 3.5%) but are much less likely to support the Moderata Samlingspartiet (19.9% to 36.6%). Finally, there are significant differences in the distribution of party vote intentions between government employees and other citizens in Switzerland (χ^2 = 27.58, p < 0.001). Swiss public-sector bureaucrats are more likely to state a vote preference for the Grune Partei (22.2% to 12.7%) and the Sozial Democratische Partei (27.3% to 23.0%) but are less likely to prefer the Schwizerische Volkspartei (9.5% to 19.9%) and the Freisinning-Demokratische Partei (17.7% to 22.1%).

The only two countries for which there is not a difference between government employees and other citizens are Germany and the United States. In these two cases there are minor differences in party vote intentions, but they are not of sufficient magnitude to achieve standard significance levels.

In the final two columns of table 8.3 we report the multinomial logit coefficients for the government employment variable in each country. Once we control for the effects of other variables related to party vote intentions, we find that differences between government employees and other citizens disappear in some cases and not in others. Indeed, for five of the eight countries in our analysis, there is at least one significant multinomial logit coefficient for the government employment variable. For instance, in Australia there are strong, significant government employment effects, even after one controls for other variables related to vote choice; in comparison to the Liberal Party, the (excluded) baseline category, government employees are more likely to vote for more liberal parties the Australian Labor Party (b = 0.645, t = 3.41), the National Party (b = 0.793, t = 1.74), the Greens (b = 0.896, t = 3.23), the Australian Democrats (b = 0.815, t = 2.14), and One Nation

Table 8.3 Party Vote Intention Preferences for Government Employees and Other Respondents in Various Countries, 2005 World Values Survey

Country / party	% Government employees	Others	Pearson's χ^2	Government employment Multinomial logit coefficients b	t-ratio
Australia (N = 1330)					
Australian Labor Party	35.7	29.9	32.40***	0.645	3.41***
Liberal Party	36.8	51.6		–	–
National Party	3.1	3.1		0.793	1.74*
Greens	13.0	6.6		0.896	3.23***
Australian Democrats	4.3	3.1		0.815	2.14*
Independents	0.9	0.7		0.259	0.34
One Nation	3.1	1.5		1.383	2.66**
Family First	3.1	3.6		0.506	1.17
Total	100	100			
Group N	(353)	(977)			
Canada (N = 1703)					
Liberal	24.1	33.7	19.59***	−0.099	−0.41
Progressive Conservative	33.8	37.2		–	–
New Democratic Party (NDP)	24.9	18.9		0.035	0.13
Bloc Québécois	17.1	10.2		0.688	2.32**
Total	100	100			
Group N	(245)	(1458)			
Finland (N = 778)					
Social Democratic Party	27.0	29.8	10.95***	−0.076	−0.18
Centre Party	25.8	25.5		0.254	0.64
National Coalition Party	16.2	18.8		–	–

(Continued)

Table 8.3 (Continued)

Country / party	% Government employees	Others	Pearson's χ^2	Government employment Multinomial logit coefficients b	t-ratio
Left Alliance	6.3	7.4		0.491	0.81
Swedish Peoples' Part of Finland	0.6	1.5		−0.748	−0.63
Green League	17.4	9.8		0.395	0.85
True Finns	1.2	3.3		−0.240	−0.27
Christian Democrats	5.4	3.9		0.868	1.33
Total	100	100			
Group N	(167)	(611)			
Germany (N = 1387)					
Christlich-Demokratische Union	35.4	36.6	10.24	–	–
Sozial Democratische Partei	35.4	31.8		0.239	1.18
Freie Demokratishe Partei	5.4	6.3		−0.372	−0.99
Die Gruenen	6.9	9.7		−0.254	−0.76
Partei des Democratishen Sozialis	16.3	12.5		−0.121	−0.41
Republickaner, NDP	0.7	3.1		−0.747	−0.75
Total	100	100			
Group N	(277)	(1110)			
Norway (N = 894)					
Labour Party	38.4	32.8	50.74***	0.203	0.71
Progressive Party	14.5	21.8		0.137	0.46
Conservative Party	12.5	21.4		–	–
Christian Democratic Party	5.4	2.8		0.618	1.26
Communist Party	2.3	0.6		1.004	1.01

Country / party	% Government employees	Others	Pearson's χ^2	Government employment Multinomial logit coefficients b	t-ratio
Center Party	7.1	7.6		0.106	0.29
Socialist Left Party	16.2	6.3		1.142	2.90**
Liberals	3.7	6.8		−0.392	−0.92
Total	100	100			
Group N	(352)	(542)			
Sweden (N = 766)					
Centerpartiet	5.0%	4.1%	37.03***	0.754	1.74*
Folkpartiet	11.9%	13.8%		0.389	1.28
Kristdemocraterna	4.6%	3.5%		0.571	1.15
Miljopartiet	10.9%	7.5%		0.684	1.65*
Moderata Samlingspartiet	19.9%	36.6%		–	–
Social Demokraterna	37.4%	31.0%		0.468	1.37
Vansterpartiet	10.3%	3.5%		1.390	2.73**
Total	100%	100%			
Group N	(302)	(464)			
Switzerland (N = 818)					
Freisinning-Demokratische Partei	17.7	22.1	27.58***	0.344	1.00
Sozial Democratische Partei	27.2	23.0		0.320	0.82
Christlich-Democratische Volkspartei	12.7	13.6		0.349	0.91
Schwizerische Volkspartei	9.5	19.9		–	–
Grune Partei	22.2	12.7		0.679	1.74*
Liberale Partei	2.3	2.4		0.595	0.94
Evangelische Volkspartei	3.2	1.8		1.375	2.03*

(Continued)

Table 8.3 (Continued)

Country / party	% Government employees	Others	Pearson's χ^2	Government employment Multinomial logit coefficients b	t-ratio
Partei der Arbeit	2.7	1.2		0.266	0.30
Christlischsoziale Partei	1.8	1.3		0.909	1.21
Lega Dei Ticinesi	0.9	2.0		−0.517	−0.47
Total	100	100			
Group N	(221)	(597)			
United States (N = 1100)					
Republican Party	36.4	35.3	0.123	–	–
Democratic Party	45.8	45.6		−0.053	−0.19
Independent	17.8	19.0		0.026	0.08
Total	100	100			
Group N	(118)	(982)			

Note: For the multinomial logit results, the omitted (comparison) group is the most conservative of the major political parties in each given political system.

***$p < 0.001$; **$p < 0.01$; *$p < 0.05$

(b = 1.383, t = 2.66). For Canada, Norway, Sweden, and Switzerland, government employees are more likely than other individuals to support at least one party over the most conservative major party. On the other hand, for Finland, Germany, and the United States, none of the coefficients for the government employee variable achieve statistical significance.

The bottom line is that government employees tend to support more liberal political parties and candidates. The empirical evidence to support this claim is not uniform – in some political systems or specific elections this expected pattern is not observed. However, there are enough differences in the voting behaviour of public-sector employees and other citizens to suggest support for this component of the bureau voting theory. Simply, in most cases government employees are more predisposed to support liberal parties and candidates than are other citizens.

Conclusion

The purpose of this chapter is to reassess the degree of empirical support for the bureau voting theory. As noted, this theory attributes growth in the size of government to the pursuit of increased spending by self-interested government bureaucrats who further their personal and policy goals through the electoral arena. The bureau voting theory contends that government employees are more liberal in their attitudes, more likely to vote in elections, and more likely to cast their votes for liberal candidates who will support an expanded public sector. The candidates who benefit from having the support of this relatively liberal, high-participation group become strong supporters of growth in the size of the public sector, and subsequently government activity and budgets increase over time. This theory can be contrasted with Niskanen's bureau information monopoly theory, a close cousin that portrays government growth as a function of the willingness of self-interested bureaucrats to use their monopoly of information in institutional settings to persuade elected officials to support larger budgets.

With a few notable exceptions, much of the research finding support for this theory was conducted during the 1990s (Garand, Parkhurst, and Seoud, 1991; Blais and Dion 1991). In our view it is important to re-evaluate empirical support for this theory in light of the availability of more recent data appropriate for testing the basic contours of the theory. We use data from the American National Election Study (2004 and 2008), the Canadian Election Study (2008), and the World Values Survey (2005) to provide a comparative test of this theory across up to sixteen countries.

On the basis of our review of the empirical evidence, we can say that the bureau voting theory stands up very well to additional empirical scrutiny. We find fairly strong evidence that government employees are more likely to cast votes for parties and candidates that are on the liberal side of the ideological spectrum. In most countries there is a discernible government employment effect on vote choice, with government employees showing a greater propensity than other citizens to oppose conservative parties and candidates and support their more liberal counterparts. These effects often remain in multivariate models that include a variety of control variables.

What Do We Not Know?

The research findings reported in this chapter go a long way towards confirming previous empirical support for the bureau voting theory. Yet there is a great deal that we still do not know about this theory and the processes that underlie it. What are the remaining unanswered questions in this research stream?

First, while we find general support for the three components of the bureau voting theory, the level of empirical support for this theory is not uniform across countries and time. What explains this spatial and temporal variation in the applicability of the bureau voting theory? To be fair, we do include country fixed effects in our pooled models, but this is no substitute for careful theoretical thinking about the sources of variation in government employment effects. Is there something about differences in the meaning of government bureaucratic service across different countries? Does variation in how government employees are selected have an effect? Are there other institutional or cultural factors that influence the relationship between public-sector employment and political attitudes and behaviour?

Second, we would be the first to admit that previous research on the bureau voting theory has been based on the rather crude survey instrument that simply differentiates government employees from other citizens in binary fashion. This is clearly an oversimplification of the world. Public-sector employees are not monolithic; rather, they differ in many important ways – e.g., the agencies or departments for which they work, the level of government (i.e., federal, state, local), their occupational prestige, educational and other qualifications. To place all types of government employees into one category prevents scholars from developing more detailed, nuanced interpretations and tests of the bureau voting theory. There may be general expectations drawn from the bureau voting theory that applies to all or most government bureaucrats, but there may also be other expectations that are specific to more detailed categories of bureaucrats. For instance, public school teachers may have stronger views towards spending on public education than, say, someone working for the federal Environmental Protection Agency, who may actually be more concerned about spending on the environment. In addition, bureaucratic self-interest may not be limited to individuals who work for the public sector. It is possible that individuals who have retired from government service (and who have hence had some of the same socialization experiences as current government employees) or who have a spouse or other close family member working for the public sector will behave in a way similar to that of current public-sector employees. It is important for scholars to develop more detailed survey instruments that measure various aspects of government employees' work experiences and other attributes related to their self-interest.

Third, considerably more work is needed on the competing processes that can create differences between government employees and other citizens. We have already mentioned self-selection and socialization, which represent two possible processes that generate the government employment effect. Do public-sector employees differ from other citizens because the agencies and departments for which they work socialize or indoctrinate them into a perception of self-interest that results in a specific set of attitudes and behaviours? Or are different kinds of individuals (i.e., liberals, advocates of active government, those with a strong sense of political participation or policy activism) drawn to government employment? Or is there a combination of these two processes at work? We have tried to provide an indirect test of these two alternate processes by estimating multivariate models that include a wide range of control variables, including variables that represent long-standing attitudes and socio-economic/demographic attributes. Yet such tests are only indirect and are a poor substitute for conducting a longitudinal analysis of individuals prior to the start of their career work lives. For instance, are high school seniors who eventually become government employees somehow different from high school seniors who pursue other career paths in the private or non-profit sectors? Or are future government employees a random draw from the population of high school seniors and develop their left-leaning attitudes and behaviour when they are socialized by their employing agencies? We contend that creating a definitive picture of the processes that generate differences between government employees and other individuals requires the development of a longitudinal research design that tracks individuals from their pre-employment to employment periods.

Finally, little is known about the working mechanisms underlying how bureau voting theory is translated into political outcomes. If government employees are more likely to hold liberal attitudes, cast votes in elections, and vote for liberal candidates, how does this matter? How, exactly, do bureaucrats use the electoral process to influence public spending and government policymaking and, subsequently, increase the size of the public sector? For instance, we are intrigued by the possibility that government employees represent a relatively coherent interest that can affect the behaviour of elected officials through their ideological or policy positions, their greater propensity to vote, and their greater likelihood of voting for liberal candidates who are more likely to support an active government. A case in point is the work of Blair (2003), who explores the degree to which the roll-call behaviour of U.S. House members is affected by the presence of government employees in their districts. Blair finds that House members are significantly less likely to exhibit spending constraint as the percentage of government employees in their congressional districts increases. We suggest that this finding is consistent with the bureau voting theory, insofar as it appears that House members shift their behaviour in a pro-spending direction as government employees represent a larger share of their district electorates. This is the kind of extension of the bureau voting theory that is important for scholars to consider in future research.

Appendix 1: Description of Variables Used in 2004 and 2008 American National Election Studies

Variable	Description
Government employment	1 = government employee; 0 = otherwise
Republican presidential vote	1 = R voted for Republican presidential candidate; 0 = R voted for Democratic presidential candidate
Republican House vote	1 = R voted for Republican House candidate; 0 = R voted for Democratic House candidate
Republican Senate vote	1 = R voted for Republican Senate candidate; 0 = R voted for Democratic Senate candidate
Partisan identification	7-point partisan identification scale (6 = strong Republican)
Liberal-conservative ideology	7-point liberal-conservative scale (6 = extremely conservative)
Retrospective economic evaluation	Evaluation of national economic performance in past year (4 = much better)
Retrospective unemployment evaluation	Evaluation of national unemployment in past year (4 = much better)

Variable	Description
Working	1 = R is working; 0 = otherwise
Education	Educational attainment (2004: 7 = graduate degree; 2008: years of education completed, ranging from 0 to 17)
Household income	Household income (2004: 23 = high income; 2008: 25 = high income)
Gender	1 = R is a woman; 0 = R is a man
Black	1 = R is black; 0 = otherwise
Hispanic	1 = R is Hispanic; 0 = otherwise
Asian	1 = R is Asian; 0 = otherwise

Appendix 2: Description of Variables Used in 2005 World Values Survey

Variable	Description
Government employment	1 = government employee; 0 = otherwise
Party preference: USA	1 = Republican; 2 = Democrat; 3 = Independent
Party preference: Australia	1 = Australian Labor Party; 2 = Liberal Party; 3 = National Party; 4 = Greens; 5 = Australian Democrats; 6 = Independent; 7 = One Nation; 8 = Family First
Party preference: Canada	1 = Liberal Party; 2 = Progressive Conservative Party; 3 = New Democratic Party; 4 = Bloc Québécois
Party preference: Finland	1 = Social Democratic Party; 2 = Centre Party; 3 = National Coalition Party; 4 = Left Alliance; 5 = Swedish People's Party of Finland; 6 = Green League; 7 = True Finns; 8 = Christian Democrats
Party preference: Germany	1 = Christlich-Demokratische Union; 2 = Sozial Demokratische Partei; 3 = Freie Demokratishe Partei; 4 = Die Gruenen; 5 = Partei des Demokratishen Sozialis; 6 = Republickaner, NDP
Party preference: Norway	1 = Labour Party; 2 = Progressive Party; 3 = Conservative Party; 4 = Christian Democratic Party; 5 = Communist Party; 6 = Center; Party; 7 = Socialist Left Party; 8 = Liberals
Party preference: Sweden	1 = Centerpartiet; 2 = Folkpartiet; 3 = Kristdemocraterna; 4 = Miljopartiet; 5 = Moderata Samlinspartiet; 6 = Social Demokraterna; 7 = Vansterpartiet

(Continued)

Appendix 2: (Continued)

Variable	Description
Party preference: Switzerland	1 = Freisinning-Demokratische Partei; 2 = Sozial Democratische Partei; 3 = Christlich-Demokratische Volkspartei; 4 = Schweizerische Volkspartei; 5 = Grune Partei Liberale Partei; 6 = Evangelische Volkspartei; 7 = Partei der Arbeit; 8 = Christlichsoziale Partei; 9 = Lega Dei Ticinesi
Liberal-Conservative ideology	10-point ideology scale (10 = strong conservative; ... ; 0 = strong liberal)
Union membership	1 = union member; 0 = otherwise
Age	Respondent's age
Age^2	Respondent's age squared
Education	Education level in 9 categories
Religiosity	1 = R is religious; 0 = R is not a religious person or is an atheist
Church attendance	Church attendance (0–6 scale): 6 = more than once a week; ... ; 0 = never)
Upper class	1 = upper class; 0 = otherwise
Upper middle class	1 = upper middle class; 0 = otherwise
Lower middle class	1 = lower middle class; 0 = otherwise
Working class	1 = working class; 0 = otherwise

Appendix 3: Description of Variables used in the 2008 Canadian Election Study

Variable	Description
Government employment	1 = government employee; 0 = otherwise
Vote choice	For which party did you vote in the 2008 federal election? (0 = Other parties-base category; 1 = Liberal Party; 2 = Progressive Conservative Party; 3 = New Democratic Party; 4 = Bloc Québécois; 5 = Green Party)
Liberal-conservative ideology	Ideological self-identification (0 = extreme left; ... ;10 = extreme right)
Gender	Gender of respondent (0 = female; 1 = male)
Age	Age of respondent
Age^2	Age squared

Variable	Description
Satisfaction with democracy	Satisfaction with the way democracy works in Canada (0 = not at all; ... ; 3 = very satisfied)
Interest in federal elections	How interested are you in the federal election? (0 = not at all; ... ;10 = a great deal)
Interest in politics	How interested are you in politics in general? (0 = not at all; ... ; 10 = a great deal)
Sociotropic economic evaluations	Has the economy got better last year? (–1 = worse; 0 = the same; 1 = better)
Pocketbook economic evaluations	Are you better off financially than a year ago? (–1 = worse; 0 = the same; 1 = better)
Union membership	Do you belong to the union? (0 = no; 1 = yes)
Married	Marital status (1 = married or partnered; 0 = single, separated, divorced, or widowed)
Employment status	1 = work with pay, i.e., full time or part-time; 0 = without pay, i.e., retired, student, unemployed, etc.)
Ideology extremism	0–5 scale: 0 = neutral or moderate; ... ; 5 = extreme left or right.
Education	Years of education
Family income	Family income (in thousands)

NOTES

1 Hereafter we use public-sector employees, government employees, and (government) bureaucrats interchangeably.
2 Importantly, this theory suggests a central role for both turnout and vote choice, but not always at the same time. This arguably calls for the kind of integrated study of both advocated for in the introduction of this volume.
3 Future studies might also employ the Comparative Study of Electoral Systems, as highlighted in chapter 9.

References

Aberbach, Joel, Robert Putnam, and Bert Rockman. 1981. *Bureaucrats and Politicians in Western Democracies*. Cambridge, MA: Harvard University Press.
Aberbach, Joel, and Bert Rockman. 1976. "Clashing Beliefs within the Executive Branch: The Nixon Administration Bureaucracy." *American Political Science Review* 70:456–68.

Blair, William. 2003. "Bureaucratic Influence in Congressional Roll-Call Voting." PhD diss., Louisiana State University.

Blais, André, Donald Blake, and Stéphane Dion. 1990. "The Voting Behavior of Bureaucrats." In *The Budget-Maximizing Bureaucrat: Appraisals and Evidence*, edited by André Blais and Stéphane Dion, 205–30. Pittsburgh: University of Pittsburgh Press.

– 1997. *Governments, Parties and Public Sector Employees*. Pittsburgh: University of Pittsburgh Press.

Blais, André, and Stéphane Dion. 1990. "Are Bureaucrats Budget Maximizers? The Niskanen Model and Its Critics." *Polity* 22:655–75.

– , eds. 1991. *The Budget-Maximizing Bureaucrat: Appraisals and Evidence*. Pittsburgh: University of Pittsburgh Press.

Blake, Donald. 1991. "Policy Attitudes and Political Ideology in the Public Sector." In *The Budget-Maximizing Bureaucrat: Appraisals and Evidence*, edited by André Blais and Stéphane Dion, 231–56. Pittsburgh: University of Pittsburgh Press.

Corey, Elizabeth C., and James C. Garand. 2002. "Are Government Employees More Likely to Vote? An Analysis of Turnout in the 1996 U.S. National Election." *Public Choice* 111:259–83.

Dolan, Julie. 2002. "The Budget-Minimizing Bureaucrat? Empirical Evidence from the Senior Executive Service." *Public Administration Review* 62:42–50.

Downs, Anthony. 1967. *Inside Bureaucracy*. Boston: Little, Brown.

Garand, James C., Catherine Parkhurst, and Rusanne Jourdan Seoud. 1991a. "Bureaucrats, Policy Attitudes, and Political Behavior: An Extension of the Bureau Voting Model of Government Growth." *Journal of Public Administration: Research and Theory* 1:177–212.

– 1991b. "Testing the Bureau Voting Model: A Research Note on Federal and State-Local Employees." *Journal of Public Administration: Research and Theory* 1:229–33.

Jensen, Jason L., Paul E. Sum, and David T. Flynn. 2009. "Political Orientations and Behavior of Public Employees: A Cross-National Comparison." *Journal of Public Administration: Research and Theory* 19:709–30.

Lewis, Gregory B. 1990. "In Search of the Machiavellian Milquetoasts: Comparing Attitudes of Bureaucrats and Ordinary People." *Public Administration Review* 50:220–7.

Lowery, David, and William Berry. 1983. "The Growth of Government in the United States: An Empirical Assessment of Competing Explanations." *American Journal of Political Science* 27:665–94.

Niskanen, William. 1971. *Bureaucracy and Representative Government*. Chicago: Aldine Atherton.

- 1991. "A Reflection on *Bureaucracy and Representative Government.*" In Blais and Dion, *Budget-Maximizing Bureaucrat*, 13–32.
Putnam, Robert. 1973. "The Political Attitudes of Senior Civil Servants in Western Europe: A Preliminary Report." *British Journal of Political Science* 3:257–90.
Sears, David O., and Jack Citrin. 1982. *Tax Revolt: Something for Nothing in California.* Cambridge, MA: Harvard University Press.

PART III

Electoral Systems

9 How Electoral Systems Shape What Voters Think about Democracy

CHRISTOPHER J. ANDERSON

When they fail to offer choices, elections lose their meaning as instruments of democracy (Powell 2000). Yet, despite their centrality for the quality of democratic elections, little is known about how the variety of options voters have on Election Day affect people's views of the political system. Are the choices available to citizens connected to consent? The literature suggests that they are, but scholars disagree about whether more and more distinct choices are good or bad for the legitimacy of political systems. On one hand, scholars have reported higher levels of support for political systems with more proportional election rules and expansive party systems. On the other, a long-standing concern in comparative politics has been with the corroding effects of polarized and fragmented party systems, which often are thought to be the natural by-product of proportional electoral systems. Who, if anyone, is right?

To answer the question of whether fragmented and polarized party systems are good for or inimical to democratic support requires that we differentiate the key dimensions of electoral supply and delineate the logic by which they are expected to shape voters' attitudes about the political system.[1] It also requires that we examine the connection between the kinds of choices democratic elections provide at the level of countries on one hand and the attitudes of individual voters on the other. Below, I do so by arguing that the menu of choices on hand at election time shapes citizen attitudes about democratic political systems, but that it does so with distinct consequences for different groups of voters. Electoral supply in the form of party system polarization and the number of viable parties influences citizens who are likely to take a dim view of the political system – i.e., those who voted for the losers in the last election – differently from those who are among the winners and have reason to be content with the status quo. In particular, I posit that party systems act as safety valves for political discontent.

Analyses of data from twenty-four democracies around the world by the Comparative Study of Electoral Systems project show that overall levels of political polarization or the number of electoral options does not help to predict whether people, on average, express more positive or negative views of the political system. The only macro-level variables that reveal significant effects are the level of democracy and the age of the party system. Citizens in more democratic countries and in countries with older party systems express greater satisfaction with the working of the political system and are more likely to endorse democracy as their preferred system of government. Importantly, the analyses reveal that countries' macro-level supply of choices and individuals' predispositions interactively shape citizen consent such that more and distinct partisan options diminish the negative views held by disenchanted segments of the electorate. In contrast to analysts pessimistic about the consequences of electoral fragmentation, the results reported below suggest that distinct and abundant choices diminish the discontent of citizens with more negative views of the democratic order.

Below, I first discuss the competing theoretical and empirical claims made in the literature on electoral institutions, party systems, and system support. I then develop a model of contingent contextual effects on attitudes about the political system, which I subsequently test with the help of multivariate multilevel regression estimations. After reporting the results, I discuss the findings and avenues for future research.

Electoral Supply and System Support

While students of democratic politics have long agreed that a country's electoral and party systems condition the stability and legitimacy of democratic political systems, they have developed conflicting expectations and evidence about how this works in practice (for a nice overview, see also Blais 1991). On one side is what one could term the "classical" view, which suggests that proportional representation and polarized party systems are bad for citizen support of electoral democracy because they signal and exacerbate competing and conflicting pressures that require peaceful accommodation within the body politic. On the other side, scholars have theorized that political systems characterized by proportional electoral rules and plentiful choices can function as a safety valve for political discontent and thus, ultimately, produce higher levels of legitimacy.

The classic position regarding the connection between electoral systems and legitimacy has been that, compared to single member district systems, proportional electoral systems may be hazardous for a democracy's health. In his famous "Proportional Representation and the Breakdown of German Democracy," Ferdinand Hermens, for example, argued that the Weimar Republic's proportional electoral system was a necessary (though not sufficient) condition for the breakdown of the German Republic (Hermens 1936, 1941).[2] Or, as Finer (1956, 623) observed, "PR kept both Nazism and Communism alive so that together they could murder the Weimar Republic" (see also Quade 2006). This general argument has been made and contested countless times (see, e.g., the review in Kreuzer 2001); its underlying logic is that proportional electoral systems provide incentives and opportunities for extremist parties to gain an electoral foothold and mobilize opponents of democracy, only to undermine it once the opportunity arises.

The position about the corroding effects of more proportional electoral systems was perhaps made most famous in political science by Giovanni Sartori's conjecture that party systems characterized by a small number of relevant parties and limited ideological distance between them will help produce a more stable political system and a higher quality of democracy (Sartori 1976, 131–216). In Sartori's view, party systems characterized by "polarized pluralism" were the least desirable because, in such systems, extreme elites can attain power on the backs of relatively small slivers of disenchanted electorates; at a minimum, political elites in polarized party systems have few incentives to cooperate.

Compared to Hermens's legal and constitutional perspective, Sartori's argument is less about formal institutions in the form of electoral laws and more about their consequences for elite incentives to accommodate. As such, it also is to a greater extent focused on party system fragmentation and polarization as a proxy for elite polarization and polarized polities built on structurally fragmented societies and unresolved, antagonistic cleavages. But, like Hermens, Sartori foresees inferior performance of democratic systems with extensive and polarized party systems. The shared logic underlying the presumed relationship between electoral laws and legitimacy specified by Hermans and Sartori on the basis of the paradigmatic cases of Weimar Germany and post–Second World War Italy is thus twofold: (1) that the party system acts as a transmission belt for political grievances and extreme ideological positions and ultimately an expression of the level of political consensus in society; and (2) that electoral systems that allow a lack of consensus to be manifested in party systems lead to less cohesive democracy.

In contrast to this classic perspective, which focuses on the opportunities electoral systems provide political elites for mobilizing anti-system voters, a more recent, alternative perspective has focused on the ways in which voters perceive the offerings that elections provide, and how these may affect what voters think about the political system. That is, instead of focusing on how elites vying for power use electoral systems and party systems to mobilize discontent from above, this perspective focuses on the psychology of voters themselves.

Like the classic perspective, this bottom-up perspective starts from the classic empirical regularity that PR systems produce more parties. When there are more parties, they have incentives to distinguish themselves ideologically in order to target identifiable segments of the electoral market. Rooted in a spatial, rather than socio-structural conception of electoral competition, it presumes that voters are motivated to make choices consistent with their self-interest as it can be represented in an ideological space. Like Hermens or Sartori, this perspective assumes that the performance of electoral systems shapes the reputation of the political system in citizens' eyes. However, it comes to very different predictions about the potential downsides of proportional representation (PR) and multipartism.

Specifically, the logic underlying this approach presumes that citizens value choices (Iyengar and Lepper 2000; see also Sen 1988). That is, more choices are seen as normatively appealing in a democracy and reflective of freedom. Moreover, it presumes that a greater number of more distinct parties increase the odds that voters' views will find articulation, leading them to experience and feel that their preferences can be represented through existing political channels. In this way, a more numerous and diverse menu of choices can enhance support for the existing political arrangements, including the political system, and this effect should be especially pronounced among citizens with a political axe to grind (see also Anderson 2011; Blais and Loewen 2007).

Given their broad similarities, what can explain the different positions and findings between the classic view and its alternative? One possibility is that differing findings are due to case selection on the dependent or independent variable, the time period investigated, or perhaps the methodology employed. Another possibility is that the root cause is theoretical. I suspect it is a little bit of both. At the empirical level, it is apparent that case selection matters for the inferences that are drawn about the role of electoral institutions. While the classic view selects what most would consider new or failed democracies – thus selecting countries that score low on the dependent variable of legitimacy – the more recent perspective has typically selected countries that have highly stable and legitimate democratic systems.

Specifically, the traditional view relied heavily on a set of model cases of troubled democracies like Weimar Germany, the Spanish Republic of the 1930, post-war Italy, France Fourth Republic, or Chile in the 1960s to provide evidence of the corroding effects of proportional representation and multipartism. In contrast, the emerging literature on the positive effects of proportional electoral systems for system legitimacy has relied on a mix of single country studies and broader cross-national studies of stable democracies to make its case. Thus, Miller and Listhaug (1990) examined the connection between party systems and trust in government in Sweden, Norway, and the United States in the 1980s, arguing that flexible party systems, which allow small parties to be represented, are better for government trust because they allow the discontented to voice their frustration within the existing democratic framework (see also Miller and Listhaug 1999).[3] Consistent with this, several aggregate level, cross-national studies of advanced industrialized countries have reported that citizens in systems with more proportional electoral systems express higher levels of satisfaction with the functioning of the democratic system (Anderson 1998; Lijphart 1999; Norris 1999).[4]

Aside from case selection, theories and empirical tests may come to varying conclusions about the connection between electoral systems and legitimacy because of a mismatch between the theories they articulate and the tests they conduct. First, their analyses tend to confound the varied consequences of electoral systems that deserve empirical separation. Specifically, they conflate the nature of the electoral system, as well as the number and distinctiveness of parties in a system – that is, they treat the multipartism and polarization facilitated by proportionality as symbiotic and reflecting a similar underlying cause. Good examples are Weimar Germany or Republican Italy, where polarization and party system fragmentation went hand in hand. And aggregate studies that simply examine the impact of electoral system proportionality on support for the political system without specifying the mechanisms by which the effects are produced are similarly indeterminate.

Second, theories about electoral system effects really are theories of heterogeneous electorates and require testing as such. Specifically, they specify that the effects of electoral systems differ for voters who are and who are not (or who feel and do not feel) represented in the democratic process. Specifically, the hazards of proportional representation articulated in the traditional view are really the hazards of elite manipulation of disenchanted mass publics – and therefore not all voters – while the hazards of proportional representation in the revisionist view similarly are the hazards of preventing disenchanted voters from voicing their grievances effectively at the ballot box. Thus, both views pay special attention to the critical role played by malcontented segments of the electorate, though they differ in the motivations they ascribe to them: in one (the traditional view) they seek to undermine democracy; in the other (the revisionist view), they seek to be represented in the democratic process in order to air their grievances.

To specify the effects of electoral systems on system support, the challenge thus is to disentangle these conceptual issues and test them empirically on a set of countries with varied democratic traditions, to test them in a way that examines the impact of macro-level electoral conditions on individual beliefs, and to test them in a way that takes into account the heterogeneity in macro-level effects across different individuals. This is the task I turn to next.

A Model of Electoral Supply, Losing, and System Support

The analyses reported below make use of data collected by the Comparative Study of Electoral Systems (CSES) project. The CSES is a collaborative research program among election studies conducted in democracies around the world (for more information, see www.cses. org). Participating countries include a common module of survey questions in their post-election studies, all surveys must meet certain quality and comparability standards, and all are conducted as nationally representative surveys. The CSES also compiles ancillary data on the political systems, electoral systems, and parties in each election and that are combined with the survey data. The analyses below are based on Module 2 of the CSES, fielded between 2001 and 2006.[5] From this module, twenty-four countries provided the necessary individual and country level information.[6]

To bring some order to the thicket of competing claims about the connections between electoral laws, electoral options, and voters' views and behaviours that can be tested empirically, I develop a model that connects individual citizens and the electoral environment in which they make choices and judge their system on the basis of several assumptions. First, it assumes that people judge the performance and desirability of democratic institutions in part from their experiences with electoral processes and institutions. That is, democratic political systems are judged by how well their electoral processes and institutions work. Second, it assumes that voters are not political scientists – that is, it does not presuppose that voters must have a lot of detailed information about electoral rules or how these affect election outcomes and the quality of representation. Instead, institutions are causally anterior and become visible to voters in the form of outcomes that constitute and constrain the choice they are called on to make in elections. Third, it assumes that electoral context has heterogeneous effects on citizen beliefs about the political system.

Variation in Electoral Supply

Starting from these assumptions, I contend that electoral laws influence people's opinions about the political system by shaping the nature of the electoral supply – defined here as the extent to which elections provide voters with meaningful choices. This supply is observed by voters and most proximately affects their behaviour. The term "meaningful choices" implies that the electoral supply is differentiated (Klingemann and Weßels (2009) and Weßels and Schmitt 2008). Differentiation of the electoral supply has two structural characteristics that should be observable by voters: first, the number of choices; and two, how distinct they are.[7] Operationally, these correspond to the number and distinctiveness of partisan choices.

The number and distinctiveness of partisan choices arise from the strategic choices political elites make by choosing to organize political parties and where to position them politically. And while it is commonly believed that polarization – that is, the location of parties in the policy space – and fragmentation – the numbers of parties competing in the space – are correlated – hence Sartori's idea of "polarized pluralism" – this does not have to follow. To examine whether this is the case requires information about both the number and distinctiveness of choices.

Measuring the number of parties is relatively straightforward, though it is more than simply a count of parties that appear on the ballot since many (if not most) parties are typically listed without a significant chance of winning votes or legislative representation. Thus, to measure the number of viable choices available to voters, I calculated the well-known *effective number of parties*, which weights the number of parties by their size (Laakso and Taagepera, 1979; Taagepera and Shugart 1999; see also Rae 1971).

The distinctiveness of choice is slightly more complicated. Previous research often presumed that the distinctiveness of choice was also related to the effective number of parties in a political system. Following Sartori and a long line of electoral researchers, the assumption was that party choices also reflected the social cleavages that exist in a society (see also Lijphart 1999).[8] That is, the assumption was that ideological polarization was greater when larger numbers of parties compete because of numerous cleavages. Conversely, following Downs, a smaller number of parties will all gravitate towards the middle, reducing ideological polarization.

However, this would be true only if the number and diversity of choice were synonymous. To gauge whether the number of choices in fact reflects the nature ideological or socio-structural divisions in society, it is important to consider the extent to which the choices are differentiated along some important dimension – that is, whether more parties also means more polarized choices. Conceptually, the distinctiveness of choices should capture the relative position of each party along a dimension of contestation, as well as weight the party's position by size, since a larger party at an extreme end of this dimension would indicate greater polarization than a splinter party in the same position (see Dalton 2008).

Party system polarization reflects the dispersion of political parties along an ideological or policy dimension. Sartori (1976) focused attention on this concept when he compared the consequences of centripetal and centrifugal party systems. Similarly, many of Downs's (1957) theoretical arguments on the consequences of party system competition were based on parties' presumed distribution along an ideological continuum. The logic of party system polarization thus implies that it should reflect the dispersion of parties along an ideological dimension; most commonly, this it taken to be a single Left-Right dimension.

The use of a Left/Right scale does not require that citizens possess a sophisticated conceptual framework or theoretical understanding of political philosophy. It simply assumes that positions on this scale summarize the issues and cleavages that structure political competition in a nation.[9] The CSES asked respondents to position themselves along a Left-Right scale and then position the parties in their nation on this same scale. These placements of the parties provide the basis for measuring polarization for the party system as a whole.[10] I employ the index developed by Dalton (2008; see also Dalton 2011), which measures the dispersion of parties along the Left-Right scale.[11] This index is comparable to a measure of the standard deviation of parties distributed along the dimension.

Figure 9.1 shows the two dimensions of the electoral supply – the number and distinctiveness of electoral options – across the twenty-four countries included in the analysis. Regarding the number of electoral options, measured here as the effective number of electoral parties, the numbers reveal wide variation across countries, ranging from close to 2 in the United States to over 6 in Norway. Countries with more numerous viable options also include the Netherlands, Slovenia,

Figure 9.1 Differentiation of the Electoral Supply

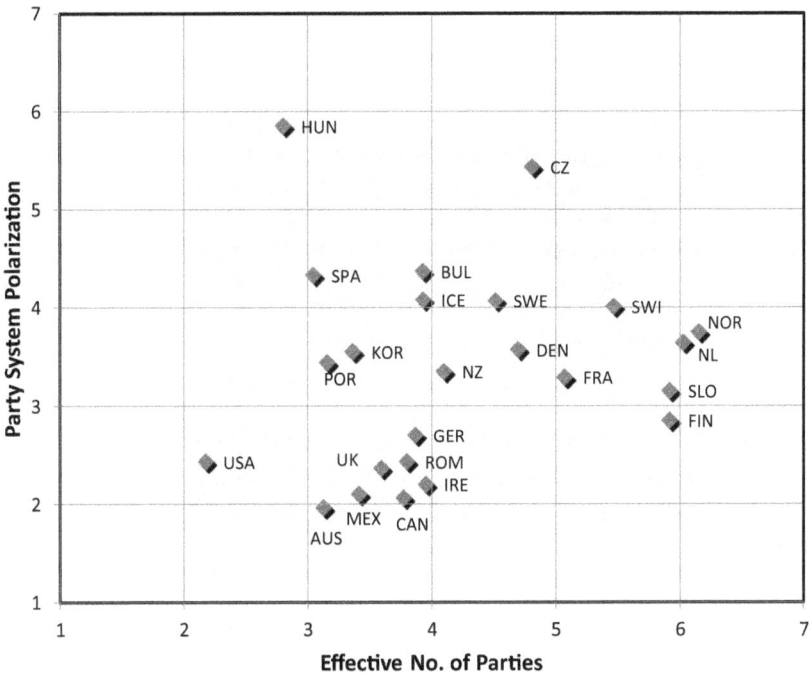

Finland, Switzerland, France, the Czech Republic, Denmark, Sweden, and New Zealand at between 4 and 6; countries with few options also include Hungary, Spain, Australia, Portugal, Korea, Mexico, and the United Kingdom, at around 3 to 3.5 parties.

When it comes to the distinctiveness of electoral options, here measured as the ideological polarization of party systems, Hungary and the Czech Republic lead the pack (at around six), followed by Bulgaria, Spain, Iceland, Sweden, and Switzerland (at around four). In contrast, voters in Australia, Canada, Mexico, Ireland, the United Kingdom, the United States, and Romania face much less distinct options at around two.

As the data also demonstrate clearly, the number and distinctiveness of choices constitute separable dimensions – multipartism and party system polarization are separate traits. The graph shows, for example, the well-known fact that electoral offerings in majoritarian systems – such as Australia, the United States, or the United Kingdom Great Britain – are marked by a relatively small number of effective electoral parties and comparatively low levels of polarization. But a small number of parties do not necessarily imply convergence towards the median voter. For example, while Hungarian and Spanish voters, too, have relatively few effective options, these are much more distinct.

Conversely, Finland, the Netherlands, Norway, and Slovenia have a relatively large number of effective electoral parties, but only modest levels of ideological polarization on the level of Portugal or South Korea, countries with significantly smaller party systems.[12] Thus, numerous options do not have to be particularly distinct. And voters in Spain, Bulgaria, and Iceland, for example, have a moderate number of options that are moderately distinct.[13] Together, the two dimensions of the electoral supply provide a set of offerings that are quite distinct across countries and not easily categorized as belonging to one type or another.[14]

The Heterogeneous Consequences of Electoral Supply

When considering the impact that these dimensions of the electoral supply may have on voters' beliefs, one critical question in light of the theoretical discussion above is whether all voters should be expected to be equally sensitive to the nature of the (cross-nationally variable) electoral supply. Consistent with recent scholarship, I argue that they should not; specifically, I presume that those who have reason to be discontented with the existing political arrangements are most likely to be affected by the nature of the available choices, because these shape their opportunities to voice that discontent through electoral channels. That is, instead of assuming that more or fewer parties or more or less polarization is equally good or bad for everyone, I posit that the electoral supply is most critical for shaping legitimacy beliefs among the discontented. In particular, I argue that a more abundant and differentiated electoral supply allows those who dislike the existing arrangements more distinctive opportunities to voice that discontent clearly. Thus, in contrast to the scenario implicit in the work of Hermens and in Sartori, I expect the electoral supply to act as a safety valve for political discontent.

In the context of how elections and electoral context affect legitimacy beliefs, one obvious way to identify voters with a negative predisposition towards the political system is to focus on political losers. Recent work on electoral losers has shown consistently that voters who supported parties or candidates that failed to win power report more negative attitudes about the political system (for a summary, see Anderson et al. 2005). By definition, these voters' views are not represented in government and they are, at least until the next election, political outsiders.

Consistent with this literature, I hypothesize that electoral losers exhibit more negative attitudes about the political system. Moreover, I hypothesize that the size of this negative effect varies as a function of the electoral supply. Specifically, I posit that the connection between losing and system support is contingent on the electoral supply, such that a more numerous and differentiated supply reduces the negative impact that losing has on system attitudes because it provides the next best thing to winning outright: having one's political voice articulated clearly and tangibly.

While the finding that electoral losers have more negative attitudes about the system has been replicated in a number of contexts (Banducci and Karp 2003; Karp and Bowler 2001; Henderson 2008; Blais and Gélineau 2007; Craig et al. 2006; Criado and Herreros 2007; Ginsberg and Weisberg 1978; Loewen and Blais 2006), an important but largely unanswered question in this emerging literature has been whether this effect is due mostly to being in or out of power, or whether it is about being shut out of having one's policy positions represented in government. For example, we can imagine voters supporting parties that ultimately do not end up forming the government, yet those same voters having their policy positions represented in the policy process because they are close to the government's. Similarly, while voters may well have cast their ballot for a governing party, the government's position can end up being quite distant from the voter's own – for example, because of co-alition or legislative bargaining (Kedar 2005). And regardless of which party or candidate people voted for, the government's position is not equally close to all voters'. As a result, I would expect voters whose policy positions go unrepresented – or what we could call "policy losers" – to express more negative opinions about the functioning of the political system than those whose own position is close to the government's, regardless of whether their party is in government. That is, aside from coming out on the losing side in elections, incongruence between voter and government policy positions should foster negative attitudes about the political system (see also Paskeviciute 2006).

Similarly to the conjecture that the electoral supply should condition the effects of electoral losing, I hypothesize that the size of the negative effect of policy losing should vary as a function of the electoral supply. Thus, I posit that the connection between policy losing and system support is contingent on the electoral supply, such that a more numerous and differentiated supply reduces the negative impact that losing has on system attitudes. In the next section, I turn to investigating this hypothesized contingent effect of the electoral supply on system attitudes.

Attitudes towards the Democratic Political System

To assess citizens' attitudes towards the political system, I examine responses to two survey questions. First, respondents were asked to report how satisfied they were with the way democracy works in their country; second, they were asked to report whether they thought democracy was better than other forms of government. These questions allow us to tap into different dimensions of attitudes about the political system. The democracy satisfaction indicator gauges system support at a low level of generalization. It does not refer to democracy as a set of norms, but to the functioning of the democratic political system (see Anderson and Guillory 1997). Thus, it gauges people's responses to the process of democratic governance; that is, a country's "constitution in operation" (Lane and Ersson 1991, 194) or its "constitutional reality" (Fuchs, Guidorossi, and Svensson 1995, 328; see also Klingemann 1999; Anderson et al. 2005).

As such, it is a useful indicator for connecting the performance of electoral institutions to what people think about the political system. It also bridges David Easton's (1965) distinction between diffuse and specific support. Diffuse support is typically considered a long-standing predisposition that "refers to evaluations of what an object is or represents – the general meaning it has for a person – not of what it does" (273). Specific support derives from citizens' evaluations of system outputs; it is performance-based and may be more short term.

The second indicator examined here, support for democracy as a form of government, asked respondents whether they agreed or disagreed with the following statement: "Democracy may have problems but it's better than any other form of government." This question does not tap into democracy as an ideal – rather, it asks respondents to compare democracy as a form of government to other forms of government. In this way, the indicator does not ask about current performance of the political system but explicitly taps into the rejection of undemocratic alternatives. This "Churchillian" support concept is especially relevant for the purposes of the analyses reported here, as the sample of countries includes states with a recent undemocratic past, where such comparisons between democracy and other types of government are particularly relevant and salient (see Rose, Mishler, and Haerpfer 1998). Together, these two indicators should allow us to cover the different and relevant dimensions of system attitudes for the purposes of this analysis.[15]

Variation in System Support across Countries and across Individuals

Using the positive responses to the survey questions, figures 9.2a and 9.2b show the distribution of these measures of system support across the twenty-four countries included in this study for which the relevant variables included in the multivariate analyses described below are available.[16] Satisfaction with democracy is systematically higher in the older democracies, relative to the younger ones. Though there are exceptions, satisfaction levels are generally higher in the United States and the Scandinavian countries relative to newer democracies, including the Central-East European states, Mexico, and Korea. In countries such as Denmark, Ireland, Australia, the United States, Norway, Spain, and Switzerland, for example, around 80 per cent of respondents (and over 90 per cent in the case of Denmark) express satisfaction with democracy. In stark contrast, only 20 to 30 per cent of citizens in Bulgaria, Korea, and Mexico express such sentiments about their country's politics.

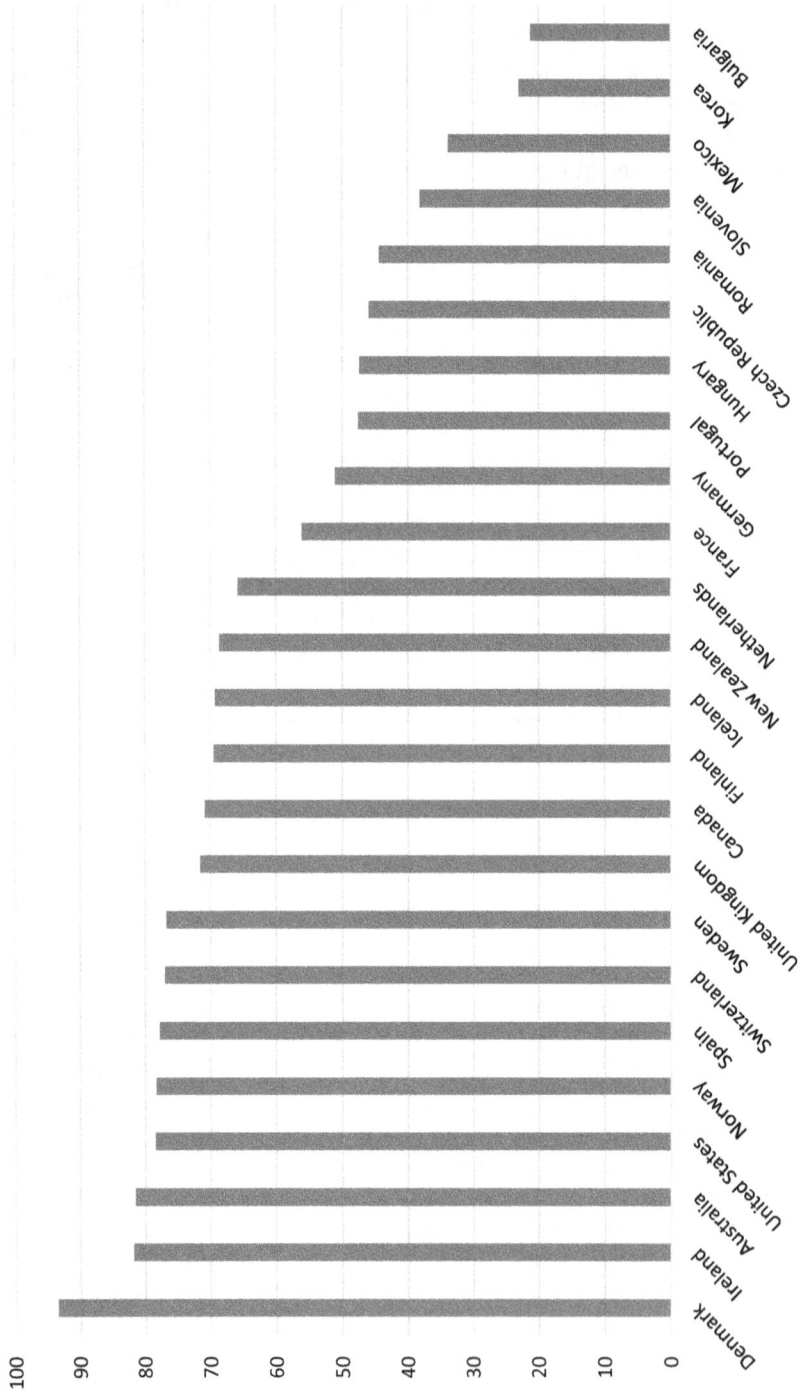

Figure 9.2a Democracy Satisfaction

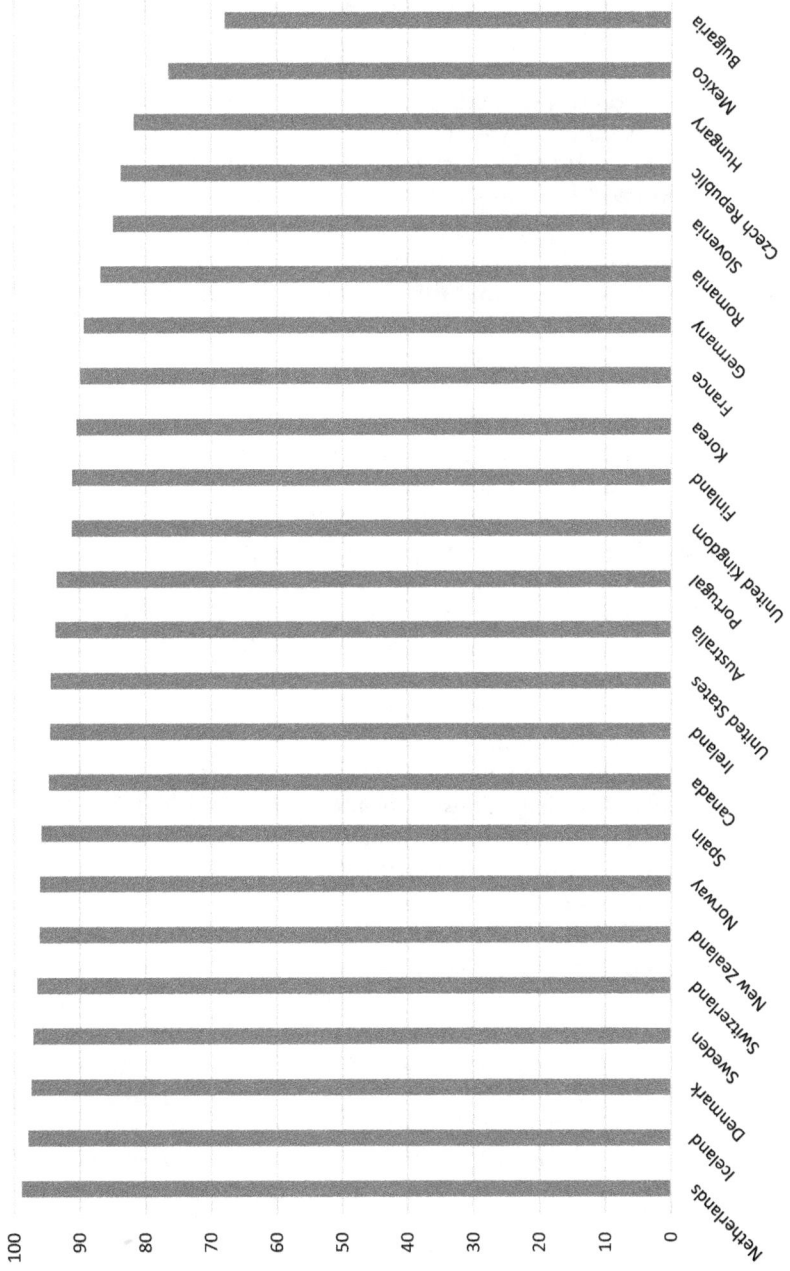

Figure 9.2b Preference for Democracy

Levels of support for democracy as a form of government also are very high, especially in the older democracies. In fact, in these countries, democracy is considered the only game in town, with around 90 per cent of respondents indicating support for democracy over undemocratic alternatives (though respondents in all countries make use of the full scale to express their attitudes about democracy). But in stark contrast, respondents in the newer democracies, including Bulgaria, Mexico, Hungary, the Czech Republic, or Romania express more ambivalent attitudes about democracy. This is consistent with related research, which shows that diffuse support tends to be lower in new relative to old democracies (Klingemann 1999; Tóka 1995).

The first critical question for the purposes of my analysis is whether the nature of the variation we see in citizens' responses to questions about the political system requires a set of explanations both at the level of individuals and at the level of countries. That is, do the data support the contention that support is both a function of individual characteristics and the nature of the political context that varies across countries? To determine whether there is significant variation in attitudes about the political system at the individual and country levels, I estimated multi-level regression models that decompose the variance in the dependent variables.[17] The argument that both levels of analysis are important for understanding each of our dependent variables is supported if both variance components are statistically significant (see Steenbergen and Jones 2002).

Table 9.1 shows estimates of the variance components. Both variance components are statistically significant for all dependent variables, suggesting that there is significant variance in levels of satisfaction with democracy and acceptance of democracy at both levels of analysis. Results of the variance component models show that country-level variance is proportionally smaller than individual-level variance for all three dependent variables. Specifically, individual-level variance constitutes 68.5 per cent of the total variance in satisfaction with democracy and 73.3 per cent in support for democracy.[18] Given that these data are measured at the individual level, this is not entirely surprising (Steenbergen and Jones 2002, 231), but it is interesting that there is relatively more variance at the macro level in the model of satisfaction with democracy (31.5 per cent) than in the model of preference for democracy (26.7 per cent). At the same time, the results of the models indicate clearly that there is significant variation in the sources of system support at both levels of analysis, but much more (more than twice as much) at the level

Table 9.1 Variance Decomposition in System Support

	Satisfaction with democracy	Preference for democracy
Fixed effects	2.616***	3.316***
Constant	(.069)	(.048)
Variance components Country-level	.328***	.236***
	(.048)	(.035)
Individual-level	.714***	.648***
	(.003)	(.002)
−2Log likelihood	38467.9	34099.2
Macro *N*	24	24
Micro *N*	35497	34534

Notes: Entries are maximum likelihood estimates; standard errors in parentheses.
$*p < 0.05$; $**p < 0.01$; $***p < .001$.

of individuals. Thus, I now turn to the question of whether the model I have specified can account for some of this variance.

Multi-level Models of Attitudes about the Political System

To see whether the electoral supply as conceptualized and measured here affects people's attitudes, the next step in the analysis requires that we merge information about the country-level electoral supply with the individual survey data and construct estimation models that include important individual-level and country-level predictors of system support. At the individual level, most importantly, establishing that political losers take a dim view of the political system requires categorizing respondents as electoral and policy losers. I classified respondents as electoral losers with the help of a survey question that asked which party the individual voted for in the election. I then combined these responses with information about the party or parties that controlled the executive branch after the election. If the respondent's reported vote choice did not match the actual party in power, I scored that individual as 1 (electoral loser); all others were scored 0.

To categorize voters as policy losers, I measured the distance between the respondent's self-placement on the Left-Right scale and the government's Left-Right position, calculated as a weighted average of the governing parties' Left-Right positions. Thus, individuals further removed from the government's position received a higher score than individuals closer to the government's position.[19]

To ensure that the multivariate models were well specified, I also controlled for a number of important individual-level and country-level predictors of system support. Including these variables avoids drawing faulty inferences due to spuriousness that can result from omitting relevant variables. At the individual level, I included a standard set of demographic variables (age, gender, education, income, marital status), political ideology (Left-Right placement), electoral participation,[20] and identification with a political party. At the level of countries, I controlled for level of economic development, level of democracy, age of the party system, and government ideology. The age of the party system is a particularly important control variable because it measures the predictability of electoral choices from one election to the next. The argument here is that there is little point in talking about electoral supply if voters cannot learn about them because they change rapidly and unpredictably from one electoral contest to the next. At the same time, the stability of the choices, registered in the age of the party system, could also be taken to be an indicator of legitimacy and thus be considered endogenous to system support attitudes (see also Mainwaring 1999). Because of its importance but ambiguous causal connection to the dependent variables examined here, this variable is included as a control variable.

Direct Effects of Losing and Electoral Supply on System Support

To estimate the effect of macro-level variables, such as the electoral supply, on individual-level outcomes requires the estimation of multi-level models (see Steenbergen and Jones 2002). Table 9.2 reports the results of a multivariate, multilevel random intercept, random slopes model estimating the direct effects of electoral supply on system attitudes. The random slopes portion of the estimation model is designed to ascertain whether the effects of electoral and policy losing vary systematically across countries.

The results show that the measures of electoral supply do not have a direct effect on people's views of the political system. That is, knowing that polarization is high or low or that electoral options are numerous or few does not help to predict whether people, on average, express more positive or negative views of the political system. The only macro-level

Table 9.2 Random Intercept Models of System Support in 24 Countries

	Satisfaction with democracy	Preference for democracy
Electoral loser	−.117***	−.025**
	(.010)	(.009)
Policy loser	−.007*	.004
	(.003)	(.003)
Effective number of parties	.027	.007
	(.045)	(.025)
Polarization	−.003	.026
	(.054)	(.030)
Electoral participation	.162***	.125***
	(.014)	(.013)
Close to party	.118***	.112***
	(.009)	(.008)
Respondent ideology (Left-Right)	.023***	.015***
	(.002)	(.002)
Age	−.017***	.044***
	(.005)	(.004)
Female	−.012	−.043***
	(.009)	(.008)
Education	.013*	.097***
	(.006)	(.005)
Married	−.000	−.017†
	(.010)	(.009)
Income	.026***	.046***
	(.004)	(.003)
Level of development	.036	.064
	(.446)	(.249)
Level of democracy	.247†	.243**
	(.139)	(.078)
Age of party system	.004*	.002*
	(.002)	(.001)

(Continued)

Table 9.2 (Continued)

	Satisfaction with democracy	Preference for democracy
Government ideology	.002	.012
	(.042)	(.023)
Constant	2.244***	2.602***
	(.572)	(.319)
Variance components Country-level	.231	.128
Individual-level	.692	.627
ρ	.10	.04
R^2 (overall)	.16	.15
Macro *N*	24	24
Micro *N*	26105	25724

Source: Comparative Study of Electoral Systems, Module II.

Notes: Random intercept multilevel regression models; standard errors in parentheses.

[†] $p < .1$; *$p < .05$; **$p < .01$; ***$p < .001$.

variables that reveal significant effects are the level of democracy and the age of the party system. Citizens in more democratic countries and in countries with older party systems express greater satisfaction with the working of the political system and are more likely to endorse democracy as their preferred system of government.

In contrast, a number of individual level variables have significant effects on system support. Among them, most importantly, we find that electoral losers are less satisfied with how well democracy works, and they are less likely to prefer democracy. At the same time, the variable measuring policy losing exerts such a direct effect only on satisfaction with the way democracy works. Thus, consistent with earlier work on electoral losers, election outcomes significantly shape voters' views of the political system, but this direct effect is more pronounced for electoral losing than for policy losing.[21]

The other individual level variables exert results consistent with past research. Thus, people who voted, who feel close to parties, and locate themselves on the right express more positive attitudes about the political system. As well, the results show that older respondents report less satisfaction with the way democracy works but value democracy more. As expected, individuals with higher levels of education and income express significantly more positive attitudes about the performance of the political system (democracy satisfaction) and a more pronounced preference for democracy.

Taken together, these results suggest two preliminary conclusions: individuals whom the electoral process has placed on the losing side express systematically more negative views of the performance and desirability of democratic political systems. Moreover, electoral options in the form of the number and distinctiveness of political parties do not shape attitudes about the political system independently. Whether they do so in interaction with electoral or policy losing is the question I turn to next.

Contingent Effects of Losing and Electoral Supply on System Support

To establish whether the electoral supply is a more critical variable for shaping system support among some segments of the electorate – that is, whether electoral supply has contingent effects, as I have hypothesized above – I examine the interactive effects of losing and electoral supply on system support in a series of multi-level random intercept models. These models are identical to those reported in table 9.2, with the exception that they also include two interaction terms – losing by polarization and losing by effective number of electoral parties. The results of such models examining the interactions of electoral losing and electoral supply are shown in table 9.3.

The multi-level contingent effects models of electoral losers, electoral supply, and system support reported in table 9.3 show that there are indeed systematic contingent effects. As before, losers are less satisfied with how democracy works and less likely to prefer democracy. And as in the models shown in table 9.2, the electoral supply does little to shape system support (among winners). What is notable, however, is that the independent effect of electoral losing are much larger than in the direct effects model, and that there are consistently significant effects for policy losers on system support once a contingent effects model is estimated.

Most importantly for the purposes of this chapter, there are highly significant interaction effects between the variables measuring political losers and the electoral supply. Specifically, electoral losers living

Table 9.3 Multi-level Contingent Effects Models of Political Losers, Electoral Supply, and System Support in 24 Countries

	Satisfaction with democracy			Preference for democracy		
Electoral loser	−.705***	−.131***	−.615***	−.236***	−.029**	−.192***
	(.044)	(.010)	(.046)	(.041)	(.009)	(.042)
Policy loser	.014***	−.159***	−.114***	.001	−.064***	−.048***
	(.003)	(.015)	(.015)	(.003)	(.013)	(.014)
Number of parties	.012	.008	.002	.001	−.006	−.008
	(.052)	(.041)	(.050)	(.028)	(.018)	(.021)
Polarization	−.058	−.078	−.100†	.007	.002	−.006
	(.062)	(.050)	(.060)	(.034)	(.021)	(.024)
Electoral loser	.039***	–	.034***	.015*	–	.010
* no. of parties	(.008)		(.008)	(.007)		(.007)
Electoral loser	.133***	–	.108***	.046***	–	.038***
* polarization	(.009)		(.009)	(.008)		(.008)
Policy loser	–	.009***	.006*	–	.007***	.006**
* no. of parties		(.002)	(.002)		(.002)	(.002)
Policy loser * polarization	–	.033***	.023***	–	.011***	.008**
		(.003)	(.003)		(.002)	(.002)
Electoral participation	.164***	.165***	.165***	.125***	.126***	.126***
	(.014)	(.014)	(.014)	(.013)	(.013)	(.013)
Close to party	.157***	.118***	.116***	.111***	.112***	.111***
	(.010)	(.009)	(.009)	(.008)	(.008)	(.008)
Respondent ideology (Left-Right)	.022***	.020***	.020***	.015***	.015***	.015***
	(.002)	(.002)	(.002)	(.002)	(.002)	(.002)
Age	−.016***	−.016***	−.015***	.044***	.044***	.044***
	(.005)	(.005)	(.004)	(.004)	(.004)	(.004)
Female	−.012	−.012	−.012	−.043***	−.043***	−.043***
	(.009)	(.009)	(.009)	(.008)	(.008)	(.008)
Education	.013*	.012*	.012*	.097***	.096***	.096***
	(.006)	(.006)	(.006)	(.005)	(.005)	(.005)
Married	−.002	.000	−.001	−.017†	−.016†	−.017†
	(.010)	(.010)	(.010)	(.009)	(.009)	(.009)

	Satisfaction with democracy			Preference for democracy		
Income	.026***	.026***	.026***	.046***	.046***	.046***
	(.004)	(.004)	(.004)	(.003)	(.003)	(.003)
Level of development	.039	.002	.015	.065	.054	.058**
	(.514)	(.408)	(.498)	(.279)	(.172)	(.202)
Level of democracy	.237	.250*	.241	.239**	.247***	.242***
	(.160)	(.127)	(.155)	(.087)	(.054)	(.063)
Age of party system	.004*	.004**	.004*	.002*	.002**	.002**
	(.002)	(.002)	(.002)	(.001)	(.001)	(.001)
Government ideology	.002	.009	.007	.012	.014	.013
	(.049)	(.038)	(.047)	(.026)	(.016)	(.019)
Constant	2.493***	2.589***	2.682***	2.690***	2.750***	2.779***
	(.660)	(.523)	(.639)	(.358)	(.222)	(.261)
Variance Components Country-level	.267	.211	.258	.144	.087	.102
Individual-level	.689	.690	.688	.626	.627	.626
ρ	.13	.09	.12	.05	.02	.03
R^2 (overall)	.170	.170	.174	.155	.155	.156
Macro N	24	24	24	24	24	24
Micro N	26105	26105	26105	25724	25724	25724

Source: Comparative Study of Electoral Systems, Module II.

Notes: Random intercept multilevel regression models; standard errors in parentheses.

†: $p < .1$; *: $p < .05$; **: $p < .01$; ***: $p < .001$.

in countries with a more clearly differentiated electoral supply express significantly more faith in the workings of the political system and democracy as a preferred political system. These results support the contention that the electoral supply shapes the system views of electoral losers, rather than the electorate writ large. Moreover, there is a significant effect for the interaction between electoral losing and the number of parties on democracy satisfaction: this suggests that living in a country with a greater number of choices reduces the negative effect of losing on system support. Taken together, these results speak in favour of the safety valve hypothesis, rather than the notion that polarized party systems are inimical to legitimacy.

The results for the interactive effects of policy losing and electoral supply on system support also show consistent support for the safety valve hypothesis. Another way to think about this is to ask whether the electoral supply has a stronger or weaker support among policy winners and losers. As previously, the estimation models contain two interaction terms – policy losing by polarization and policy losing by effective number of electoral parties. These contingent effects models of policy losers, electoral supply, and system support reveal that there are indeed contingent effects of electoral supply on system support. As before, these models, too, show that electoral losers report lower levels of satisfaction with how democracy works and are less likely to prefer democracy as a system of government. In a departure from the results in table 9.2, the results in table 9.3 show that policy losers are also significantly more likely to be dissatisfied with the performance of the political system, or less likely to express a preference for democracy.

Since it is unsatisfactory to report the direct effects of variables that are part of interaction terms, the results for the interaction analyses are

Figure 9.3a Electoral Supply and Democracy Satisfaction among Electoral Winners and Losers

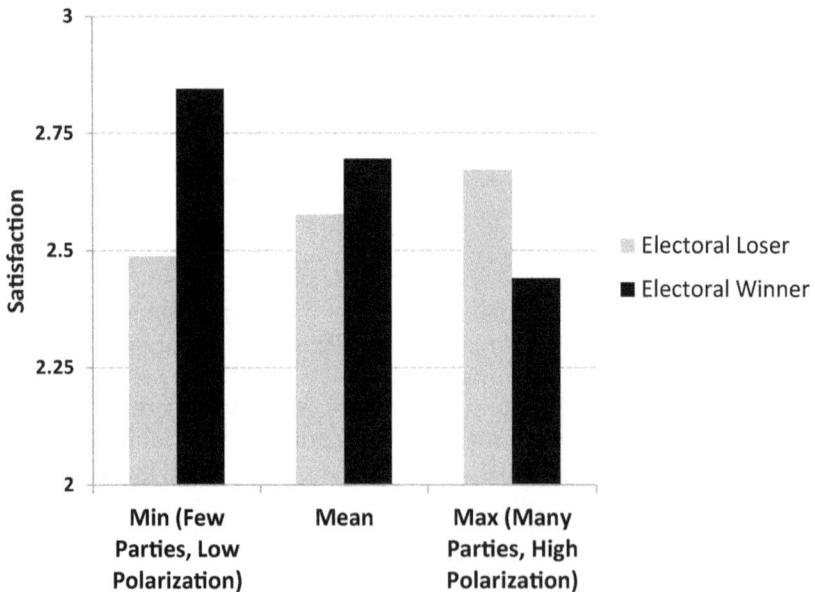

Figure 9.3b Electoral Supply and Democracy Satisfaction among Policy Winners and Losers

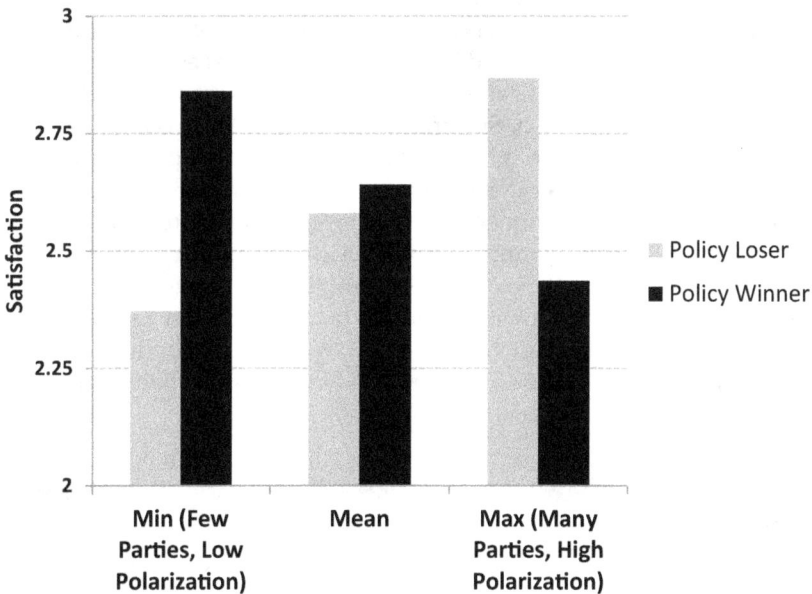

the key test of my safety valve hypothesis. The results shown in table 9.3 demonstrate highly significant interaction effects between policy losers and polarization. This implies that policy losers living in countries with a more clearly differentiated electoral supply have more faith in the workings of the political system and democracy as a system of government. Put another way, the negative effect of being a policy loser is significantly diminished in countries that provide a more distinct set of choices.

As in the case of electoral losers, there is a significant effect for the interaction between policy losing and the number of parties on preference for democracy. This suggests that living in a country with greater number of meaningful choices reduces the negative effect of losing on preference for democracy. All around, these estimation results clearly speak in favour of the safety valve hypothesis; or put more conservatively, nothing in these results suggests that there is a significant downside to a distinct and numerous electoral supply when it comes to legitimacy beliefs among voters with reasons to be discontented.

These results can also be expressed substantively as predicted changes in the dependent variables for different values of the independent variables. Figures 9.3 and 9.4 use table 9.3 model estimates to chart system support for political losers and non-losers, conditioned across values of political context. Specifically, I simulate three scenarios: first, an electoral context marked by few choices and low polarization; second, at mean levels of electoral supply; and third, in an electoral context characterized by abundant choices and high levels of polarization.

The results shown in figures 9.3 and 9.4 are straightforward. Electoral and policy losers like their political system better if there are more parties that offer more distinct options to choose from on Election Day. Conversely, losers are much less enamoured with the political system when they live in countries with few and indistinguishable options on

Figure 9.4a Electoral Supply and Preference for Democracy among Electoral Winners and Losers

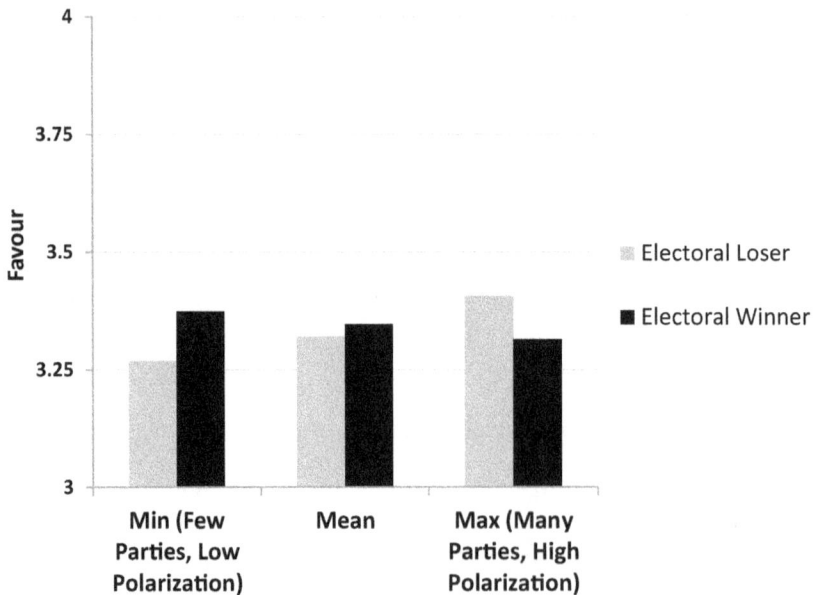

Figure 9.4b Electoral Supply and Preference for Democracy among Policy Winners and Losers

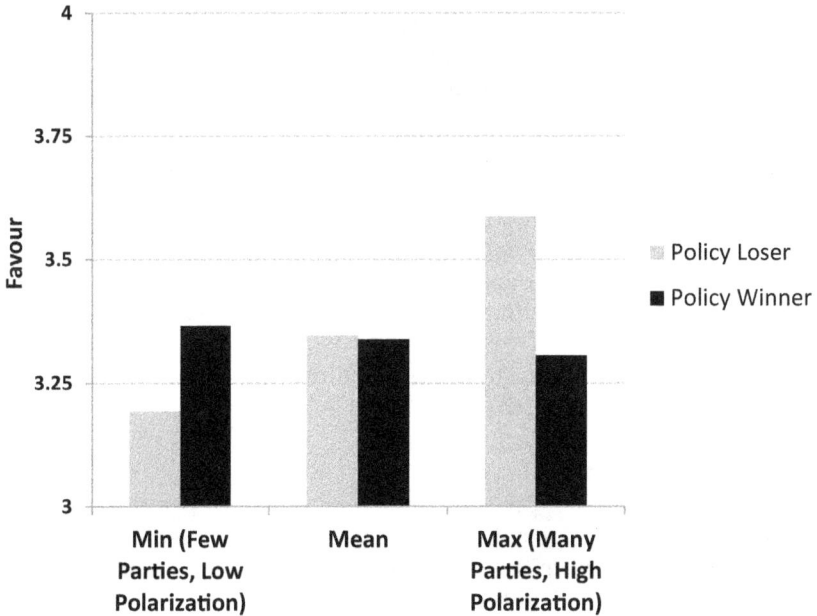

Election Day. While winners are happier than losers in countries with few options that are located near each other in the ideological space, losers are happier than winners in countries with many and differentiated options. Thus, it appears that living in a Downsian world of two parties that fail to offer distinct choices is agony for policy and electoral losers, but bliss for winners. In contrast, living in a country with a multitude of distinct parties elevates the level of system support among losers and diminished it among winners.[22] Worth noting is also the fact that this pattern of effects is somewhat more pronounced with regard to evaluations of the democratic system's performance than for people's preference for democracy as a system of governance. Thus, electoral supply coupled with individual status as political winner or loser has stronger effects on evaluations of system performance than the desirability of democracy.[23]

Conclusion

In recent years a number of contemporary democracies have sought to reform their electoral systems, typically with very specific goals in mind. Among them has frequently been the desire to increase the legitimacy of the political system by enhancing citizens' sense that voting matters and their voices are represented. Yet how exactly electoral systems help to produce citizen consent has long been subject to debate and oftentimes without the requisite evidence that would allow us to adjudicate among competing perspectives. One long-standing debate has to do with the consequences of proportional representation systems. By serving as transmission belts for political grievances, does PR act as a safety valve for democracy or does it allow extreme voices to undermine democracy?

In this chapter I set out to examine the impact of electoral rules by examining their consequences in the form of the volume and distinctiveness of the electoral supply has corroding or salutary effects on how people view the political system. The results are in, and they suggest that a differentiated supply and a more numerous supply have positive effects on system support. But these effects are not present for all voters; instead, they exist chiefly among voters whom the political system has left unrepresented, either in government or in the policy process. Thus the electoral supply shapes system support, but it is most critically important for those with a political axe to grind. Put simply, differentiation begets legitimation among political losers.

These findings run counter to Sartori's conjecture; they reveal that the quantity and quality – fragmentation and polarization – are separable traits of the electoral supply. Moreover, to the extent that they coincide, polarized pluralism begets happier political losers. Whether these results are the result of the times we live in, and thus perhaps not as contradictory to the analyses of Hermens and Sartori as they seem, is unclear. And absent direct comparisons between this set of countries at this point and an earlier one, it will be difficult to find out. But at a minimum, we can say that there is no indication that a more differentiated and more numerous electoral supply has negative consequences for how citizens view the political system. This is reassuring, but it does raise the question of whether the more limited electoral supply in countries such as the United States is at least partially responsible for the erosion of public support for the political system there (see Dalton 2007). Speaking more generally, the findings suggest that parties' incentives to place themselves in the political centre may be useful for winning votes but have the undesirable by-product of undermining people's faith in elections and democracy (Weßels n.d.). Yet again, absent further and more detailed and systematic analyses of the connection between changes in electoral supply and system support, this remains conjecture.

The analyses reported here rely on conceptualizations and measurement of the electoral supply at the level of the nation-state. One interesting and unanswered question is whether the supply of electoral choices at the sub-national level may exacerbate or attenuate the effects I have demonstrated here. Research on economic voting and losers' consent suggests that subnational politics is a fertile area for answering such questions (Anderson 2006; Loewen and Blais 2006). Moreover, these findings raise interesting potential questions about the extent to which polarization can help orient voters and supply important information about the political system.

The results also speak to open questions in the growing literature on how losers view the political system. They show that disentangling electoral and policy losing is important; they reveal that policy losing and electoral loss have separable consequences. Moreover, they suggest that some findings in that literature – e.g., that losers like consensual democracy (Anderson and Guillory's 1997) – may be combining a set of structural and institutional factors – e.g., party systems, polarization, and coalition government – that require conceptual and empirical separation in order to adequately identify the ways in which electoral and policy losers react to the political context. Moreover, they provide a potential explanation for the legitimacy puzzle of why dissatisfied citizens continue to support a political system (Booth and Seligson 2009).

Taken together, the results presented in this paper show that the nature of the available choices influences the attitudes of those citizens who already have strong incentives to take a dim view of the political system such that distinct partisan offerings diminish the negative views electoral and policy losers hold. This means that countries' macro-level supply of choices and individuals' predispositions interactively shape citizen consent, complicating the story of how electoral contexts shape consent. But they also clearly suggest that polarization and multiparty systems do not delegitimize the state, as is commonly believed. Misery loves choices, making the electoral supply a potential safety valve for democracy.

NOTES

1 Chapter 10 provides a very useful review of how the various factors within electoral systems shape the supply of parties provided to voters. Chapter 11 similarly provides a review of how these same systemic features are related to the decision to vote strategically.

2 Hermens was certainly not the first to discuss the virtues and disadvantages of electoral systems, but his argument took on particular significance after the failure of the Weimar Republic. Prior scholarship on the topic extends to Jean-Charles de Borda, Marquis de Condorcet, J.S. Mill, and Walter Bagehot, and a number of others.

3 But, as Listhaug, Aardal, and Ellis (2009) note, this explanation may not work in Sweden after the party system there underwent significant changes in 1988–91.

4 Consistent with the general tenor of the positive effects of proportional representation and multipartism, Huber et al. argue that, as the party system offers more electoral choices to voters, individuals should be better able to identify which parties represent their views and thus navigate the political system. Critically, to Huber et al., more parties are expected to send better, clearer, and therefore more easily identifiable signals (Huber, Kernell, and Leoni 2005). Related to this, a recent individual level study based on CSES surveys by Banducci and Karp (2009) argued that the logic of PR systems leads supporters of smaller parties to feel as if they are not wasting their votes.

5 Unlike other modules of the CSES, Module 2 contains a critical dependent variable of interest (preference for democracy) and allows the analysis of a larger sample of democracies.

6 Australia, Bulgaria, Canada, Czech Republic, Denmark, Finland, France, Germany, Hungary, Iceland, Ireland, Korea, Mexico, Netherlands, New Zealand, Norway, Portugal, Romania, Slovenia, Spain, Sweden, Switzerland, United Kingdom, United States.

7 Fortuitously, these properties of the electoral supply are also the critical dimensions of party systems identified by earlier research on the connection between electoral and party systems on one hand, and system support on the other.

8 Along similar lines, one could measure the diversity of choice by the number of distinct party families that exist in the party system.

9 Inglehart (1990, 273), for instance, showed that people in most nations can locate themselves on the Left-Right scale, and he described the scale as representing "whatever major conflicts are present in the political system"

(also see Fuchs and Klingemann 1989; Huber and Inglehart 1995; Knutsen 1999).

10 For a discussion of other measures of party ideological positions see Dalton (2008).

11 This index has a value of 0 when all parties occupy the same position on the left/right scale, and 10 when all the parties are split between the two extremes of the scale.

12 This does not mean, of course, that there are not other lines of political division not captured by the Left-Right ideological polarization score.

13 The value of differentiating between the number of options and the nature of those options is also apparent when we compare the numbers in figure 9.2 to those reported by Klingemann and Weßels (2009, 263–4) on the differentiation of the electoral supply, which is based at its core on the number of party and candidate offerings. While the Klingemann and Weßels measure, for example, identifies Hungary as having a relatively lower differentiation of electoral supply, figure 9.2 reveals that this is true only with regard to the number of offerings, but not their distinctiveness. Similarly, to use another example, they identify Spain as having a relatively high differentiation of electoral supply; as the numbers in figure 9.2 show, this is primarily true with regard to the distinctiveness of choices. This is meant to be illustrative, since our measures and theirs are not strictly comparable.

14 The form of the electoral system, PR v. majoritarian system, is related to the number of effective number of parties (.48) and the level of polarization in a party system ($r = .38$), but the correlation between the effective number of parties and polarization is .02.

15 The Pearson correlation between the two items is .28.

16 The analyses focus on legislative elections only.

17 Where Support ij = $\gamma 00$ + $\delta 0j$ + ϵij. In this model, $\gamma 00$ is the grand mean on the support indicator. The sources of cross-national variation, which cause particular countries to deviate from this mean, are in $\delta 0j$, and ϵij contains the sources of inter-individual variation.

18 These calculations are based on the ratios of each variance component relative to the total variance in system support (see Bryk and Raudenbush 1992; Snijders and Bosker 1999).

19 Electoral and policy losing are not synonymous, as the Pearson correlation between the two is .27.

20 Following the argument that participation enhances feelings of trust and external efficacy (and vice versa) (see Finkel 1987), I included a variable distinguishing voters and non-voters to control for differences attributable to having participated in the election. I expect that those who participated

in the election (coded 1) will have more positive attitudes toward the political system than those who did not (coded 0).
21 This difference according to partisanship and policy preferences reflects the important distinction between cognitive and emotional processes outlined in chapter 8.
22 While the size of these effects is not overwhelming, it is worth keeping in mind for comparison, that they are on the same order as or larger than the effects of other important independent variables, such as education, income, or ideology.
23 Part of the reason for this in all likelihood lies in the more restricted range of responses to the question about the desirability of democracy.

References

Anderson, Cameron D. 2006. "Economic Voting and Multilevel Governance: A Comparative Individual-Level Analysis." *American Journal of Political Science* 50 (2): 449–63.

Anderson, Christopher J. 1998. "Party Systems and Satisfaction with Democracy in the New Europe." *Political Studies* 46 (4): 572–88.

– 2011. "Electoral Supply, Median Voters, and Feelings of Representation in Democracies." In *Citizens, Context, and Choice: How Context Shapes Citizens' Electoral Choices*, edited by Russell J. Dalton and Christopher J. Anderson, 214–40. New York: Oxford University Press.

Anderson, Christopher J., André Blais, Shaun Bowler, Todd Donovan, and Ola Listhaug. 2005. *Losers' Consent: Elections and Democratic Legitimacy*. New York: Oxford University Press.

Anderson, Christopher J., and Christine A. Guillory. 1997. "Political Institutions and Satisfaction with Democracy: A Cross-National Analysis of Consensus and Majoritarian Systems." *American Political Science Review* 91 (1): 66–81.

Banducci, Susan A., and Jeffrey A. Karp. 2003. "How Elections Change the Way Citizens View the Political System: Campaigns, Media Effects, and Electoral Outcomes in Comparative Perspective." *British Journal of Political Science* 33 (3): 443–67.

– 2009. "Electoral Systems, Efficacy, and Voter Turnout." In *The Comparative Study of Electoral Systems*, edited by Hans-Dieter Klingemann, 109–36. New York: Oxford University Press.

Blais, André. 1991. "The Debate over Electoral Systems." *International Political Science Review* 12:239–60.

Blais, André, and François Gélineau. 2007. "Winning, Losing, and Satisfaction with Democracy." *Political Studies* 55:425–41.

Blais, André, and Peter Loewen. 2007. "Electoral Systems and Evaluations of Democracy." In *Democratic Reform in New Brunswick*, edited by Bill Cross, 39–57. Toronto: Canadian Scholars'.

Booth, John A., and Mitchell A. Seligson. 2009. *The Legitimacy Puzzle in Latin America: Political Support and Democracy in Eight Nations*. New York: Cambridge University Press.

Bryk, Anthony S., and Stephen W. Raudenbush. 1992. *Hierarchical Linear Models*. Newbury Park, CA: Sage.

Craig, Stephen C., Michael D. Martinez, Jason Gainous, and James G. Kane. 2006. "Winners, Losers, and Election Context: Voter Responses to the 2000 Presidential Election." *Political Research Quarterly* 59 (4): 579–92.

Criado, Henar, and Francisco Herreros. 2007. "Political Support: Taking into Account the Institutional Context." *Comparative Political Studies* 40 (12): 1511–32.

Dalton, Russell J. 2007. *Democratic Challenges, Democratic Choices: The Erosion of Political Support in Advanced Industrial Democracies*. New York: Oxford University Press.

– 2008. "The Quantity and the Quality of Party Systems: Party System Polarization, Its Measurement and Its Consequences." *Comparative Political Studies* 41 (7): 899–920.

– 2011. "Left-Right Orientations, Context, and Voting Choices." In *Citizens, Context, and Choice: How Context Shapes Citizens' Electoral Choices*, edited by Russell J. Dalton and Christopher J. Anderson, 103–25. New York: Oxford University Press.

Downs, Anthony. 1957. *An Economic Theory of Democracy*. New York: Harper.

Easton, David. 1965. *A Systems Analysis of Political Life*. New York: John Wiley and Sons.

Finer, Herman. 1956. *Governments of Greater European Powers*. New York: Henry Holt.

Finkel, Steven E. 1987. "The Effects of Participation on Political Efficacy and Political Support." *Journal of Politics* 49:441–64.

Fuchs, Dieter, Giovanna Guidorossi, and Palle Svensson. 1995. "Support for the Democratic System." In *Citizens and the State*, edited by Hans-Dieter Klingemann and Dieter Fuchs, 323–53. New York: Oxford University Press.

Fuchs, Dieter, and Hans-Dieter Klingemann. 1989. "The Left-Right Schema." In *Continuities in Political Action*, edited by M. Kent Jennings and Jan van Deth, 203–34. Berlin: de Gruyter.

Ginsberg, Benjamin, and Robert Weisberg. 1978. "Elections and the Mobilization of Popular Support." *American Journal of Political Science* 22 (1): 31–55.
Henderson, Ailsa. 2008. "Satisfaction with Democracy: The Impact of Winning
and Losing in Westminster Systems." *Journal of Elections, Public Opinion, and
Parties* 18 (1): 3–26.
Hermens, Ferdinand A. 1936. "Proportional Representation and the Break-
down of German Democracy." *Social Research* 3 (4): 411–33.
– 1941. *Democracy or Anarchy? A Study of Proportional Representation.* Notre
Dame, IN: University of Notre Dame Press.
Huber, John, and Ronald Inglehart. 1995. "Expert Interpretations of Party
Space and Party Locations in 42 Societies." *Party Politics* 1 (1): 73–111.
Huber, John D., Georgia Kernell, and Eduardo L. Leoni. 2005. "Institutional
Context, Cognitive Resources and Party Attachments across Democracies."
Political Analysis 13 (4): 365–86.
Inglehart, Ronald. 1990. *Culture Shift in Advanced Industrial Society.* Princeton,
NJ: Princeton University Press.
Iyengar, Sheena S., and Mark R. Lepper. 2000. "When Choice Is Demotivating:
Can One Desire Too Much of a Good Thing?" *Journal of Personality and Social
Psychology* 79 (6): 995–1006.
Karp, Jeffrey A., and Shaun Bowler. 2001. "Coalition Politics and Satisfaction
with Democracy: Explaining New Zealand's Reaction to Proportional Rep-
resentation." *European Journal of Political Research* 40 (1): 57–79.
Kedar, Orit. 2005. "When Moderate Voters Prefer Extreme Parties: Policy Balanc-
ing in Parliamentary Elections." *American Political Science Review* 99 (2): 185–99.
Klingemann, Hans-Dieter. 1999. "Mapping Political Support in the 1990s: A
Global Analysis." In *Critical Citizens: Global Support for Democratic Gover-
nance,* edited by Pippa Norris, 31–56. New York: Oxford University Press.
Klingemann, Hans-Dieter, and Bernhard Weßels. 2009. "How Voters Cope
with the Complexity of Their Political Environment." In *The Comparative
Study of Electoral Systems,* edited by Hans-Dieter Klingemann, 237–68. New
York: Oxford University Press.
Knutsen, Oddbjörn. 1999. "Left-Right Party Polarization among the Mass
Publics." In *Challenges to Representative Democracy,* edited by Hanne Narud
and Toril Aalberg, chap. 9. Bergen: Fagbokforlaget.
Kreuzer, Marcus. 2001. *Institutions and Innovation: Voters, Parties, and Interest
Groups in the Consolidation of Democracy – France and Germany, 1870–1939.*
Ann Arbor: University of Michigan Press.
Laakso, Markku, and Rein Taagepera. 1979. "'Effective' Number of Parties: A
Measure with Application to West Europe." *Comparative Political Studies* 12
(1): 3–27.

Lane, Jan-Erik, and Svante Ersson. 1991. *Politics and Society in Western Europe.* 2nd ed. London: Sage.

Lijphart, Arend. 1999. *Patterns of Democracy: Government Forms and Performance in Thirty-Six Countries.* New Haven, CT: Yale University Press.

Listhaug, Ola, Bernt Aardal, and Ingunn Opheim Ellis. 2009. "Institutional Variation and Political Support: An Analysis of CSES Data from 29 Countries." In *The Comparative Study of Electoral Systems,* edited by Hans-Dieter Klingemann, chap. 14. New York: Oxford University Press.

Loewen, Peter, and André Blais. 2006. "Testing Publius' Federalism: Losers Consent, Winners Lament?" Paper prepared for conference on the Comparative Study of Electoral Systems, Seville, Spain, 23 March 2006.

Mainwaring, Scott. 1999. *Rethinking Party Systems in the Third Wave of Democratization: The Case of Brazil.* Palo Alto, CA: Stanford University Press.

Miller, Arthur H., and Ola Listhaug. 1990. "Political Parties and Confidence in Government: A Comparison of Norway, Sweden and the United States." *British Journal of Political Science* 29 (3): 357–86.

– 1999. "Political Performance and Institutional Trust." In *Critical Citizens: Global Support for Democratic Governance,* edited by Pippa Norris, chap. 10. New York: Oxford University Press.

Norris, Pippa. 1999. "Institutional Explanations for Political Support." In *Critical Citizens: Global Support for Democratic Governance,* edited by Pippa Norris, chap. 11. New York: Oxford University Press.

Paskeviciute, Aida. 2006. "Elections, Policy Representation, and System Legitimacy in Contemporary Democracies." Paper prepared for presentation at the annual meeting of the American Political Science Association 2007, Philadelphia.

Powell, G. Bingham. 2000. *Elections as Instruments of Democracy: Majoritarian and Proportional Visions.* New Haven, CT: Yale University Press.

Quade, Quentin L. 2006. "PR and Democratic Statecraft." In *Electoral Systems and Democracy,* edited by Larry Diamond and Marc Plattner, 92–7. Baltimore, MD: Johns Hopkins University Press.

Rae, Douglas. 1971. *Political Consequences of Electoral Laws.* New Haven, CT: Yale University Press.

Rose, Richard, William Mishler, and Christian Haerpfer. 1998. *Democracy and Its Alternatives: Understanding Post-Communist Societies.* Baltimore, MD: Johns Hopkins University Press.

Sartori, Giovanni. 1976. *Parties and Party Systems: A Framework for Analysis,* vol. 1. Cambridge: Cambridge University Press.

Sen, Amartya. 1988. "Freedom of Choice: Concept and Content." *European Economic Review* 32 (2–3): 269–94.

Snijders, Tom A.B., and Roel J. Bosker. 1999. *Multilevel Analysis: An Introduction to Basic and Advanced Multilevel Modeling*. London: Sage.

Steenbergen, Marco R., and Bradford S. Jones. 2002. "Modeling Multilevel Data Structures." *American Journal of Political Science* 46 (1): 218–37.

Taagepera, Rein, and Matthew Soberg Shugart. 1999. *Seats and Votes: The Effects and Determinants of Electoral Systems*. New Haven, CT: Yale University Press.

Tóka, Gábor. 1995. "Political Support in East-Central Europe." In *Citizens and the State*, edited by Hans-Dieter Klingemann and Dieter Fuch, chap. 12. New York: Oxford University Press.

Weßels, Bernhard. n.d. "Performance and Deficits of Present-Day representation." In *The Future of Representative Democracy*, edited by Sonia Alonso, Wolfgang Merkel, and John Kean, 96–123. Cambridge: Cambridge University Press.

Weßels, Bernhard, and Hermann Schmitt. 2008. "Meaningful Choices, Political Supply and Institutional Effectiveness." *Electoral Studies* 27 (1): 19–30.

10 Party Strategies, Institutions, and Electoral System Effects

ROMAIN LACHAT

1. Introduction

We know at least since the classical study of Duverger (1951) that electoral systems influence the distribution of seats as well as the behaviour of parties and voters. Political actors anticipate the consequences of the rules used to transform the votes cast into seats (Cox 1997; Lijphart 1994). Three effects of electoral systems usually are distinguished: a mechanical effect and two psychological effects. The *mechanical effect* of an electoral system is a direct consequence of the electoral formula. Depending on the distribution of votes and on the degree of proportionality of the electoral formula, the share of seats received by each party in competition will match more or less closely its share of votes. Given the limited number of seats to be distributed, however, even the most proportional electoral system will create disparities, with some parties receiving a disproportionally high share of seats, and others receiving less seats than votes or even no seats at all. This mechanical effect leads voters and parties to strategically adapt their behaviour. This is reflected in two indirect electoral system effects. The *psychological effect on voters* means that some citizens will vote in a strategic way.[1] They will avoid wasting their votes by not supporting parties or candidates who have no real chances of winning a seat (Alvarez and Nagler 2000; Blais et al. 2001). The *psychological effect on parties*, finally, means that some parties will refrain from entering the race and spending resources in electoral districts in which their chances of success are too thin. The general expectation formulated in the literature is that less proportional electoral systems have stronger effects. That is, a less proportional electoral system will lead to more parties deciding not to enter the race, to more frequent strategic desertion from non-viable parties, and to larger disparities between the distributions of votes and seats.

Although these effects have been known for quite a long time, research has long been hampered by the difficulties of identifying and quantifying these effects. This is particularly true of the "elusive" psychological effects on voters and parties (Blais and Carty 1991; Clark and Golder 2006). However, Blais et al. (2011) have suggested a methodology for disentangling and measuring the three effects of electoral systems. This method is based on the comparison of parallel elections that differ only in the electoral system used. It allows determining how differences in the partisan distribution of seats between the two elections can be attributed to a psychological effect on parties, on voters, or on the mechanical effect of the electoral system.

This new approach offers interesting possibilities for measuring electoral system effects.

Furthermore, as the effects are measured using the same metric, their size can be compared to one another. Most important, this methodology also offers new possibilities for explaining differences in the size of electoral system effects. Several studies have already dealt with the size of the mechanical effect, which can be more easily quantified, using, for instance, a measure of the disproportionality of the allocation of seats, compared to the distribution of votes (e.g., Gallagher 1991; Lijphart 1990). But quantitative analyses dealing with all three effects and with their relative importance are largely missing so far.

This chapter analyses electoral system effects in Switzerland, which is one of the two countries on the basis of which the methodology of Blais et al. (2011) was developed.

The focus is on the difference between the outcomes of the election of the lower house (National Council) and upper house (Council of States) of the Swiss federal parliament, in the nine elections that took place from 1971 to 2003. For both councils, the electoral districts correspond to the twenty-six cantons, the units of the federal state. The National Council is elected with a PR system, for which district magnitude ranges from one to thirty-five. The Council of States election is a two-round majority election, with districts of magnitude one or two. The two elections differ only in the electoral system used. The two houses of the federal parliament have exactly the same powers, and the same citizens have the right to vote in both elections (Kriesi and Trechsel 2008; Lachat 2006). Any difference between the two outcomes can thus be attributed to an effect of the electoral system.[2]

Several possible explanations for the relative size of the electoral system effects will be investigated. I will first consider the relations between the three partial effects, that is, the degree to which the strength of one electoral system effect depends on the strength of the others. Second, I will focus on the role of institutional and strategic factors. I will test hypotheses about the role of district magnitude, about the presence of incumbents and of small party challengers, and about differences in the degree of coordination of left-wing and right-wing parties. The rest of this chapter is structured as follows. The method used to measure the total effect of the electoral system and its three components is introduced in section 2. Section 3 discusses the hypotheses about the effects of district magnitude and of the partisan configuration of candidates. The empirical results are presented in the following three sections. First, descriptive results about the distribution of the electoral system effects are introduced in section 4. Section 5 discusses the relation among the electoral system effects. Finally, the hypotheses about the role of institutional and partisan factors are tested in section 6.

2. Measuring Electoral System Effects

This study aims to explain the difference in the outcome of two parallel elections, which differ from one another only in the electoral system used. Taking the PR election of the National Council as the reference point, the electoral system effect is defined as the effect on the election outcome of using a majority rule and small districts rather than a PR rule with districts of varying magnitude. That is, the effect of the majoritarian electoral system is defined not in comparison with a hypothetical perfectly proportional system, but by comparing its outcome with that of another, more proportional electoral system.

The majoritarian electoral system of the Council of States elections leads to a concentration of votes and seats on a smaller number of parties, compared to the outcome of the National Council election. Following the logic of Duverger, three partial effects can be distinguished: a psychological effect on parties, a psychological effect on voters, and a mechanical effect. To better understand how these three partial effects can be disentangled and measured, it is important to emphasize two important properties. First, the effects are sequential, that is, they take place one after the other and not simultaneously. Second, they influence other aspects of the electoral process.

The sequence of electoral system effects is presented in figure 10.1. The difference between the outcomes of the two elections corresponds to the total effect of the electoral system. This total effect is the cumulative result of three partial effects. First in the sequence is the psychological effect on parties. It takes place before votes are cast and it influences the number of parties in competition. The majoritarian electoral system of the Council of States election is less permissive, meaning that it makes it more difficult for small parties to gain representation. As a consequence, some parties who compete for the National Council will prefer not to do so for the Council of States.

The second effect is the psychological effect on voters. It takes place at the moment of the vote and influences how votes are distributed. Some supporters of parties who have only weak chances of winning a seat in the Council of States will prefer supporting another candidate, choosing from among the viable candidates. The psychological effect on voters should thus lead to a concentration of votes on the front-runners. Last of all, the mechanical effect takes place after votes were cast. It influences how votes are transformed into seats. The majoritarian electoral system should lead to larger disparities between parties' shares of votes and their shares of seats. In the Council of States election, only

Figure 10.1 Sequence of Psychological and Mechanical Effects

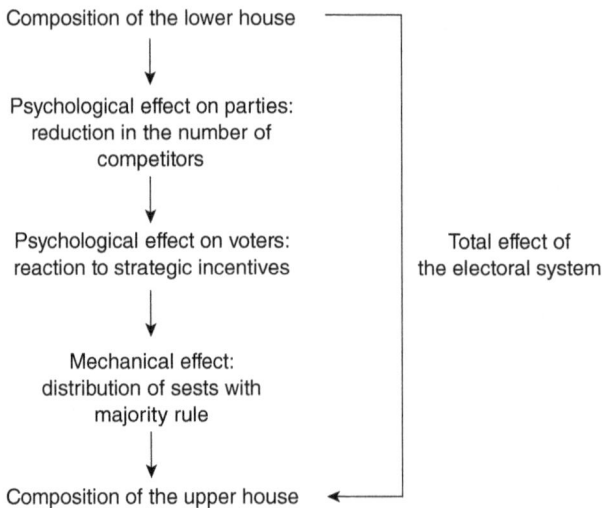

Composition of the lower house

↓

Psychological effect on parties:
reduction in the number of
competitors

↓

Psychological effect on voters:
reaction to strategic incentives

Total effect of
the electoral system

↓

Mechanical effect:
distribution of sests with
majority rule

↓

Composition of the upper house

one or two parties will win a seat in a given canton, and all others will receive none.

In order to be able to compare more easily the various electoral system effects with one another, they must be expressed using the same metric. Blais et al. (2011) suggest expressing each effect as a change in the effective number of parliamentary parties (ENPP; Laakso and Taagepera 1979). This is relatively straightforward as far as the total effect is concerned: to compare the outcomes of the two elections, one can summarize the distribution of seats in each council using the ENPP, and take the difference between these two figures:

Total effect = ENPPnonpr – ENPPpr

To measure the mechanical effect, one needs to compare the outcome of the Council of States election (i.e., after all three partial effects played their role) with the outcome that would have resulted from having both psychological effects but no mechanical effect. The latter hypothetical outcome corresponds to distributing the Council of States votes with the electoral formula and districts of the PR election. Following the notation of Blais et al. (2011), the latter outcome is called simulation 1.

Mechanical effect = ENPPnonpr – ENPPsim1

It follows that the total psychological effect (the sum of the psychological effects on both parties and voters) is equal to the difference between the total effect and the mechanical one, which can be expressed as

Total psychological effect = ENPPsim1 – ENPPpr

Next, the psychological effect on voters corresponds again to the difference between two (hypothetical) electoral outcomes: when voters respond to strategic incentives and when they do not. Both of these outcomes are derived from a regression model of the votes received by the various parties competing in the Council of States election. Parties' vote shares are regressed on their electoral strength in the PR election of the National Council, on their viability in a majoritarian election, and on an interaction term between the two. Using this regression model, one can predict parties' vote shares under two scenarios: when citizens respond to parties' viability (simulation 2), that is, when the psychological effect on voters plays, and when all parties are considered to be viable (simulation 3), that is, cancelling the psychological effect on voters. These votes are then transformed into seats using the rules of the PR election. The corresponding distributions of seats are summarized with the ENPP, which allows computing the effect on voters:

Psychological effect on voters = ENPPsim2 – ENPPsim3

The psychological effect on parties, finally, corresponds simply to the difference between the total psychological effect and the effect on voters:

Psychological effect on parties = (ENPPsim1 – ENPPpr)
                                         – (ENPPsim2 – ENPPsim3)

The method and data used to compute these effects are identical to those of Blais et al. (2011), who also offer a more detailed presentation of the method. The results from the regression model used to perform simulations 2 and 3 can be found in the same article.[3]

These estimated electoral system effects can be conceived of in both absolute and relative terms. In absolute terms, they simply express the corresponding change in the effective number of parties. The total effect in a given electoral district and election could, for instance, be of reducing the effective number of parties by 3. This effect corresponds to the sum of the three partial effects. These could take different values, for instance a reduction of 1.5 parties due to the psychological effect on parties, of 0.5 parties due to the effect on voters, with the rest being a consequence of the mechanical effect.

When expressed in relative terms, the effects correspond to the proportion of the total effect explained by the corresponding partial effect. In the above example, the effect on parties would represent half of the total effect, the effect on voters 17 per cent and the mechanical effect 33 per cent. In relative terms, thus, the three partial effects sum by definition to one. Both absolute and relative effects are useful and they allow answering different questions, as we will see below. All this is relatively straightforward, but one small complication must be emphasized: as will be shown below in the presentation of the results, the estimated electoral system effects can sometimes be positive, that is, in the opposite direction of the total effect. This may appear to be counterintuitive and I will offer below some examples and additional explanations to show why this can happen. For the purpose of computing relative electoral system effects, however, I have simply set positive effects to 0. Positive effects then have a relative effect of 0 (they do not contribute at all to the total reduction in the effective number of parties). When partial effects are negative, which happens in the vast majority of cases, their relative impact is computed as their size divided by the sum of all negative effects.[4]

3. Explaining Electoral System Effects

The goal of this chapter is to analyse the role of a series of factors likely to influence the size of electoral system effects. Three types of explanatory factors will be considered. First, I will look at the relations among effects, that is, the degree to which earlier effects constrain or influence subsequent effects. Second, the role of electoral institutions will be considered. In the Swiss context, the most important institutional variable is district magnitude: it varies considerably in the PR election of the National Council while being almost constant in the majoritarian election of the Council of States. Third, the chapter will consider the role of party strategies and of the partisan configuration of candidates. As the latter factors already are part of the effect on parties, this last series of analyses will be limited to how these variables affect voters and the mechanical effect of the electoral system.

3.1 Relation among Effects

As mentioned above, the effects are sequential. This is likely to lead to strong relations among the three partial effects. The size of the psychological effect on parties, for instance, should constrain the size of the subsequent effects. If parties strongly respond to the anticipated mechanical effect, so that no weak candidate takes part in the majoritarian election, the further effects can only be small. In more general terms, one would expect that there is less room for subsequent effects if previous effects are strong. This hypothesis may appear to be relatively trivial, and it would indeed be quite surprising to find no such relationship. However, some questions remain open. For instance, it is a priori unclear if the effect on parties constrains both the effect on voters and the mechanical effect, or only one of these. Also, when focusing on absolute effects, rather than relative ones, the relation among electoral system effects may or may not be strong. In some cantons, all effects could be large, while in others, they could all be small.

3.2 *District Magnitude*

The second type of explanatory factor that will be considered is district magnitude. There is much variation in this respect between the electoral districts. As mentioned above, district magnitude for the National Council election varies from one to thirty-five. In the Council of States election, most cantons have two seats, while a few cantons have a single seat. This means that in some cantons there a large differences in district magnitude between the PR and the majoritarian election, while in other cantons the difference is small. This variation allows testing the impact of district magnitude on the size of electoral system effects. To this end, I start from the *difference* between the PR district magnitude and the majoritarian district magnitude. This difference is positive in most cases, as district magnitude is normally larger in the PR election than in the majoritarian one. But it is equal to 0 in a few cases, and even negative (–1) in one case. The latter is for a canton that has two seats in the upper house but a single one in the lower house.[5] As the distribution of this difference is strongly asymmetric (mean value 8.6 with the median at 6), I take its logarithm (after having added 2 to all values in order to have only positive values).

As proportionality and the fear of wasted votes are the factors that drive electoral systems effects, the difference in the district magnitude of the two elections should have a strong effect. Here, too, it would be surprising to find no relation. The larger the difference in the magnitude of the districts, the stronger should be the absolute electoral system effects. However, it is an open question as to which of the effects is most strongly influenced by district magnitude. That is, it is more difficult to formulate a clear hypothesis about the impact of district magnitude on the *relative* electoral system effects. It could be, for instance, that parties strongly react to district magnitude but that voters do so only to a lesser extent.

3.3 *Party Supply*

The third group of explanatory factors pertains to the type and configuration of parties that compete in the election of the Council of States. As this is a consequence of parties' decision to enter or not to enter this race, it forms part of the psychological effect on parties. As a consequence, such factors can be considered only when explaining subsequent electoral system effects, that is, the effect on voters and the mechanical effect. The first relevant characteristic of the partisan configuration is the presence and number of incumbents. Incumbency sends voters a strong signal about the viability of a candidate. When one or both of the councillors of states decide not to run again, it may be more difficult for voters to know which of the candidates are viable. Accordingly, I expect the psychological effect on voters to be smaller – and the mechanical effect to be larger – when one or both of the incumbents decide not to compete for an additional mandate.

The second relevant aspect of the party configuration is the presence of small challengers. The upper house of the Swiss parliament is largely dominated by the main four Swiss parties: the Social Democratic Party (SPS), the Christian Democratic Party (CVP), the Liberal Party (FDP), and the Swiss People's Party (SVP). These four parties formed the federal government from 1959 to 2008. In the elections considered in this article, these parties won all but one or two seats in the Council of States. Nonetheless, challengers from smaller parties are often competing in this election. I expect the presence of small party challengers to increase the relative importance of the psychological effect on voters, compared to the mechanical effect.

When only candidates from large parties are running, it may be quite difficult for voters to sort out viable from non-viable candidates. By contrast, when candidates who are clearly non-viable in a majoritarian election also enter the race, these candidates should be recognized more easily by citizens. The variable used to capture this aspect of the partisan configuration simply counts how many candidates in the Council of States election are from a party other than the main four parties.[6]

Finally, I consider the degree of coordination in the various political camps. In particular, I look at differences between the left-wing and right-wing camps. There are strong incentives for parties of similar ideological orientation to coordinate around common candidatures. In most cantons, it is for instance virtually impossible for left-wing parties to claim both seats. If two left-wing candidates enter the race, the chances that any of them will win a seat will be reduced. Such coordination failures are all the more important when they are unilateral. That is, if left-wing parties coordinate successfully but right-wing parties do not, the latter will be in a more difficult position, as they face the risk that the votes from their supporters will be divided between several candidates (Kriesi 1998a, 1998b). However, this situation may also strengthen the incentives for strategic voting. In the situation sketched above, right-wing supporters may recognize the increased need for strategic voting and concentrate on the stronger candidates from their political camp. Accordingly, I expect a unilateral coordination failure to reinforce the psychological effect on voters.

To identify such cases of "coordination failures," I start from the difference between the number of left-wing candidates and the number of right-wing candidates in each canton and each election year. I then take the median value of this difference in each canton. In some cantons, for instance, right-wing parties usually present two candidates and left-wing parties a single one, resulting in a median difference of 1. In other cantons, both left-wing parties and right-wing parties usually present two candidates, leading to a median difference of 0. In other words, this gives me the "baseline" or usual difference between the numbers of candidates presented by each camp. Then, for each canton/election, I compute how the left-right difference differs from the baseline. Take, for example, the canton of Neuchatel. In most elections, there were an equal number of candidates on the left and on the right, resulting in a median difference of 0. In 1999, however, six left-wing candidates entered the race, against only two right-wing candidates. This indicates a strong coordination failure on the left: the difference between the two camps in the number of candidates was higher than the median difference by a value of 4.

4. The Distribution of Electoral System Effects

The analyses are divided into three parts. First, I discuss some descriptive results on the distribution of absolute and relative electoral system effects. Second, I turn to the question of how effects constrain each other. Finally, I present results on the effects of both district magnitude and the partisan configuration of candidates.

Figure 10.2 summarizes the distribution of the total effect of the electoral system and of its three components. The left-hand panel shows the distribution of absolute effects, and the right-hand panel of relative effects. Considering first absolute effects, one can note a substantial variation in the size of the total effect (the fourth boxplot in the left-hand panel). It ranges from a value of 0 to a value of −5. A value of 0 corresponds to the weakest possible effect. It means that the effective number of parties in a given canton/year is the same in both houses of the parliament, despite the difference in the electoral system. The strongest effect observed is a reduction of five effective parties between the National Council and the Council of States. The median value is −1.6.

Figure 10.2 Distribution of Absolute and Relative Electoral System Effects

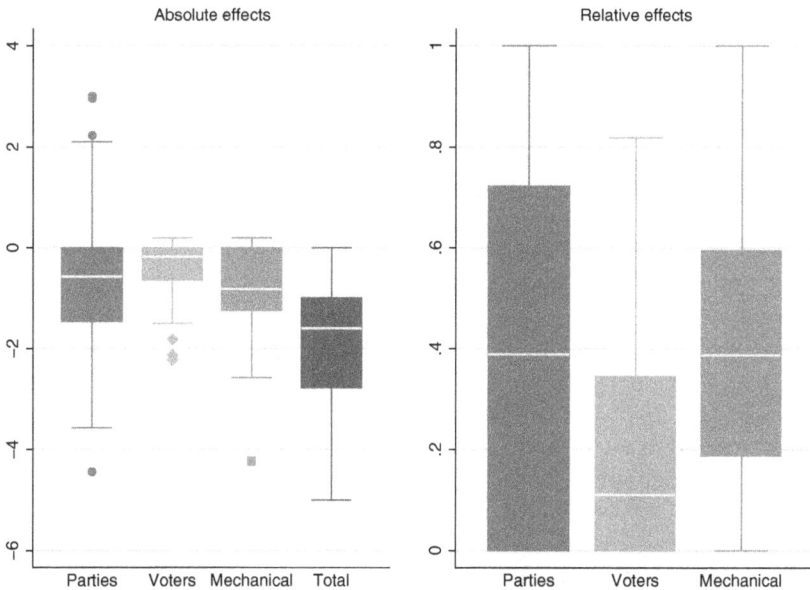

Based on the median values of the effects, the strongest of the partial effects is the mechanical one (−0.8), followed by the psychological effects on parties (−0.6) and the effect on voters (−0.2). The distribution of the partial effects expressed in relative terms, in the right-hand panel, confirms that the psychological effect on voters contributes least to explaining the smaller number of effective parties observed in the Council of States. At the same time, this figure shows considerable variation across cantons and elections in the relative importance of the three partial effects. For each of them, there are cases in which they do not contribute at all to the total electoral system effect. On the other hand, there are cases in which the entire electoral system effect is due either to the psychological effect on parties or to the mechanical effect.

Apart from the strong variation in the size of effects, another striking result in figure 10.2 is that the partial effects can be positive. This finding may be counterintuitive and it requires some explanation. The estimated effects show the difference in terms of the ENPP resulting from the use of a majoritarian system (with small districts) rather than a PR system (with districts of varying magnitude). One would expect the effective number of parties always to be smaller (or at least not to be larger) under a majoritarian rule, as this system leads to a concentration of votes and seats on the strongest competitors. While this is the case for the total effect, its components may in some cases work in opposite directions.

Consider first the mechanical effect. This is the simplest case, as it involves only a change of the seat allocation rule, based on the same distribution of votes. While this effect has the expected negative value in most cases, it is positive in 13 out of 145 cases. The largest value is an increase in the ENPP of 0.2 in the canton of Schwyz in the 1991, 1995, and 1999 elections. That is, the effective number of parties is higher with the majoritarian rule (and two seats) than if the Council of States votes had been distributed using the same rules as for the National Council election, that is, a PR rule with a district magnitude of 3. In the Council of States election, votes were heavily concentrated on the main three candidates, two from the CVP and one from the FDP. The ENPP in the upper chamber was equal to 2, as each of these parties received one seat. But with a PR rule, the CVP would have won two of the three seats, and the FDP one, resulting in a smaller ENPP of 1.8. The use of a PR electoral rule would thus have decreased the effective number of parties, compared to the majoritarian rule and a slightly smaller district magnitude.

Psychological effects also can be positive. For the effect on voters, this happens however in only two cases: Thurgau in 1971 and Luzern in 1975. In both cases, the psychological effect on parties was already so strong that only the two front-runners presented candidates for the Council of States. In both of those cases, the distribution of votes simulated by cancelling the impact of strategic factors led to a slightly higher share of votes for the strongest party, which reduces the ENPP (from about 2 to 1.8 in both cases). Positive values are more frequent for the psychological effect on parties (40 out of 145 cases), and a few of them are relatively large. Such positive effects are most likely to occur when some large parties refrain from presenting any candidate for the Council of States, while many small parties decide to do so (see Blais et al. 2011). This type of configuration has become particularly frequent in recent elections. It implies an increase in the effective number of parties, because small parties would benefit from the withdrawal of some of the major competitors. This situation, of course, is in reality compensated for later by the psychological effect on voters and by the mechanical effect, which will both reduce the effective number of parties.

5. Relations among Effects

Having presented some descriptive statistics on the distribution of the effects, I can now turn to the first part of the analysis, considering the relations among effects. Table 10.1 presents the correlations among both absolute and relative effects. As expected, the effects are related to one another. But there are important differences in the strength of these associations. It is more interesting to consider the associations between the relative effects. One would expect strong negative relations: when one effect is larger, there is less room for further effects to influence the distribution of votes and seats. Such relations can be observed with respect to the first effect in the sequence, that is, the effect on parties. The larger the effect on parties, the weaker the effect on voters and the mechanical effect. The association between the effect on voters and the mechanical effect, by contrast, is not significant. A larger effect on voters does not necessarily imply a weaker mechanical effect. This means that voters do not compensate entirely for the lack of coordination among parties. A large effect on voters is possible only when the effect on parties is relatively weak, that is, when parties without realistic electoral chances nonetheless decide to field candidates for the upper house election. In such a situation, voters' response to strategic incentives is more consequential, but not to the point of making the mechanical effect irrelevant.

Table 10.1 Correlations among Absolute and Relative Effects

	Total	Parties	Voters
Absolute effects ($N = 145$)			
Parties	0.62***		
Voters	0.07	−0.64***	
Mechanical	0.46***	−0.37***	0.59***
Relative effects ($N = 139$)			
Voters	–	−0.69***	
Mechanical	–	−0.84***	0.18*

$^*p < 0.05$; $^{**}p < 0.01$; $^{***}p < 0.001$

6. Impact of Institutions and Party Strategies

The first potential explanatory factor to be considered is related to the institutional context: it is the (log of the) difference between the district magnitude for the PR election and the district magnitude for the majoritarian election. Table 10.2 shows how this difference is related to the size of the electoral system effects. First, one can notice a negative association with the total effect. This is not surprising and just confirms a general property of electoral system effects. The decrease in the ENPP resulting from using a majoritarian rather than a proportional electoral system is all the more important, as the district magnitude of the PR election is large. Also, the first column in table 10.2, which shows the associations with the *absolute* partial effects, reveals that the associations are negative. Again, this was to be expected.

More interesting are the relations between district magnitude and the *relative* effects, shown in the right-hand column of table 10.2. In cantons with larger districts for the National Council election, the effect on parties represents a smaller part of the total effect, while the mechanical effect represents a larger part. The relative importance of the effect on voters, by contrast, does not appear to vary systematically with district magnitude. These results point to a difference in the nature of electoral system effects between smaller and larger cantons. In small cantons, i.e., cantons with a limited number of seats in both councils, the number of parties that can gain representation is limited. This is likely to reduce the coordination problems in the various political camps and is therefore linked with a stronger partisan effect. In large cantons, by contrast,

Table 10.2 Correlations between the Seats Difference (Log) and the Electoral System Effects

	Absolute effects	Relative effects
Total effect	−0.59***	
Psychological effect on parties	−0.12	−0.26**
Psychological effect on voters	−0.26**	0.10
Mechanical effect	−0.57***	0.28***
N	145	139

*$p < 0.05$; **$p < 0.01$; ***$p < 0.001$

the larger number of parties competing in the PR election makes coordination more difficult. Even parties that have virtually no chances of success in the upper chamber may still decide to compete, in order to be more visible and to try to increase their electoral prospects in the parallel PR election (Kriesi 1998a). This relatively weaker effect on parties in larger district is compensated mainly by a larger mechanical effect – but not by a larger effect on voters. While larger districts are characterized by larger electoral effects in absolute terms, the relative importance of the psychological effects is smaller.

Turning to the role of partisan factors, table 10.3 shows the average relative effects for different configurations of incumbents and challengers. In cantons with a single seat, I distinguish the cases where the incumbent is running again and those where he or she does not. In cantons with two seats in the upper house, the effects are summarized separately for elections with zero, one, or two incumbents. The presence of incumbents increases the relative size of the psychological effect on parties. In cantons with a single seat in the upper chamber, the effect on parties accounts for 57 per cent of the total effect when the incumbent is not running again, and this effect increases to 83 per cent when the incumbent runs for an additional mandate. In the latter situation, there is very little room left for the other effects. An incumbent running again apparently sends a strong signal to the other parties, and many of them refrain from entering the race.

Table 10.3 Average Total Effect and Average Relative Effects by Number of Incumbents

	Total	Parties	Voters	Mechanical	n
Cantons with 1 seat					
No incumbent	−2.28	0.57	0.21	0.21	6
1 incumbent	−2.52	0.83	0.03	0.14	19
Cantons with 2 seats					
No incumbent	−1.84	0.26	0.23	0.50	12
1 incumbent	−1.83	0.29	0.24	0.46	47
2 incumbents	−1.76	0.44	0.17	0.40	61

A similar effect can be observed in cantons with two seats in the Council of States. The effect on parties makes up a larger share of the total effect when both incumbents are running again than when none of them is running again. The increase in the relative size of the psychological effect on parties (from 26 to 44 per cent) is even larger than in the first group of cantons.

The other two characteristics of the partisan configuration are the presence and number of candidates from small parties, on the one hand, and coordination failures among left-wing or right-wing parties, on the other. I expected both of these variables to reinforce the psychological effect on voters, compared to the mechanical effect. As both hypotheses are based on a similar logic, I will discuss the corresponding results simultaneously. Table 10.4 presents the size of the electoral system effects for different numbers of candidates from small parties, and table 10.5 presents the same type of results for different "coordination differentials" between the main two political camps. As explained above, both a larger number of small party candidates and a unilateral coordination failure mean that the effect on parties has been smaller. It is thus simply logical to observe that these variables are very strongly related with the relative importance of the psychological effect on parties.

The interesting results are those pertaining to the effect on voters and to the mechanical effect. When the relative effect on parties becomes smaller, both subsequent effects become larger. The psychological effect on voters, however, is more strongly influenced. It is quite small when no small party fields a candidate in the upper house election (representing 10 per cent of the total effect, table 10.4) or when both political camps are equally coordinated (accounting then for 15 per cent of the total effect, table 10.5). Yet it increases rapidly as small party candidates enter the race or as coordination failures become more evident. In every case, it remains smaller than the mechanical effect. As we have already

Table 10.4 Average Total Effect and Average Relative Effects by Number of Small Party Candidates

Candidates from small parties	Total	Parties	Voters	Mechanical	n
0	−1.75	0.63	0.10	0.27	73
1	−1.88	0.31	0.21	0.48	38
2 or more	−2.28	0.15	0.32	0.53	34

Table 10.5 Average Total Effect and Average Relative Effects by Coordination Differential between Left-Wing and Right-Wing Camps

Absolute difference from median	Total	Parties	Voters	Mechanical	n
0	−1.84	0.49	0.15	0.36	96
1	−2.09	0.36	0.22	0.42	41
2 or more	−1.82	0.14	0.32	0.54	8

seen before, the effect on voters generally is weaker than the other electoral system effects. But it comes closer to the mechanical effect in situations that make strategic voting easier. In table 10.4, for instance, we see that the effect on voters is almost three times smaller than the mechanical effect when small parties keep out of the majoritarian election.

In contrast, when two or more small party candidates compete, the mechanical effect is "only" about one and a half times larger than the effect on voters. A similar increase in the relative importance of the psychological effect on voters can be observed in table 10.5, when comparing races with and without coordination failures.

7. Conclusion

The method proposed by Blais et al. (2011) to quantify electoral system opens up new possibilities for examining how parties and citizens react to the strategic incentives linked with different electoral rules. Although this method is limited to the special case of having two parallel elections based on different electoral systems, it represents an interesting opportunity for analysing which factors may influence the relative importance of the three electoral system effects, that is, the psychological effects on parties and voters, as well as the mechanical effect. This chapter focused on the case of Switzerland in order to estimate how these effects were influenced by district magnitude as well as by various characteristics of the configuration of parties in competition. In the Swiss context, the effects on voters and parties and the mechanical effect can be measured by contrasting the outcome of the National Council election, based on a PR system with districts of varying magnitude, with that of the Council of States election, involving a majoritarian election with small districts. The analysis of these elections in 1971–2003 has shown that both the effect on parties and the mechanical effect are strong, while the psychological effect on voters is comparatively less important. Parties and voters do anticipate the effects of the majoritarian rule used in the Council of States election. Some parties refrain from presenting candidates in that election, and voters tend to concentrate on the more viable parties. However, these psychological effects account only for a part of the total effect of the electoral system. The psychological effect on voters, in particular, appears to be relatively limited. It is also less strongly related to the effect on parties than is the mechanical effect. The effect on parties is weak when many non-viable parties compete in the majoritarian election, leaving more room for subsequent effects to influence the electoral outcomes. But the relative importance of the mechanical effect increases more strongly than that of the psychological effect on voters. Citizens' limited capacity to compensate for a weak effect on parties was also evident from the analysis of the role of district magnitude. In cantons with a larger number of seats in the lower house, more parties tend to compete for both the National Council and the Council of States. The psychological effect on parties is thus negatively related with district magnitude. While this means there are more opportunities for citizens to vote in a strategic way by deserting weak candidates, the relative importance of the effect on parties does not significantly vary with district magnitude.

On the other hand, the analysis of the role of partisan factors has revealed that voters do respond to specific strategic situations. The psychological effect on voters is clearly stronger when small parties field candidates in the majoritarian election of the upper house. Similarly, the impact of strategic voting is more pronounced when left-wing or right-wing parties fail to coordinate on a small number of common candidatures. In both situations, the configuration of parties in competition makes it easier for citizens to identify non-viable candidates or reinforces the incentives to defect from such non-viable candidates. Voters do respond to this type of strategic incentives, increasing the relative importance of the psychological effect on voters, compared to the mechanical effect.

NOTES

1 The next chapter systematically reviews the factors that lead to variation in this rate of strategic voting.
2 Some cases – that is, canton by year combinations – were however excluded from the analysis because of additional differences between the two

elections. This pertains to cantons that use a different electoral system for the upper house election (different electoral rule or elections in a popular assembly or through the cantonal parliament) and to cantons in which the elections take place on different days.

3 A step-by-step example of the method can be found in the online appendix of Blais et al. (2011), http://www.romain-lachat.ch/cps_2011/index.html.

4 In the rare event that all effects are equal to zero, relative effects are set to missing.

5 In this case, as well as in the five cantons/years in which district magnitude is the same in both elections, the total electoral system effect turns out to be equal to zero.

6 I made one exception to this rule. In the canton of Zurich, the League of Independents (LdU) won a seat in the Council of States in five of the nine elections under study. As a consequence I did not count the LdU candidate as a small party candidate in that canton.

References

Alvarez, R. Michael, and Jonathan Nagler. 2000. "A New Approach for Modelling Strategic Voting in Multiparty Elections." *British Journal of Political Science* 30 (1): 57–75.

Blais, André, and R.K. Carty. 1991. "The Psychological Impact of Electoral Laws: Measuring Duverger's Elusive Factor." *British Journal of Political Science* 21 (1): 79–93.

Blais, André, Romain Lachat, Airo Hino, and Pascal Doray-Demers. 2011. "The Mechanical and Psychological Effects of Electoral Systems: A Quasi-Experimental Study." *Comparative Political Studies* 44 (12): 1599–621.

Blais, André, Richard Nadeau, Elisabeth Gidengil, and Neil Nevitte. 2001. "Measuring Strategic Voting in Multiparty Plurality Elections." *Electoral Studies* 20:343–52.

Clark, William Roberts, and Matt Golder. 2006. "Rehabilitating Duverger's Theory: Testing the Mechanical and Strategic Modifying Effects of Electoral Laws." *Comparative Political Studies* 39 (6): 679–708.

Cox, Gary W. 1997. *Making Votes Count: Strategic Coordination in the World's Electoral Systems*. Cambridge: Cambridge University Press.

Duverger, Maurice. 1951. *Les partis politiques*. Paris: Seuil.

Gallagher, Michael. 1991. "Proportionality, Disproportionality and Electoral Systems." *Electoral Studies* 10 (1): 33–51.

Kriesi, Hanspeter. 1998a. "Straightforward and Strategic Voting in the Elections for the Swiss Council of States in 1995." *Electoral Studies* 17 (1): 45–59.

– 1998b. "Wählen aus Überzeugung und strategisches Wählen bei den Ständeratswahlen 1995." In *Schweizer Wahlen 1995*, edited by Hanspeter Kriesi, Wolf Linder, and Ulrich Klöti, 193–218. Bern: Haupt.

Kriesi, Hanspeter, and Alexander H. Trechsel. 2008. *The Politics of Switzerland: Continuity and Change in a Consensus Democracy.* Cambridge: Cambridge University Press.

Laakso, Markku, and Rein Taagepera. 1979. "'Effective' Number of Parties: A Measure with Application to West Europe." *Comparative Political Studies* 12 (1): 3–27.

Lachat, Romain. 2006. "A Tale of Two Councils: Explaining the Weakness of the SVP in the Upper House of the Federal Parliament." *Schweizerische Zeitschrift für Politikwissenschaft* 12 (4): 77–99.

Lijphart, Arend. 1990. "The Political Consequences of Electoral Laws, 1945–1985." *American Political Science Review* 84 (2): 481–96.

– 1994. *Electoral Systems and Party Systems.* Oxford: Oxford University Press.

11 When Do Voters Act Strategically? Institutional and Individual Variation in the Incidence of Strategic Voting in Democracies

JOHN ALDRICH AND LAURA B. STEPHENSON

The single most obvious observation that flows from the earliest survey research on voting (Berelson, Lazarsfeld and McPhee 1954; Lazarsfeld, Berelson, and Gaudet 1944; Campbell et al. 1960) is that voters tend to be remarkably ill-informed about the fundamentals of politics, and, as Converse famously showed (1964), they are often perceived to be what has become known as "innocent" of ideology. While there is variation to that, the basic outlines of these points are invariably true across the decades and among nations.

It seems a short step from those observations to the claim that the voter is best understood as making very simple decisions using very simple decision rules (as suggested by Kelley and Mirer 1974), quite different from the complex reasoning attributed to candidates, party leaders, and the like. One reason, for example, that rational choice models of politics are often thought more appropriate and useful for studying the actions and choices of the political elite is that game theoretic and strategic decision-making seem more at home with those whose livelihoods depend upon the outcome than with those who are mostly inattentive to the day-to-day workings of politics.

And yet economic theory often treats consumers as strategic actors. Should we expect citizens to act strategically as consumers but to totally disavow acting to advance their interests as voters? Perhaps we should, because, after all, livelihoods do depend in part on consumption decisions. Conversely, however, game theoretic models are meant to apply to conventional, regular, small-scale actions such as daily purchases of bread and milk. Is that really all that different from decisions about casting a vote in a media-rich national election?

258 Duty and Choice

Indeed, strategic voting (sometimes referred to as "sophisticated voting") is one such case in which theorists (e.g., Duverger 1963; Cox 1997), empiricists (e.g., Black 1978; Cain 1978; Abramson et al. 1992; Stephenson, Aldrich, and Blais 2018), and non-academic observers (journalists seeing the avoidance of "wasted voting" by the public) find at least relatively rudimentary forms of strategic reasoning in the public's voting choices. Most of the time, this reasoning is indeed seen in a simple strategic environment. Most of the time, that is, it is seen in the actions of voters in a predominately two-party system embedded (not coincidentally) in first-past-the-post (FPTP) systems. And theory does show that the nature of strategic choices in two-party, FPTP systems, and especially in plurality systems in particular, as we have in the cases we use, is quite straightforward to discover and easy to implement. As Niou (2001) and Kselman and Niou (2010) show, in a plurality system strategic voters always vote for their most preferred party if it is in first or second place and will defect from their most preferred party only if it is in third place or lower, to avoid wasting their vote where it cannot make a difference in determining who wins or loses. Perhaps, then, voters *can* reason, but only under the highly stylized and simplified setting of two-party elections in plurality systems.

Yet we know that plurality is not the only electoral system vulnerable to strategic reasoning. Theoretically, as Gibbard (1973) and Satterthwaite (1975) have shown, all systems are vulnerable to strategic reasoning. Systems do vary in the ease with which such reasoning can be understood and implemented, with plurality certainly at the easiest end of that continuum. But perhaps voters can figure out (possibly with assistance from parties and candidates) how to do so in other systems. Empirically, the system that seems to stand at the other end of the continuum, PR, appears just about as vulnerable to actual strategic reasoning by voters (see, for example, Abramson et al. 2010; Blais et al. 2006).

In this chapter we examine the incidence of strategic voting across nations, and thus across electoral and party systems.[1] We do so using Comparative Study of Electoral Systems (CSES) data. In this, we follow in the footsteps of Blais and Gschwend (2011), adding to and elaborating on their findings. Like them, we find that what appears to be strategic voting is quite widespread. And, like them, we find a mixture of individual and national variables affecting the incidence of strategic voting. We consider the effects of variables related to political sophistication and specific institutional features, and find that our results do not consistently align with our understanding of how voter behaviour should be influenced. We thus conclude with some intriguing puzzles that provide avenues for further research.

Our Empirical Measure of Strategic Voting

Blais and Gschwend (2011) study the effects of defecting from one's most preferred party for strategic reasons, by which they mean defecting from one's most preferred choice to win the immediate election for the purpose of seeking to achieve one's ends.[2] Their definition of a "strategic voter" is one in which voters consider both their preferences over parties and their expectations about outcomes. There are, therefore, two other sorts of voters.[3] One is the voter who votes only on the basis of preferences, known as the "sincere voter." The other bases the vote exclusively on expectations, ignoring her own preferences, which they call the "momentum voter." Their conservative approach is to count only those who defect from their party preference as clearly strategic, because those who vote for their most preferred party when it is running well in the polls might be doing so for either strategic reasons (choosing to support a front-runner) or sincere reasons (expressing a preference), as these two are observationally equivalent under those conditions, that is, predict the same empirical patterns.

Here we begin by examining four sets of voters, using the "rules" for strategic and sincere voting in FPTP found in Niou (2001) and Kselman and Niou (2010). A sincere voter is one who votes for the most preferred party, without considering any other information, including expectations. We categorize these voters as *Purely Sincere*. However, the largest possible set of sincere voters is all of those who voted for their most preferred party, including those for whom considering expectations made it still rational to vote sincerely (i.e., those who preferred one of the top two parties). We call this the *Total Sincere* set. Thus, in practice, the Purely Sincere group includes only those who prefer parties that are not one of the two largest, as only those voters are clearly not factoring expectations into their vote choice.

Conversely, those who "defected" from their most preferred party to support a leading (but lower-ranked) party to defeat an even lower-ranked leading party apparently defected so as to avoid wasting their vote. We call these voters – who are included in Blais and Gschwend's strategic defectors – the *Purely Strategic* set of voters. These voters are most certainly not sincere, because they did not vote for their most preferred party. But there are other voters who find it strategically wise, that is, rational, to vote for their most preferred party, because it may be the leading or second-leading party and voting for it is not wasting one's vote. Although these voters are strategic in that they take rational expectations into account, they have what is often referred to as a "straightforward decision" and are observationally indistinguishable from sincere voters. So if we add the total number who voted for their most preferred party that was in first or second place to the Purely Strategic set of voters, we have the largest number of voters who could have taken expectations into account and voted strategically. We call this the *Total Strategic* set.[4]

Like Blais and Gschwend (2011), we use data from module 2 of the CSES project. The CSES data include a common module of survey questions that are collected in post-election studies around the world. These individual-level data are augmented with district- and system-level information, such as the number of candidates that competed in a district and the electoral rules of the system. Thus, the data set is extremely rich and contains the ideal information for our project, as we are interested in understanding differences and similarities in individual-level behaviour across electoral and party systems.

In order to evaluate voter behaviour, we first need to understand preferences. We use the "feeling thermometer" evaluation of parties to create measures of preferences. With an eleven-point thermometer scale, we face the possibility of a number of ties in rank order, and we considered several procedures to deal with this issue. Here, we report data that exclude all ties for first preferences.[5]

We next turn to three sets of analyses.[6] First, we detail the proportion of respondents in each of the four categories detailed above (Purely Sincere, Purely Strategic, Total Sincere, and Total Strategic) and examine how the proportions vary across electoral systems. In particular, we consider the differences among Plurality, Majority, PR, and Mixed systems. We then look more closely at those who voted for their most preferred party, sorting by those who most preferred the largest, the second-largest, or a "third" party,[7] again comparing this cross tabulation across our four electoral systems. These two sets of analyses reveal the extent of similarity across systems. Finally, we turn to a multivariate analysis to consider how a range of individual- and institutional-level variables affects who votes strategically and sincerely.

Strategic and Sincere Voters

In table 11.1 we report the percentage of voters who are Purely Strategic, Purely Sincere, in the Total Sincere category, and in the Total Strategic category. Obviously many, those who most prefer one of the two largest parties and vote for that party, are in both of the latter two categories.[8] We report these percentages for voters within each of the electoral system types. Those who believe that voters are not capable of strategic reasoning at all will be disappointed by the observation of a small but significant number of voters who clearly are voting strategically. And those who believe that voters are capable of limited strategic reasoning, and therefore strategic voting is confined to plurality systems, will be disappointed to observe that purely strategic reasoning is no more common in plurality than in other electoral systems. Indeed, majority and mixed systems contain significantly more purely strategic voters.

Table 11.1 offers two important lessons. The most important is that there is a great deal of potentially sincere voting, but there is nearly as great an amount of potentially strategic voting, because the two "Total" categories are similar in size. Thus, how one understands and categorizes the observationally equivalent portions of the data has important consequences. Perhaps it is precisely because so many voters face choices that are identical, whether they reason sincerely or

Table 11.1 Strategic and (Total) Sincere Voting by Electoral System

Electoral system	% purely strategic	N	% purely sincere	N	% total strategic	N	% total sincere	N	Total N (by electoral system type)
Plurality	2.9	140	13.7	668	55.3	2688	66.1	3216	4864
Majority	5.3	84	7.0	111	56.7	905	58.4	932	1595
PR	2.7	596	18.8	4162	47.4	10503	63.5	14069	22164
Mixed	5.0	358	14.9	1076	43.4	3135	53.4	3853	7222
Total N	3.3	1178	16.8	6017	48.1	17231	61.6	22070	35845

Notes: Some voters (12,597, or 35.1%) did not fit into our classification scheme. "Total N" represents all voters who indicated their vote choice.

strategically, that this discipline has been able, for over a generation, to have one large stream of research concluding that voters are massively ill-informed and another, often using the same data, that concludes that voters cast strategic votes.

The second important finding in table 11.1 is that it is not obvious that institutional rules make a great deal of difference. This finding is tentative, and we move to examine this point more carefully and systematically next. It does, however, point to a genuine puzzle for strategic voting theory. The strategic voter appears to reason consistent with how the theory says he or she should in plurality systems, but also appears to reason just the same in PR and other non-plurality systems, and the theory does not sustain that (Aldrich, Blais, and Stephenson 2018). This point is assessed more fully in the next section.

Preferences and Choices

The empirical leverage in testing strategic voting theory in plurality systems comes from differentiating between supporters of the two largest parties and those supporting any "third" party. This is so because the first rationally do not differ from sincere voters in that they always should support their most preferred party. Conversely, those who support any "third" party might – but might not – rationally defect from their most preferred party and vote for another. Of course, this is not only the most theoretically interesting observation, it is also the most empirically interesting aspect of strategic voting, and it is therefore what the media focus on – for example, people defecting from supporting the Liberal Democrats in Britain in 2010 or from voting for Ralph Nader for U.S. president in 2000 to avoid casting a "wasted vote."

In table 11.2, we present the relationship between the percentage who reported voting for the party they preferred the most, depending upon whether that party was the largest party in that election, the second-largest, or stood behind first and second place. Most of the "action" is along the main diagonal, that is, most voters who most liked the largest party voted for it, similar to those who preferred the second-largest, and, as well, those who most liked some other party. Just shy of nine in ten who most liked one of the two largest parties voted for it, while about seven in ten who most liked some other party were faithful to it on Election Day. We can compare these results to theoretical

Table 11.2 Preference and Vote Choice

Most preferred party	Party voted for				
	Largest	Second-largest	Same other	Different other	N
Largest	86.9	4.3		8.8	10770
Second-largest	4.6	87.6		7.7	6582
Other	9.1	8.8	70.9	11.3	9795

expectations. If everyone were a sincere voter, then, absent measurement or some other random source of variation in voting report, 100 per cent of respondents would support their most preferred party. If everyone were a strategic voter, then only the first and second-largest parties would have such high levels of support, as defections should rationally occur among those who most prefer some other party, at least in plurality electoral systems. Indeed, nearly 20 per cent of the set of voters who most preferred a party in third (or lower) place "defected" to support one of the top two contenders and therefore acted consistently with the strategic voting hypothesis.

Of course, this table was designed to test an implication about plurality systems. We present the same data in table 11.3, dividing our sample by electoral system. Here, we can see that there is variation. Conveniently, the PR system has the highest proportion of apparently sincere voting among third party supporters. Somewhat inconveniently, the set of nations using a plurality system comes next, while the majority system category is about as close to a perfect illustration of the expected pattern – in plurality systems, at least – as survey data are likely to afford (and it is very similar to that found in studies of strategic voting in U.S. presidential elections, such as in Abramson, Aldrich, and Rohde 2002; and Abramson et al. 2010).

This part of our inquiry has shown that voting patterns strongly support the notion that voters are often able to reason and act strategically in reaching their voting decisions. It also modifies the theoretical challenge of explaining why voters vote the way they do – voting behaviour is remarkably similar, whether it takes place in a plurality voting system or one that uses another method, which calls into question Duvergerian incentives. Of course, there are many reasons that one might

Table 11.3 Preference and Vote Choice by Electoral System

A. Plurality

Most preferred party	Party voted for				
	Largest	Second-largest	Same other	Different other	N
Largest	83.0	9.2		7.9	1693
Second-largest	7.7	87.3		5.0	1310
Other	10.9	12.9	69.2	7.0	966

B. Majority

Most preferred party	Party voted for				
	Largest	Second-largest	Same other	Different other	N
Largest	93.0	3.5		3.5	513
Second-largest	3.3	94.5		2.2	364
Other	17.8	29.9	48.1	4.3	231

C. Proportional representation

Most preferred party	Party voted for				
	Largest	Second-largest	Same other	Different other	N
Largest	87.7	3.7		8.6	6382
Second-largest	3.7	89.1		7.2	3798
Other	6.4	6.7	74.0	13.0	6879

D. Mixed

Most preferred party	Party voted for				
	Largest	Second-largest	Same other	Different other	N
Largest	86.2	2.3		11.5	2182
Second-largest	4.6	80.8		14.6	1110
Other	17.5	12.2	62.6	7.7	1719

choose to cast a vote that appears sincere or one that appears strategic that are not captured in variables so far included in the analysis. So before turning to consider the theoretical challenges remaining to investigate, we turn to a multivariate analysis of voting types to sort out some of those reasons.

Who and Where Are the Sincere and Strategic Voters?

In this section we develop and estimate a statistical model to explain who engages in what appears to be sincere and strategic voting. We have already hinted at the two most obvious sources of hypotheses: variables that differentiate those most interested and engaged in – or "sophisticated" about – politics, and variables that differentiate nations by virtue of their electoral and party systems. The standard voting behaviour and public opinion literature suggests that more sophisticated reasoning should be reserved for those with a more sophisticated interest in and understanding of politics. As we have detailed more directly, electoral and party system measures are also expected to matter, in particular because plurality and two-party systems offer the easiest and clearest avenues for strategic voting. Similar to the other chapters in this book, then, our analysis considers the effects of both individual and contextual factors.

The CSES data are limited (by virtue of the project) in data at the individual level, compared to what those who use such large-scale survey projects as the American National Election Study, British Election Study, or Canadian Election Study are used to. Still, there are a base set of measures that are gathered by all participating nations, and we include in our model as many as could reasonably be considered related to the level of political sophistication as possible. These include the demographic variables of age, sex, income, and whether one's residence is urban. It also includes partisanship, which we include on the grounds that holding a partisan preference is likely to deter one from defecting from that partisanship to support another party, wasted vote or not. We also include two more direct measures of political engagement: an index of political information and one of political participation. Finally, we include two attitudinal measures that might prove relevant to willingness to engage in strategic versus sincere behaviour: how much the respondent believes it matters who is in power; and how much the respondent believes that voting matters in affecting politics.

Institutionally, we have emphasized throughout our discussion so far that plurality systems have a simple, easily understood and implemented strategic decision, and that, at least from Duverger (1963) onward, the importance of strategic voting has been theoretically and empirically (and practically) understood. We thus include a plurality dummy variable. Indeed, Duverger is relevant also for his explanation of the relevance of our next major institutional variable, the effective number of political parties in the electoral system. That is, the electoral system and the number of parties are related, and in particular, plurality systems induce a tendency towards two-party systems, according to his law. To capture the converse of Duverger's argument, and to consider the more recent work that shows strategic behaviour in PR systems, we also include a PR dummy variable. Finally, we include two other system variables, federalism and presidentialism. We do so because considerations relevant to other offices may affect choices for this office and thus may affect the extent of strategic and sincere voting.

We estimated the implied statistical model on the four measures in table 11.1, that is, on whether the respondent belongs to the set of Purely Strategic voters, Purely Sincere voters, Total Sincere voters, and/or Total Strategic voters. We used a random effects probit model to account for the multilevel nature of the data.[9] Our expectations are that, at least purely, any factor that might detract from a voter being affected by and acting upon strategic incentives will decrease strategic voting. Thus, we expect pure strategic voting to increase with political sophistication and political participation, decrease with partisanship, and be negatively related to the effective number of parties and plurality systems. Believing who is in power matters should positively affect strategic behaviour, while believing in the importance of voting should have a negative effect. The results can be found in table 11.4.

At the individual level, we see a range of similar and different effects across our dependent variables. Age has a negative effect on Purely Sincere voting, as does income. Income also has a positive effect on strategic voting, both the Pure and Total variants, while age only has a positive effect on Total Strategic voting. Urban residence has a positive effect on Purely Sincere voting. Partisanship, while significant in each of our models, affects sincere and strategic behaviour in the same way (contrary to our expectations). Partisans are less likely to engage in Purely Strategic or Purely Sincere voting (e.g., the average predicted probability of Purely Strategic voting falls to 0.030 from 0.043), but they are more likely to be included among the Total sets. Given the way our categories are constructed, this suggests that partisans are more likely to be included in the straightforward voter category.

Table 11.4 Multivariate Model of Vote Type

Variable	Purely strategic	Purely sincere	Total strategic	Total sincere
Age	−0.001	−0.005***	0.003***	0.001
	0.002	0.001	0.001	0.001
Female	0.047	−0.002	−0.012	−0.027
	0.046	0.030	0.025	0.026
Income	0.034*	−0.030**	0.023*	−0.009
	0.017	0.011	0.009	0.010
Urban residence	0.036	0.045***	−0.019	0.001
	0.020	0.013	0.011	0.011
Partisanship	−0.166***	−0.100**	0.418***	0.426***
	0.048	0.031	0.026	0.027
Political Information Index	0.054	0.040*	−0.035*	−0.017
	0.030	0.019	0.016	0.017
Political Participation Index	0.038*	0.105***	−0.041***	0.020
	0.018	0.012	0.010	0.011
Who is in power matters	0.024	0.035**	−0.041***	−0.025*
	0.021	0.013	0.011	0.012
Voting matters	−0.027	−0.011	0.022	0.023
	0.022	0.014	0.012	0.012
Plurality system	−0.522***	0.177	0.361*	0.739***
	0.118	0.350	0.147	0.160
PR System	−0.159	0.073	0.327**	0.469***
	0.092	0.266	0.113	0.123
Effective number of parties	−0.017	0.063	−0.188***	−0.120***
	0.026	0.072	0.031	0.033
Federalism	0.150	−0.482*	0.039	−0.221*
	0.077	0.239	0.100	0.109
Presidential system	0.063	−0.659**	0.067	−0.300**
	0.085	0.236	0.099	0.108
Constant	−1.879***	−0.916**	0.182	0.433**
	0.200	0.308	0.153	0.163

(Continued)

Table 11.4 (Continued)

Variable	Purely strategic	Purely sincere	Total strategic	Total sincere
lnsig2u	−4.519***	−1.557***	−3.371***	−3.186***
	0.706	0.343	0.343	0.330
rho	0.011	0.174	0.033	0.040
N (individual)	11478	11478	11478	11478
N (election)	23	23	23	23

Note: Standard errors are noted underneath coefficients.

$*p < 0.05$; $**p < 0.01$; $***p < 0.001$

Political information, which was expected to increase one's ability to cast a strategic ballot, is significant (positively) only for Purely Sincere voting and (negatively) for Total Strategic voting. Political participation has similar effects for these models, but it is also significant for the Purely Strategic model (positively) and has an opposite sign (although insignificant) for Total Sincere voting. Finally, attitudes about the importance of who is in power are positively related to Purely Sincere voting and negatively related to both Total Strategic and Total Sincere voting (contrary to expectations).

Among the institutional variables included in the model, we see the surprising result that the plurality variable has similar effects to the PR variable across each of the models, although it is uniquely significant in the Purely Strategic model. This unique effect is the most interesting result – plurality systems have *less* Purely Strategic voting. This is consistent with our earlier analyses yet still unexpected, given the theoretical literature. Although the common understanding is that plurality systems provide the most frequent and easily understood incentives for strategic voting, this appears to be incorrect.

Turning to our remaining institutional variables, the effective number of parties variable is significant only for Total Strategic and Total Sincere voting, and it is similarly signed in both cases. As the variable is not significant in either the Purely Strategic or Purely Sincere vote models, this suggests that a higher number of effective parties has a depressive effect on straightforward voting. Indeed, going from two to eight effective parties decreases the average predicted probability of belonging to the set of Total Strategic voters from 0.646 to 0.238, and changes the average predicted probability of being in the Total Sincere group from 0.729 to 0.472. Finally, federalism and presidentialism lead to significantly less sincere voting (both Pure and Total) and have positive (although insignificant) effects on strategic behaviour.

All together, these findings suggest that our expectations were misinformed. Not all variables that affect the incentives and opportunity for strategic voting matter. Political information, political participation, and attitudes about electoral outcomes do emerge as significant factors for some types of voting behaviour, but not as we expected. Similarly, the anticipated institutional effects are not clear. The multivariate results are, however, consistent with the patterns that we see in our other analyses and suggest an interesting interpretation. Although the effects of information, participation, electoral systems, and party systems on voting behaviour can be easily theorized, our results suggest that the differences between sincere and strategic voting are much fewer than expected. The divide between expressing preferences and casting non-wasted votes is not very clear, hinting that voters do not see or do not react to the strategic incentives and opportunities as clearly as researchers theorize. Nonetheless, we do see that accounting for both individual- and institutional-level variables is important if one wishes to understand strategic and sincere voting behaviour.

Conclusion

The results obtained in the analyses in this chapter suggest that voters across the world are able to engage in at least a limited amount of strategic politics; at least, that is, with respect to voting in a major national election contest. This is no mean feat, and perhaps especially telling for the newer democracies and those in less developed nations, where it is common to hear politicians claim they cannot implement fully democratic procedures as a result of the inability of the citizenry to respond to them meaningfully. It is also comforting to know that the public can be active participants in the "game" of politics, so to speak, and thus have credible odds of holding their own against elites seeking to win, hold, and use political power.

The evidence also suggests that the extent to which voters engage in strategic or sincere voting is a function of two types of considerations. One is variation among individuals. In particular, a variety of measures related to political sophistication affect sincere and strategic voting.

Partisanship appears to be important, as are political participation, information, attitudes, and demographics.

The second set of considerations is institutional, and in particular the electoral and/or party system variables. That is, the use of a plurality system is strongly related to the incidence of strategic or sincere voting, and PR and the effective number of parties are also related to voting behaviour. Residence in a nation with a federal or presidential system also is relevant.

As sanguine as these comments are, they do point to some serious issues needing theoretical attention. The most important aspect of the multivariate results is that they do not support the existing theoretical understanding of strategic voting. The effects we observe are, in many cases, similar for Purely Strategic and Purely Sincere voters, or for belonging to the Total Strategic and Total Sincere sets. The latter finding is less troubling in that the overlap in the sets points to the importance of identifying those for whom a vote decision is straightforward in terms of preferences and rational considerations. The former, however, suggests that how we understand the incentives faced by voters during elections needs to be completely rethought.

The evidence also suggests that voters are acting strategically in all kinds of voting systems. However, the theory really is fully developed only for plurality and majority systems in the way estimated here, and difficult questions need to be answered to figure out what strategic voting is, theoretically, in PR systems. In addition, finding that federalism and presidential variables are institutional correlates with sincere voting suggests two avenues needing further research. One is to expand the range of institutional variables investigated empirically. It may well be that we have yet to complete the set of substantively relevant institutional effects. The other follows immediately, which is to conduct the necessary theoretical work to better understand how and why those institutional variables shape choices.

NOTES

The authors thank Greg Schober for excellent research assistance.

1 We note that the two preceding chapters both touch on these questions. Chapter 9 considers the effects of strategic voting via the supply of parties

in different electoral systems. Chapter 10 provides an effective estimate of the aggregate effects of strategic voting.

2 They are clear in saying they mean by "most preferred party" the preference for who should win the current election, and not one's long-standing party loyalties, just as we do here. Note also that they exclude those who might defect from the most preferred party to vote for the leader of some other party who they most prefer to win as prime minister.

3 This categorization thereby excludes those who vote neither on the basis of preferences nor on expectations, whatever that would leave as the basis for choice!

4 We also created a category for "too close to call" voters, who voted sincerely for a party that was not one of the top two but whose vote share was within 3 per cent of the second highest ranked party. These individuals are included in both the Total Strategic and Total Sincere numbers as their vote choices were (within a relatively small margin of error of perception) straightforward.

5 This generally means simply that the respondent has a party uniquely most highly preferred. We should also note that our specification allows individuals to have a top preference for a party with a feeling thermometer rating of 0. We tried an alternative specification of preferences, restricting the definition of a top preference to 5 or larger on the scale, and found few substantive effects on our analyses. Analyses using this variable are available upon request.

6 All analyses were conducted with unweighted data.

7 By "third" we mean a party that was neither the largest nor the second-largest, regardless of how large that party was.

8 The number of straightforward voters in our dataset is 15,127, or 42.2 per cent. By electoral system, there are 52.4 per cent in plurality systems, 51.5 per cent in majority systems, 40.5 per cent in PR systems, and 38.5 per cent in mixed systems.

9 We used the "xtprobit" command in STATA and specified grouping by election.

References

Abramson, Paul R., John H. Aldrich, André Blais, Matthew Diamond, Abraham Diskin, Indridi H. Indridason, Daniel J. Lee, and Renan Levine. 2010. "Comparing Strategic Voting under FPTP and PR." *Comparative Political Studies* 43 (1): 61–90.

Abramson, Paul R., John H. Aldrich, Phil Paolino, and David W. Rohde. 1992. "'Sophisticated' Voting in the 1988 Presidential Primaries." *American Political Science Review* 86 (1): 55–69.

Abramson, Paul R., John H. Aldrich, and David W. Rohde. 2002. *Change and Continuity in the 2000 Elections*. Washington: CQ.

Aldrich, John H., André Blais, and Laura B. Stephenson. 2018. "Strategic Voting and Political Institutions." In *The Many Faces of Strategic Voting*, edited by Laura B. Stephenson, John H. Aldrich, and André Blais, 1–27. Ann Arbor: University of Michigan Press.

Berelson, Bernard R., Paul F. Lazarsfeld, and William N. McPhee. 1954. *Voting*. Chicago: University of Chicago Press.

Black, Jerome H. 1978. "The Multicandidate Calculus of Voting: Application to Canadian Federal Elections." *American Journal of Political Science* 22 (3): 609–38.

Blais, André, John H. Aldrich, Indridi H. Indridason, and Renan Levine. 2006. "Do Voters Vote for Government Coalitions? Testing Downs' Pessimistic Conclusion." *Party Politics* 12 (6): 691–705.

Blais, André, and Thomas Gschwend. 2011. "Strategic Defection across Elections, Parties, and Voters." In *Citizens, Context and Choice*, edited by Russell J. Dalton and Christopher J. Anderson, 176–93. Oxford: Oxford University Press.

Cain, Bruce E. 1978. "Strategic Voting in Britain." *American Journal of Political Science* 22 (3): 639–55.

Campbell, Angus, Philip E. Converse, Warren E. Miller, and Donald E. Stokes. 1960. *The American Voter*. New York: John Wiley & Sons.

Converse, Philip E. 1964. "The Nature of Belief Systems in Mass Publics." In *Ideology and Discontent*, edited by David E. Apter, 206–61. New York: Free Press of Glencoe.

Cox, Gary W. 1997. *Making Votes Count*. Cambridge: Cambridge University Press.

Duverger, Maurice. 1963. *Political Parties: Their Organization and Activity in the Modern State*. Trans. Barbara North and Robert North. New York: Wiley.

Gibbard, Allan. 1973. "Manipulation of Voting Schemes: A General Result." *Econometrica* 41 (4): 587–601.

Kelley, Stanley Jr, and Thad W. Mirer. 1974. "The Simple Act of Voting." *American Political Science Review* 68 (2): 572–91.

Kselman, Daniel, and Emerson Niou. 2010. "Strategic Voting in Plurality Elections." *Political Analysis* 18 (2): 227–44.

Lazarsfeld, Paul F., Bernard Berelson, and Hazel Gaudet. 1944. *The People's Choice: How the Voter Makes Up His Mind in a Presidential Campaign*. New York: Duell, Sloan and Pearce.

Niou, Emerson M.S. 2001. "Strategic Voting under Plurality and Runoff Rules." *Journal of Theoretical Politics* 13 (2): 209–27.

Satterthwaite, Mark Allen. 1975. "Strategy-Proofness and Arrow's Conditions." *Journal of Economic Theory* 10 (2): 187–217.

Stephenson, Laura B., John H. Aldrich, and André Blais. 2018. *The Many Faces of Strategic Voting: Tactical Behavior in Electoral Systems Around the World*. Ann Arbor: University of Michigan Press.

12 The Future of Election Studies and the Study of Elections

PETER JOHN LOEWEN, DANIEL RUBENSON,
AND ANDRÉ BLAIS

The principal goal of this volume was to understand two related decisions that voters make in each election. First, will the citizen vote? Second, if they do decide to vote, for whom will they cast their ballot? For each of these decisions, how might the electoral system in which the voter is situated matter? The answers provided are as varied as they are interesting.

The first set of chapters in our volume addressed voter turnout. Kam, Cranmer, and Fowler show that concern for others can drive the decision to participate in an election, but that this causal force depends on the election being fought over policies that will change the distribution of wealth and create a net societal gain. Loewen, Dawes, and Arsenault demonstrate that individuals' traits – especially their tendencies to engage in behaviours not prescribed by rational choice theory – explains variation in voter turnout. Green's chapter provides a compelling picture of how social pressure and civic duty interact (and do not interact!) to affect voter turnout. Godbout and Turgeon provide evidence that voters and non-voters differ not only in their underlying commitments to electoral participation, but also in their policy views. Perhaps contrary to popular wisdom, they show slightly more conservatism around non-voters than voters. Taken together, these chapters represent well the diversity of work that is being undertaken on voter turnout.

The next set of chapters concerned vote choice. Nadeau, Bélanger, and Jérôme explore the role of the economy in influencing vote choice – a long-standing and ongoing concern of scholars of voter behaviour. In particular, they demonstrate that regional economic conditions matter in addition to national economic conditions. This is an important heterogeneity. If election campaigns turn solely on national economic performance, it is more difficult to explain why the electoral success of parties can vary so much from one region to another. However, if regional economic factors can shape electoral fortunes, we can better understand differences in vote choice.

Fournier, Cutler, and Soroka likewise find an important heterogeneity. They explore opinion formation in election campaigns, and they tell a surprising story: very few people are persuaded to change their opinions during an election campaign. Indeed, opinion change is limited to the small subset of voters who are both ambivalent on an issue or party in question but are at the same time attentive to the campaign. This helps us understand another puzzle. Canadian Election Study data suggest that in every federal election since 2000 save one (2006), the governing party has finished the election essentially where it started. The work of Fournier and colleagues can help us understand why there is so little movement during election campaigns. Voters who are open to persuasion are simply not very common.[1]

Garand and Xu take something of a different tack in their chapter. Instead of campaigns, their focus is on a key difference between voters: some voters work in the public service while others do not. Using data from multiple countries, they show that voters who work in the public service are more likely to vote for parties of the left. However intuitive this finding might be *theoretically*, it benefits greatly from an *empirical* demonstration. The variety of countries in which it applies suggests that this is a general feature of voter choice.

The final set of chapters considered how turnout, vote choice, and citizens' attitudes are affected by the electoral system in which they are situated. Using a large number of election studies, Anderson's chapter argues that when citizens are presented with a large number of ideologically distinct choices, they are more likely to express satisfaction with democracy. This is an important contribution, as it demonstrates how a factor related to electoral systems (the number of parties and their ideological clarity) can improve democratic experiences.

Aldrich and Stephenson also take advantage of a large number of election studies, in their case to examine differences in the rate of strategic voting across electoral and party systems. Importantly, they show that factors both at the level of the individual and the political system matter for the decision to vote strategically.

Finally, the work of Lachat in many ways returns the study of electoral systems to a starting point. Sixty years ago, Maurice Duverger (1959) noted that electoral systems affect the number of parties who present at elections and who eventually win office. This happens because of both mechanical effects – that arise in the translation of votes into seats – and psychological effects – parties and voters alike make strategic choices to abandon respectively some races and some candidates to vote for more viable alternatives. In this, Duverger recognized the complex interplay between citizens' senses of both obligation and strategy within the context of electoral systems. Lachat deals with this fundamental observation in his chapter, in which he provides a method for estimating empirically the characteristics that affect the relative importance of mechanical and psychological factors. He leverages important institutional variation with Swiss electoral politics to estimate the influence of these different factors.

There is impressive diversity in these chapters – geographic, temporal, and methodological. But at the core of nearly every chapter is the use of data from election studies. Indeed, all but two chapters draw at least in part on original data from election studies.[2] These studies typically take the form of a survey of a representative sample of a thousand or more voters just before or after an election. While these studies have been occurring for more than fifty years, they are currently undergoing substantial innovation – in approaches to sampling, method of fielding, and even in their epistemological underpinnings. The purpose of this chapter is to make an argument about why election studies are still necessary, to briefly consider their history, largely using Canada as a case study, and then to speculate on the form they might take in the future.

The Purpose of Election Studies

Election studies vary substantially in the methods they use to sample voters, the size of the samples they draw, and the types of questions that they pose to voters. As we articulate in the next section, there is often a close connection between the ways that election studies are conducted and the types of questions they ask. Whether one method is better than another, however, and likewise whether one set of questions is better than another, is not easily answered. Instead, it is best to think of election studies as we might think of theoretical or empirical models: they are neither true nor false. Instead, they are *purposive*, and as such we can judge them on the basis of how well they achieve the purpose or end for which they are designed (Clarke and Primo 2012). What then are the purposes or reasons for an election study?

There are three broad purposes or functions served by election studies. First, to understand how elections function, in general. Second, to make inferences about the unfolding of specific elections. Third, to ascertain the role of elections for public policy and government.

The first purpose of election studies is to help us understand how elections function, in the most general terms. What do voters know about policies and politicians? Are they well informed and able to make consistently rational decisions (Downs 1957)? Absent full information, are they able to make use of other types of information to come to an otherwise rational and defensible choice (Lupia 1994)? Are they guided by long-term loyalties (Johnston et al. 1992; Green, Palmquist, and Schickler 2004), or are their choices driven purely by short-term factors (Clarke et al. 1992)? Are voters ideological creatures, voting on the basis of their proximity to the parties that are closest to them (Merrill and Grofman 1999; Rabinowitz and Macdonald 1989)? Or do they rely mostly on assessments of leaders (Lenz 2013)? These are important questions, not least because understanding how voters behave can help us evaluate theories of normative democratic politics. Often the conclusions are far from rosy (Achen and Bartels 2016). Moreover, by comparing variations in the nature of voter choice across electoral systems (Blais 2010), we can better understand how electoral systems condition the choices voters make, why they make those choices, and how individual choices are transformed into collective decisions.

The second purpose of election studies is the mirror image of the first. If the first objective is to make general claims about elections, the second purpose is to make specific claims about single elections. Certainly, such specific claims can add up to general conclusions, but this is not necessary for this second purpose to be fulfilled. By undertaking detailed analysis of a single election, we can understand the main motivations of voters to elect one government and not another. For example, were voters motivated mainly by a desire to remove the existing government? Or were they engaging in "positive selection" in choosing one party over another to govern into the future? Were voters familiar with the promises put forward by parties, or were they instead granting an "absent mandate"? Did voters care about a single issue, as in the 1988 "Free Trade" Canadian election (Johnston et al. 1992)? Was it all about the economy? Or was the election instead about an incoherent and perhaps irreconcilable set of issue positions? This function is essential. After every election, pundits and politicians alike seek to "frame" the contest, to put their own sense onto the judgments of voters. We can test such claims by systematically understanding why voters voted the way they did in a particular election. In the process, researchers contribute to a proper understanding of how each election fits into the democratic history of the country or region.

A third purpose of election studies is to help build our knowledge of public preferences and in turn inform public policy and government action. When an election study contains substantial information about policy preferences, it provides an unparalleled insight into public preferences over public policies, general political attitudes such as views towards minority groups, evaluations of politicians, and a number of other important social indicators. Of course, polls are ubiquitous, so election studies do not provide the only means by which we can learn about public preferences. However, they do have distinct advantages. First, election studies contain information on a large number of policy preferences rather than just a few. This allows for more comprehensive analysis. Second, because these studies happen in the course of an election (since the advent of the rolling cross-section, at least), they elicit policy preferences at a time when voters are more likely to have reflected on which policies they prefer and more likely to have done so, conscious of the trade-offs that are entailed. Third, because election studies are not commercially or politically interested undertakings, we can have more confidence in the neutrality of the data they report. In short, election studies can help us understand who wants what, when, and why.

The Variety of Election Studies

The modern election study was introduced in the 1940s and 1950s. The systematic large-scale study of elections began with the "Columbia school." This group of scholars undertook a systematic collection of in-person interviews in a single county in the 1948 American general election (Berelson, Lazarsfeld, and McPhee 1954; Lazarsfeld, Gaudet, and Berelson 1968). While their design did not allow for an understanding of the national election, it still furnished an exceptional amount of information on the social bases of vote choice, indeed enough to spur decades of research (e.g., Zuckerman 2005). Soon after, the "Michigan school" began their studies. In what would eventually become the American National Election Study series, they undertook face-to-face post-election interviews with nationally representative samples comprising thousands of voters (Campbell et al. 1960). Their expansion on the work of the Columbia school was thoroughgoing. Indeed, in the context of the above stated purposes, their approach allowed them to serve all three functions, while the Columbia school studies, at least in early forms, were largely constrained to the goal of developing generalized insights about elections.

The first modern election study in Canada arguably occurred in 1965, an effort led by John Meisel. Since then, the evolution of studies first tracked trends in the United States (and other countries more broadly). However, the 1988 Canadian Election Study broke substantial methodological ground. Canadian election studies have continued this practice.

The first two election studies in Canada occurred in 1965 and 1968 (Kanji, Bilodeau, and Scotto 2012).[3] These were both single-wave cross-sectional designs conducted in a face-to-face, in-home fashion after the election. Given the large samples (~2,100 and ~2,800 respondents, respectively), these studies often took months to complete. They were, by necessity, retrospective. They were unable to capture campaign dynamics. Arguably they served the third purpose of election studies well. The degree to which they could serve the first and second purposes depends on whether one believes that campaigns matter and have the potential to change the decisions voters make and how they make them.

By the 1970s the innovation of panel studies was introduced. When Harold Clarke and colleagues (Clarke et al. 1979; Clarke et al. 1991) took over the Canadian Election Study they retained the face-to-face, in-home, post-election model. However, they made an important innovation. Noting that it was relatively easy to recontact voters even years after a first election – after all, many people do not move house – they undertook a resampling of respondents from previous elections. Over the 1974–1979–1980 set of elections, this resulted in a three-election sample of some 800 voters. It also created two-wave panels of 1,700 voters. The benefits of this innovation are difficult to overstate. In particular, these panel data raised important questions about the stability of attitudes, the consistency of partisanship, and the meaning and depth of policy preferences (Clarke et al. 1991; LeDuc et al. 1984). In short, a single methodological innovation made it possible for election studies in Canada to serve all three of their purposes.

The following election study, conducted around the 1984 election, returned to the single wave, cross-sectional format, again conducted face-to-face, and after the election. However, the next election study would genuinely change the game. In the 1988 CES, the principal co-investigators set out to test for campaign dynamics (Johnston et al. 1992). This was made possible by a move from in-home face-to-face interviews to telephone interviews. By conducting interviews on the phone, hundreds could be completed in a day. This would allow for an election study of thousands of voters to be conducted over the course of a relatively short campaign. The principal investigators contributed at least one more innovation. Since sampling was random – via a random-digit dialling procedure – a unique sample could be drawn for each day of the campaign, generating both unbiased and efficient estimates of the support levels of each party. A study conducted during an election could thus both estimate changes in support for parties and estimate changes in the factors underwriting vote choice. A post-election follow-up study and mail-back survey allowed researchers to fill in data that did not need to be collected during a campaign. In many respects, Johnston et al. were lucky to choose the 1988 election as a test case for their method. It was an "issue" election, in that it was dominated by one issue – free trade – at the expense of another issue – the Meech Lake Accord. Moreover, it was a campaign in which events – in particular, leader debates – appeared to matter a lot.

This model of a telephone-based rolling cross-section design followed by a post-election interview (and sometimes a mail-back survey) has been the standard design in the Canadian Election Study since 1988 (Nevitte et al. 2000; Blais, Gidengil, and Nevitte 2004; Gidengil et al. 2012). In the four election run of 2004–2006–2008–2011 a panel component was added, once again allowing for the study of the long-term durability of attitudes and political preferences. This combination of campaign period surveys, post-campaign surveys, and multi-wave panel data provides perhaps the most powerful election study design to date. However, innovations are still possible.

Election Studies in the Future

What is the future of election studies? We do not pretend to be able to forecast the future but we would like to point out two crucial challenges that election specialists face. The first and the most obvious concerns the interview mode. One of the most important innovations of the Canadian Election Study has been the shift from at-home to telephone interviews, making it possible to adopt the rolling cross-section design and to investigate how campaigns affect individual vote choice and ultimately election outcomes. It seems that we will not be able to continue with telephone interviews for a long time. Response rates have been declining more or less constantly since 1988. Many people, especially youth, do not have a fixed telephones, and inducing them to answer a long questionnaire on a mobile has proven difficult. The obvious alternative is the internet, and indeed most polls nowadays are conducted online. This raises tough questions about the representativeness of internet samples and about how their biases can be corrected. The corrections that will be made are bound not to satisfy the purists, but perhaps we need to acknowledge that the world of random samples is over.

The second new task that we hope election studies will agree to undertake is more normative. Elections are a core indispensable element of democracy, and election studies should contribute to a rigorous assessment of how well or badly elections perform as an instrument of representation and accountability. For very good reasons election specialists have focused on making sense of why voters behave the way they do. We argue it is time to move on to an even more ambitious goal: the evaluation of the overall performance of electoral democracies. From this perspective political scientists can learn from economists, who do not shy away from dealing with the big normative issues.

The democratic ideal is that an election leads to the formation of a government that will make as many citizens as happy as possible for the next four or five years. From that perspective, it is not enough to understand the many complex motivations that induce citizens to vote or not to vote and to choose a particular party or candidate. The most crucial question is how well or poorly the government that is formed after the election *represents* voters' preferences.

As researchers, we are deeply interested in discovering how and why voters form their preferences and how these preferences shape vote choice, as strategic considerations may also come into play. This is perfectly legitimate and very much in line with the rise of political psychology within political science. But we should not lose sight of the fact that elections are a collective instrument for dealing with collective issues and that our ultimate goal should be to rigorously ascertain the performance of that instrument, its merits and limits, as well as to propose ways to improve it.

The implication is that we need to grasp as completely and as accurately as possible the nature of citizens' obligations and their preferences. Election studies typically include many questions about citizens' values, ideology, issue opinions, and priorities, and they allow us to ascertain what citizens want their government to do and not to do, and also to point out tensions and contradictions between these desires. But perhaps we do not spend enough time carefully describing these preferences and their complexities, because our focus is on identifying the root causes of why voters think the way they do. So it may be that a more balanced approach, where description matters as much as explanation, is called for.

The other implication, if we wish to ascertain the performance of electoral democracy, is that we need to pay as much attention to parties as we do to voters. The ultimate goal of an election is to allow a government to govern for a given period of time and that government is almost always a partisan government. The challenge is to determine whether the government that is formed after the election well represents citizens' preferences. In order to address this question we need to closely examine the various options, that is, the various parties' positions on the major issues of the day as well as general ideological predispositions and to determine whether the winning party better represents citizens' preferences than the losing parties. This is of course assuming that we have a single-party government, but a similar (though more complex) exercise can be undertaken in the case of coalition governments (see Blais and Bodet 2006a). This is a daunting challenge, because voting behaviour specialists have over time become more and more informed about voters' psychology and less and less informed about parties. The solution, it seems to us, is to make sure that party specialists are involved in the study of elections.

Concluding Remarks

The science of politics has evolved significantly in the last century. New methods for learning about voters and parties have emerged, new theoretical frameworks have been developed, new statistical techniques have been created, and new approaches to research design, including randomized experiments, have been employed. We have much more systematic knowledge about how politics operates than ever before.

Some things have not changed, however. Politics is still contested by parties. Elections still occur within electoral systems. And these party structures and electoral systems would have seemed for the most part familiar to scholars a century ago. And at the core of electoral politics are human beings, constrained and animated by the same differences and forces as one hundred years past. We still have much to learn about these citizens. For some scholars of elections and electoral behaviour, this work will feel like a duty; for others, a choice. Either way, it is work well worth doing.

NOTES

1 We thank Richard Johnston for this observation.
2 The exceptions are Green, and Kam, Cranmer, and Fowler, but even those chapters make use of either a large collection of findings from election studies and closely related surveys (in the case of Green) or an original combination of survey and behavioural experimental data (in the case of Kam, Cranmer, and Fowler).
3 We note that we rely heavily on Thomas Scotto and colleagues' comprehensive history of the Canadian Election Study, found in Kanji, Bilodeau, and Scotto (2012).

References

Achen, C., and L. Bartels. 2016. *Democracy for Realists: Why Elections Do Not Produce Responsive Government*. Princeton, NJ: Princeton University Press.

Berelson, B.R., P.F. Lazarsfeld, and W.N. McPhee. 1954. *Voting: A Study of Opinion Formation in a Presidential Campaign*. Chicago: University of Chicago Press.

Blais, A. 2010. "Making Electoral Democracy Work." *Electoral Studies* 29 (1): 169–70.

Blais, A., and M.A. Bodet. 2006a. "Does Proportional Representation Foster Closer Congruence between Citizens and Policy Makers?" *Comparative Political Studies* 39 (10): 1243–62.

– 2006b. "How Do Voters Form Expectations about the Parties' Chances of Winning the Election?" *Social Science Quarterly* 87 (3): 477–93.

Blais, A., E. Gidengil, and N. Nevitte. 2004. "Where Does Turnout Decline Come From?" *European Journal of Political Research* 43 (2): 221–36.

Campbell, A., P. Converse, W. Miller, and D. Stokes. 1960. *The American Voter*. New York: John Wiley.

Clarke, H.D., J. Jenson, L. LeDuc, and J.H. Pammett. 1991. *Absent Mandate: Interpreting Change in Canadian Elections*. Toronto: Gage Educational Publishing.

Clarke, H., E. Elliott, W. Mishler, M. Stewart, P. Whiteley, and G. Zuk. 1992. *Controversies in Political Economy: Canada, Great Britain, the United States*. Boulder, CO: Westview.

Clarke, H.D., J. Jenson, L. LeDuc, and J.H. Pammett. 1979. *Political Choice in Canada*. Toronto: McGraw-Hill Ryerson.
– 1991. *Absent Mandate: Interpreting Change in Canadian Elections*. Toronto: Gage Educational Publishing.
Clarke, K.A., and D.M. Primo. 2012. *A Model Discipline: Political Science and the Logic of Representations*. Oxford: Oxford University Press.
Downs, A. 1957. *An Economic Theory of Democracy*. New York: Harper.
Duverger, M. 1959. *Political Parties: Their Organization and Activity in the Modern State*. New York: John Wiley.
Gidengil, E., A. Blais, J. Everitt, P. Fournier, and N. Nevitte. 2012. *Dominance and Decline: Making Sense of Recent Canadian Elections*. Toronto: University of Toronto Press.
Green, D., B. Palmquist, and E. Schickler. 2004. *Partisan Hearts and Minds: Political Parties and the Social Identity of Voters*. New Haven, CT: Yale University Press.
Johnston, R., A. Blais, H.E. Brady, and J. Cret. 1992. *Letting the People Decide: Dynamics of a Canadian Election*. Stanford, CA: Stanford University Press.
Kanji, M., A. Bilodeau, and T.J. Scotto. 2012. *The Canadian Election Studies: Assessing Four Decades of Influence*. Vancouver: UBC Press.
Lazarsfeld, P.F., H. Gaudet, and B. Berelson. 1968. *People's Choice: How the Voter Makes Up His Mind in a Presidential Campaign*. 3rd ed. New York: Columbia University Press.
LeDuc, L., H.D. Clarke, J. Jenson, and J.H. Pammett. 1984. "Partisan Instability in Canada: Evidence from a New Panel Study." *American Political Science Review* 78 (2): 470–84.
Lenz, G.S. 2013. *Follow the Leader? How Voters Respond to Politicians' Policies and Performance*. Chicago: University of Chicago Press.
Lupia, A. 1994. "Shortcuts versus Encyclopedias: Information and Voting Behavior in California Insurance Reform Elections." *American Political Science Review* 88 (1): 63–76.
Merrill, S., and B. Grofman. 1999. *A Unified Theory of Voting: Directional and Proximity Spatial Models*. Cambridge: Cambridge University Press.
Nevitte, N., A. Blais, E. Gidengil, and R. Nadeau. 2000. *Unsteady State: The 1997 Canadian Federal Election*. Don Mills, ON: Oxford University Press.
Rabinowitz, G., and S.E. Macdonald. 1989. "A Directional Theory of Issue Voting." *American Political Science Review* 83 (1): 93–121.
Zuckerman, A.S. 2005. "Returning to the Social Logic of Political Behavior." In *The Social Logic of Politics: Personal Networks as Contexts for Political Behavior*, edited by Zuckerman, 3–20. Philadelphia: Temple University Press.

Contributors

John Aldrich is the Pfizer-Pratt University Professor of Political Science at Duke University.

Christopher J. Anderson is a professor of economics and politics at the University of Warwick.

Gabriel Arsenault is an assistant professor of political science at the École des hautes études publiques at the Université de Moncton.

Éric Bélanger is a professor in the Department of Political Science at McGill University.

André Blais is a professor in the Département de science politique at Université de Montréal.

Skyler J. Cranmer is the Carter Phillips and Sue Henry Associate Professor of Political Science at the Ohio State University.

Fred Cutler is an associate professor in the Department of Political Science at the University of British Columbia.

Christopher Dawes is an associate professor in the Department of Politics at New York University.

Patrick Fournier is a professor in the Département de science politique at Université de Montréal.

James H. Fowler is a professor of political science in the Department of Political Science and professor in the Global Public Health Division, Department of Medicine at the University of California, San Diego.

James C. Garand is the Emogene Pliner Distinguished Professor and R. Downs Poindexter Professor of Political Science at Louisiana State University.

Jean-François Godbout is a professor in the Département de science politique at Université de Montréal.

Donald P. Green is the Burgess Professor in the Department of Political Science at Columbia University.

Maxime Héroux-Legault is an assistant professor in the Department of Political Science at Concordia University.

Bruno Jérôme is a professor in the Département de sciences économiques at Université de Paris II Panthéon-Assas.

Cindy D. Kam holds the William R. Kenan Jr Chair and is a professor in the Department of Political Science at Vanderbilt University.

Romain Lachat is an assistant professor at CEVIPOF, Sciences Po Paris.

Peter John Loewen is a professor in the Department of Political Science and the Munk School of Global Affairs and Public Policy at the University of Toronto.

Richard Nadeau is a professor in the Département de science politique at Université de Montréal.

Daniel Rubenson is an associate professor in the Politics Department at Ryerson University and affiliated researcher at the Research Institute of Industrial Economics, Stockholm.

Stuart Soroka is the Michael W. Traugott Collegiate Professor of Communication Studies and Political Science at the University of Michigan.

Laura B. Stephenson is a professor in the Department of Political Science at Western University.

Mathieu Turgeon is an associate professor in the Department of Political Science at Western University.

Ping Xu is an associate professor in the Department of Political Science at the University of Rhode Island.

Index

www.ingramcontent.com/pod-product-compliance
Lightning Source LLC
Chambersburg PA
CBHW030238030426
42336CB00009B/148